Philosophy and the Return to Self-Knowledge

PHILOSOPHY AND THE RETURN TO SELF-KNOWLEDGE

Donald Phillip Verene

Yale University Press   New Haven and London

Copyright © 1997 by Yale University.
All rights reserved.
This book may not be reproduced, in whole or in part,
including illustrations, in any form (beyond that copying
permitted by Sections 107 and 108 of the U.S. Copyright
Law and except by reviewers for the public press), without
written permission from the publishers.

Printed in the United States of America.

Library of Congress Cataloging-in-Publication Data

Verene, Donald Phillip, 1937–
Philosophy and the return to self-knowledge /
Donald Phillip Verene.
p. cm.
Includes bibliographical references and index.
ISBN 0-300-06999-5 (cloth : alk. paper)
1. Philosophy. 2. Self-knowledge, Theory of.
3. Methodology. 4. Ethics. 5. Conduct of life. I. Title.
B945.V473P48 1997
191—dc21 97-7881
CIP

A catalogue record for this book is
available from the British Library.

The paper in this book meets the guidelines
for permanence and durability of the Committee
on Production Guidelines for Book Longevity of
the Council on Library Resources.

10 9 8 7 6 5 4 3 2

And now if anything has here been said by me inconsistent with piety, with good morals, . . . or with any aspect of truth, let it be as if unsaid.

                Hugo Grotius, *On the Law of War and Peace*

Contents

Preface / ix

Introduction: Prometheus and Descartes / 1

PART 1 • THE HISTORICAL

Chapter 1 Barbarism of Reflection / 41

Chapter 2 Metaphysics of Folly / 88

PART 2 • THE HUMAN

Chapter 3 Technological Desire / 141

Chapter 4 Philosophical Memory / 192

Epilogue: The Tablet of Philosophy / 243

Notes / 261

Credits for Illustrations / 287

Index / 289

Preface

Philosophy exists because humans are mortal. It is a response to the fact of this mortality. Philosophy as the human attempt to understand the human is formulated by Socrates in the ancient question of the examined life and its tie to the assertion in the *Phaedo* that "those who rightly philosophize are practicing to die" (*hoi orthos philosophountes apothneskein meletosi*). As modern philosophy has developed since Descartes, the connection of philosophy to mortality and its accompanying concern with self-knowledge have been set aside. Philosophy as the love of wisdom that considers the true to be the whole has been replaced by the pursuit of method and the truth of the part. The Renaissance humanists' attempt to discover the connections among wisdom, eloquence, and prudence has been given up. In regard to the Socratic tradition of self-knowledge and the humanist tradition of seeking to form thought and human action as "wisdom speaking," philosophy has lost its way.

Giambattista Vico (1668–1744), after nine years in the mountains of the Cilento during which he educated himself in the works of the ancients and the humanists, returned to his home city of Naples to find himself surrounded by Cartesians and to learn that the metaphysics of Aristotle had become a laughingstock. Like Ovid in exile at Tomis on the Black Sea and like Rousseau, the "Citizen of Geneva," Vico found himself among barbarians. Vico called the barbarism he encountered the "barbarism of reflection." The Cartesianism he encountered in his day has increased in ours, such that Cartesianism is not only a doctrine of thought but a spirit equal to the present itself. As Elio Gianturco, the translator of Vico's *On the Study Methods of Our Time*, said, "We live in a Cartesian world, a world of scientific research, technology, and gadgets, which invade and condition our lives."

Technology is the best-distributed thing in the world today; it is the possession of everyone, and those who feel they do not possess it equally with others desire more of it. No one exists who is not subject to technological order. Technology is not like an ordinary possession which may be abandoned or simply rejected. Technology is the possessor of its possessor, because its possessor can possess nothing without it. Technology is the medium of the modern world. It is the reality through which knower and known exist. Thinking, acting, and speaking have but one measure of credibility and effectiveness: the degree to which they are involved with the power of the technical.

My aim in this work is both a diagnostic and a practic. My diagnosis is that the Cartesian world of the technological has come to stay. This is not a happy prospect. It is simply a fact. It is a melancholic view, but melancholy is not new to philosophy. Philosophy is dedicated to thoughts not shared with others. As Berkeley says in *Three Dialogues Between Hylas and Philonous*, "We spend our lives in doubting of those things which other men evidently know, and believing those things which they laugh at and despise." My practic is to understand philosophy as a guide to life, having within its powers a path to civil wisdom that can be taken by considering the insights held in common by the Socratic and humanist traditions.

This work asks four questions which correspond to its four chapters. First, what is the primary condition of our life today? Second, how can we gain perspective on this condition? Third, what is the permanent ground of this condition in human consciousness? Fourth, how can we philosophically confront this permanent ground?

I wish to connect these four chapters with four terms. The first chapter is connected with the *objectifying impulse*. This is the impulse the self has to pull itself out of itself, toward the object. It is the impulse the self has to locate reality in the object and avoid confrontation with its own reality. It is an anti-Socratic impulse that stems from the uncertainty of self-knowledge. It abandons the quest for the examined life to dedicate itself to the quest for science and theory. The love of wisdom becomes the love of the object and the wholly objective in thought. Cassirer says in *An Essay on Man* that modern science "is a very late and refined product that could not develop except under special conditions." These special conditions require the development of reflective understanding as the key to knowledge and to the objective in experience.

The second chapter is connected with the *speculative impulse*, which is grounded in the human phenomenon of folly. The speculative is the opposite of the impulse to theoretical and technological mastery over the world. It is an attempt by the self to engage in *speculatio*, in "spying out," looking into the secret recesses of the world and joining their nature with ours. Speculation causes us to see the opposites in the world, to see beyond the established intellectual order. At the same time it is moral because seeing the world differently is always potentially the basis for a moral tale in which the self encounters the world, not as object but as alter ego.

Speculation has been considered simply as a type of thought and has not been traced to its origin in the activity of the human self. The speculative impulse is the beginning of self-knowledge and is connected to the universal human phenomenon of folly as analyzed by such writers as Erasmus. The classic activity of the fool inverts what we are seeing and forces us to see it differently. This logic of inversion that we find in the phenomenon of folly is the key to comprehending speculation as a form of human thought. In inversion we experience an aspect of the self that is the basis of its speculative powers.

The third chapter is connected with the *technical impulse*. This is the impulse to mastery over the other. It is rooted in desire (Hegel's *Begierde*) as a basic phenomenon of the life of the self. This is selfhood as pure power, a drive to dominate whatever it is not, in an effort to prove its reality without the inconvenience of self-knowledge. Any thought of self-knowledge is weakness and is unnecessary, because for desire, to exist is to possess. Technology is the form of this desire. It is Nietzsche's will to power attached to instruments. Technology achieves the specific ends of this deep sense of desire so successfully that desire becomes the desire for technique itself. The impulses to objectifying and to technologizing support each other. The absorption in the object frees the self from any natural concern with self-knowledge. Freed of the love of wisdom, the self is immersed in action by the technical impulse.

The fourth impulse is the *mimetic impulse*. Aristotle recognizes this in the *Poetics* as primal: "Imitation is natural to man from childhood, one of his advantages over the lower animals being this, that he is the most imitative creature in the world, and learns first by imitation." This impulse has been misunderstood and largely limited to the arts. It is instead an important definition of the human and is the key to memory and to philosophy. Philosophy can offer us three things: accounts of the civil, the natural, and the divine. These are the terms of philosophy's dialectic. The speculative philosopher enacts this dialectic by imitation in language of what is already written in the soul, in the world, and in the heavens. This inner writing of the real, perceived and brought forth in words, is wisdom become eloquence. What is made in words can be imitated in action and is prudence. For philosophy to achieve its rightful place as a guide to life it must reexamine the relation between word and action that is present in the classical and humanist conception of prudence.

To learn the use of language, which is the key to all its productions, philosophy must go to school with the poets. Philosophy is not poetry, but it must maintain a dialectic with poetry, with the myth, with metaphorical thinking, in order to keep in touch with the root meanings and functions of language which it requires. Whatever philosophy does, it does through language. I say this not only objectively but personally. I began my intellectual life as a poet, and in unconscious imitation of an old story, I discovered philosophy and slowly learned its humane form that can join tongue and heart and yet engage reason. I have described these events in "A Course of Life: My Autobiography" and "On Philosophical Tetralogy," a response to my critics, in a 1994 issue of *Clio*.

The relation of philosophical or speculative truth to poetry is the question that occupied Plato. The relation philosophy has to poetry is the question by which philosophy can guide itself in any age. How philosophy understands its relation to poetry, whether this is explicitly stated or implicitly held, determines how philosophy stands to all else. The quarrel that philosophy has with the poets is connected to the tension that philosophy always has with the polis, because poetry originally purports to contain civil wisdom. The quarrel with the poets and the polis is the origin of philosophy as we know it. Philosophy must, if it wishes to be successful, build any new doctrine on the basis of more than the present, on more than common sense or the results of scientific theory. Although both of these are of great importance for philosophy in its various aspects, what is common sense or science in one age is not in another. Neither can provide a permanent starting point. To recast itself at any time, philosophy must first go back to its own origins and begin to think its position through by coming to grips with the present on the basis of its own past.

Professional philosophy today divides itself into Anglo-American and Continental. Each of these approaches has largely left behind the insights of the Latins, the Latins' reading of the Greeks, and the Italian humanists' reading of both. The understanding of these texts has been put aside in the usual study of the history of philosophy. The works of Cicero and Quintilian and those of the humanists such as Marsilio Ficino and Giovanni Pico della Mirandola have been categorized as forms of literary and popular philosophy, as lacking the power of a philosophical system. Their ideas have not become part of the understanding or the teaching of the history of philosophy.

There is a third alternative to the bipolarity of Anglo-American and Continental philosophy. This requires the recovery of the Latin and humanist ways of thinking and philosophizing that are tied to rhetoric and poetry and to forms of civil wisdom. The center of this is historical Italy, even though humanism is also part of the Renaissance of northern Europe in the works of such thinkers as Nicholas of Cusa and Juan Luis Vives. Vives, although Spanish by birth, spent his career in the north, as a friend of Thomas More and Erasmus. The tradition of humanism displays an interest in logic as the counterpart of rhetoric and in metaphysics as a counterpart to morals.

The threshold for reentering this tradition is the work of Vico. Vico is the summary figure of this way of philosophizing. Paul Hazard wrote, in *La pensée européenne au XVIIIe siècle:* "If only Italy had lent an ear to Giambattista Vico, and if, as at the time of the Renaissance, she had served as the guide to Europe, would not our intellectual destiny have been different? Our eighteenth-century ancestors would not have believed that all that was clear was true; but on the contrary that 'clarity is the vice of human reason rather than its virtue,' because a clear idea is a finished idea. They would not have believed that reason was our first faculty, but on the contrary that imagination was."

The sources from which we can form a new philosophical world in the face of what has become rote and fatigued are accessible through Vico. These sources have within them highly developed understandings of the nature of language, politics and morals, the reading of texts, imagination and perception, mind and metaphor. These are topics of interest to both the Anglo-American and the Continental approaches. But this humanist tradition cannot simply be integrated with these approaches. The insights and understandings in this tradition require a new framework of thought, new starting points in relation to knowledge, the human, and the world. To be of real value they must be approached on their own terms, not simply familiarized into other positions. My views in this book are in the spirit of this Latin and humanist tradition, from what I know of it and from what I can carry of it into the interpretation of later thinkers, such as Hegel.

There is an old principle that to say what a thing is, is to say what it is and what it is not. When philosophy loses its way it ceases to speculate and enters the night of critical thinking. It forgets the *ars topica* and fascinates itself with the *ars critica*. The philosopher wishing to return to first philosophy must begin with the nature of the current time and say what it is and what it is not. To do this philosophy must set itself off from its own time by discovering what of itself has been lost in the erosive course of history. Whether virtue and the real can once again be seen by the philosophical eye apart from the immersion of philosophy in the modern attachment to technological society and method is an open question. "Eyes and ears," Heraclitus says, "are bad witnesses for persons with barbarian souls."

Philosophy might be revived among friends, those who wish once again to cultivate the soul. Philosophy should be a human rather than simply a professional enterprise. I wish philosophy to maintain its connection with the humanities, with the liberal arts. The work that follows is constructed as an essay with several parts. The approach I have taken may be described as philosophical-literary. In this I am indebted to the father of the essay, Montaigne. There is a tendency today to present philosophical ideas only in the form of argumentation, as if this would assure their truth. But for every argument conceived there is a conceivable counterargument. Arguments are the natural stock in trade of the philosophical mind. No philosopher can afford to be a misologist. All arguments require a context in which to occur. Logic never provides its own starting points. The philosopher cannot proceed as does Descartes' speaker of *bas breton*, who has no need of eloquence.

The context for thought is supplied by the language of the narrative, the rhetorical forms of the oration, and the tropes of poetry. The philosopher must look to these modes of expression as the means to open up the paths that argument can follow. *Argument*, in its meaning as derived from Latin, is a theme set out for thought. The deductive ideal of argument, which is never perfectly employed in metaphysical or moral philosophy, nor need it be, is only one way in which the mind can follow a theme. The important thing in philosophical thinking is that words are used in the service of truth, that there is an attempt to speak the truth on a subject. Simply putting thought into one form or another will not guarantee this. My ideal in philosophy is not the attack and defense of ideas but *pensare insieme*, to think together with others concerning the truth of ideas.

Collingwood is right when he holds in his *Autobiography* that philosophy is essentially questions and answers. We may add to this that the philosopher also requires metaphors and the

Socratic likely story to forge starting points for thought and to point to aspects of the subject that cannot fully be captured discursively. Whitehead in *Process and Reality* says: "In the real world it is more important that a proposition be interesting than that it be true. The importance of truth is, that it adds to interest." There comes a time not to be the interpreter, not to think about the philosophers' doctrines, but to think about what the philosophers thought about. This is an attempt to get to the inner form of ideas. For this there is no formula. It requires us simply to use whatever ingenuity we have. What is interesting has the promise at least of taking us toward the true. My aim has been to write a book that is a pleasure to read and that engages the reader in new perspectives for further thought.

This book is divided into two parts, the historical and the human. The two-part division is intended to indicate emphasis, not hard and fast categories into which the subject matter is separated. The human does not exist apart from the historical, but the human is more than the historical conditions of its existence. The human is more than history.

The first pair of chapters focuses on two historical developments involving the production of the modern world: reflection and folly. Reflection, as an act through which the mind defines itself, has shaped modern thought and society from the seventeenth century to our own day. The experience of reflection as an optical property is a universal human phenomenon, but as a fundamental term applied to the mind's activity it is uniquely modern. Folly rises up in the late Middle Ages and dies out in the sixteenth century, when its valuable picture of the human is lost. Folly and the fool are universal phenomena. My concern is with the consequences of their disappearance as an active force in modern consciousness and the reduction of the speculative impulse that is connected to this aspect of the self.

The second pair of chapters focuses on two elements of the

human: desire and memory. As mentioned above, by the word *desire* I mean the specific sense of the passion of the self to prove its own worth and reality by the domination of all that is other. The self desires to put all that there is at its own disposal. Memory is the master key to fulfilling the ancient aim of self-knowledge. The schools of modern philosophy have abandoned both memory and self-knowledge, and in so doing they have abandoned the love of wisdom. I wish to revive the humanist's love of memory and self so that it may act as a charm against the modernist's love of the object.

The themes of this work go back many years, to my conversations over nearly a decade and a half with the great humanist Ernesto Grassi (1902-91) at his villa on the island of Ischia, near Naples, and to the many sessions of the *Zürcher Gesprache* (1977-), or Zurich conversations, which Grassi created with the aim of reviving a *sensus communis* among thinkers of diverse fields and backgrounds. My view of Renaissance humanism as philosophical derives from Vico and from Grassi.

Much of Grassi's position is summed up in *Rhetoric as Philosophy: The Humanist Tradition* (1980). It is an approach different from that of Cassirer or Paul Oskar Kristeller. Cassirer's *The Individual and the Cosmos in Renaissance Philosophy* is a classic text for anyone interested in the subject. Kristeller's work is of the greatest importance and has been the basis for a generation or more of Renaissance scholars. I have also benefited greatly from the unequalled scholarly work on humanism of Eugenio Garin and from the works of Paolo Rossi. My approach to the humanist tradition is highly selective, focusing often on Platonic and neo-Platonic ideas and on a concern with the connections among rhetoric, poetic, and philosophy. My use of the term *humanist* throughout is normative, not historically descriptive.

My writing of this work was supported in part by the University Research Committee of Emory University and by a sabbatical leave during the 1995–96 academic year. I thank those colleagues who are friends of philosophy and with whom I have enjoyed that part of the great conversation given to us by the Muses. When the Muses are invoked they relieve the mind of all care. Those students who have found a home in the library of the Institute for Vico Studies at Emory and who have participated in its discussions have heard many of these ideas. If they have benefited from these in any way or have at least been done no harm by them, I am thankful. I am happy for the ears they have lent me.

This book has its own odyssey. I began thinking about it in 1988 while I was visiting fellow at Pembroke College, Oxford University. I began writing it during the spring semester of 1994 while directing a seminar on barbarism, rhetoric, and memory at the Folger Library and Institute in Washington, D.C. In May 1994 I presented some of these ideas in a course of lectures on Vico and the modern world at the Istituto Italiano per gli Studi Filosofici in Naples. I continued work while teaching a seminar on Vico, Descartes, and autobiographical knowledge during a visiting appointment in the Department of Italian Studies at the University of Toronto in the summer of 1994.

The first chapter and the epilogue were presented on two occasions at Yale University, in the fall of 1994 and the spring of 1996. Many of the ideas discussed here were the themes of my seminar on art and truth, taught at Emory during the spring semester of 1995. The book has benefited greatly from the library of the Warburg Institute in London during the summer of 1995 and from my time on visiting appointment at the University of Rome "La Sapienza" in the spring of 1996.

I thank Andrea Battistini, Thora Bayer, Nancy du Bois, James Gouinlock, Dan Harrell, Ann Hartle, Donald Livingston, David Lovekin, Marco Olivetti, Carl Page, and David Parry for reading the whole manuscript, chapter by chapter. I am honored to have such helpful readers. I thank Carl Page for the many fine conversations we had while I was writing this work. For her generous hospitality in London, I thank my good friend and former student Jean Arundale. I thank, finally, Molly Black Verene, bibliographer, mistress of the Institute for Vico Studies, and companion to the text.

Philosophy and the Return to Self-Knowledge

Introduction: Prometheus and Descartes

> Prometheus or the Promise of Provision
> —James Joyce, *Finnegans Wake*

Cicero in the *Tusculan Disputations* asks, "Can we scorn pain, seeing that we find the mighty Hercules bear it so impatiently?" (II. 22). His reference is to Hercules' call for the "gleaming thunderbolt" to release him from his final torments, as portrayed in the *Trachiniae* of Sophocles. To answer this question, Cicero says, "Let Aeschylus come forward, not merely a poet but a Pythagorean as well, for we are told he was; how does Prometheus in Aeschylus's play bear the pain which he suffers for the theft of Lemnos!" (II. 23).

Cicero then quotes lines from Aeschylus's play. They remind us of the ancient myth: Prometheus, one of the Titans, stole fire from Vulcan's island of Lemnos and gave it as a gift to the race of humans. Zeus in his anger bound him to a rock in the Caucasus. Daily an eagle gnawed Prometheus's liver, and every night it grew again, in a continuous cycle. "For age-long centuries massed in stern array / This dolorous doom is fastened on my body." Prometheus can see no end to this vital pain, yet his name means "foresight." Cicero concludes, "We seem then scarcely able to say that one so afflicted was not wretched, and if we pronounce him wretched assuredly we admit that pain is an evil" (II. 25). Cicero says that pain is an evil in that it is among those things that are unpleasant and unnatural. But he asserts that pain, although an evil, is not a great evil and can be "eclipsed by virtue." When pain is enduring and unbearable, death provides an ultimate refuge (II. 66-67).

Myths are the language of the passions. They form what is innermost in the human condition. Regardless of how we understand the meaning of the Prometheus myth, we are impressed with its portrait of intense suffering and pain. Prometheus is bound to the rock as Ahab later is bound by his own harpoon rope to the whale in Melville's *Moby-Dick*. Ahab's suffering is mortal, since he will be drowned. Prometheus will not be provided with the ready refuge of which Cicero speaks; since he is a god he will never die.

We live in a Promethean age in which our mastery of method and technical process seems to give us the power of the gods. The gift we have to control the conditions of our life has not come directly from Prometheus. It has come from Descartes, who has passed the fire taken from the gods on to the modern world in a particular way. To understand who we are as moderns requires us to understand Descartes. We must approach Descartes not simply as the author of certain philosophical arguments and ideas but as a cultural figure, an embodiment or symbol of the paradoxes of modern society in the way that Prometheus is an embodiment of the paradoxes of ancient society and the beginning of human society itself.

Who is Descartes? He is the modern Prometheus, who supplies fire in the form of method. To know who Descartes is we must know who Prometheus is. Who is Prometheus? Everyone has in mind the essentials of the Prometheus myth, which can be expressed in several sentences, but there are many complexities in the figure of Prometheus as it exists and influences Western consciousness. These complexities have some precise parallels with what can be called the myth of Descartes, the myth Descartes made of himself and that has been actively taken up in modern thought. Understanding Cartesianism as a form of Prometheanism is a guide for the analysis of modernity.

Prometheus the Bringer of Fire

Any myth can take the mind to the *archai* of consciousness that guide it at any moment. The version of the Prometheus myth that shows us its greatest truth for modern life is portrayed in Rousseau's frontispiece to the *First Discourse*. This engraving is Rousseau's own picture of the question of the Academy of Dijon, to which his *Discourse* is a response: "Has the restoration of the sciences and arts tended to purify morals?"[1] In the center of the scene stands a nude young man with his right arm outstretched at a downward angle. His right hand is open as if to accept the burning torch that Prometheus, in his descent from the heavens, is offering him. Prometheus, hovering slightly above the ground in a trail of clouds on the man's right side, holds the torch above and in front of the man's head so the man can gaze upon it before it is placed in his open palm.

On the left side stands a satyr, with beard, horns, hairy thighs, and cloven hooves, waving an arm above his head and pushing his way into the scene, his eyes fixed intently on the torch. The human figure stands passively in the middle, between the god Prometheus and the half-human, half-beast figure of the satyr. The human stands willing to receive the flaming fennel stalk. The satyr is rushing to grab it or at least to participate in the event.

Below the engraving Rousseau places the words: "Satyr, you do not know it." Rousseau begins the second half of the *First Discourse* with the sentence: "It was an ancient tradition, passed from Egypt to Greece, that a god who was hostile to the tranquility of mankind was the inventor of the sciences."[2] Rousseau adds to this a footnote relating Prometheus to the Egyptian god Thoth as the source of mankind's inventions. He then elaborates the motto of the frontispiece: "'The satyr,' an ancient fable relates, 'wanted to kiss and embrace fire the first time he saw it; but Prometheus cried out to him: Satyr, you will mourn the beard on your chin, for fire burns when one touches it.' This is the subject of the frontispiece."[3] Rousseau is quoting almost word for word from Plutarch's *Moralia* (II. 2). Rousseau's motto "Satyre, tu ne le connois pas" refers to a line Plutarch quotes from Aeschylus: "You, goat, will mourn your vanished beard" (*Prometheus Pyrphoros;* compare Nauck, *Trag. Graec. Frag.*, Aeschylus, no. 207).

There are no satyrs in the play by Aeschylus that has survived: *Prometheus Bound* (*Prometheus Desmotes*). This play was likely the second in a tetralogy. *Prometheus Bound,* portraying Prometheus bound to the rock in the Caucasus, disclosed the state of affairs under Zeus that was set in motion by events in a first play—*Prometheus the Fire-Bringer* (*Prometheus Pyrphoros*)—which portrayed how Prometheus committed the theft of fire itself. A third play, which Cicero quotes in the *Tusculan Disputations,* was *Prometheus Delivered* (*Prometheus Lyomenos*), which had a chorus of Titans. The fourth play, a satyr play —*Prometheus the Fire-Kindler* (*Prometheus Pyrkaeus*)—had a chorus of satyrs and concerned Prometheus showing the satyrs, as first men, how to kindle fire.[4] Its theme was reflected in fifth-century Greek vase paintings, in which satyrs with torches are shown dancing around Prometheus. Satyrs and men had to learn how to handle fire, for satyrs, nymphs, and men inhabit a common world.

In a response to his critic Claude-Nicolas Le Cat, Rousseau explains the frontispiece in terms of three factors: the torch of Prometheus is that of the sciences, formed to animate great geniuses; the satyr is the vulgar man who is fascinated by the brilliance of letters and who would pursue study thoughtlessly; and Prometheus, who cries out to them a warning of the danger, is the "Citizen of Geneva."[5] Rousseau claims Prometheus is himself, at least insofar as he is the author of the *First Discourse,* since its title page states it is written "by a Citizen of Geneva." Rousseau says that this allegory is just, beautiful, and sublime. He asks what we should think of a writer who, having meditated on it, cannot attain an understanding of it. Le Cat is not too bright, and Rousseau has given him a clever answer.

Left open in Rousseau's comment is the question of the identity of the human figure in the center of the engraving. An unstated text in Rousseau's frontispiece is the Prometheus fable of Plato's *Protagoras* (320D-322A). As told there, the gods decided to make all mortal creatures out of earth, fire, and the "substances which are compounded from earth and fire." When all the creatures of the world were so fashioned, the gods charged Prometheus and his brother Epimetheus with allotting to each type of creature the proper powers it needed to survive. Epimetheus begged Prometheus to allow him to do this distribution himself. He bestowed the proper powers on each creature, but not being truly clever, he forgot to provide for the human race.

At the last minute, just as the creatures were to emerge from the earth into daylight, Prometheus saw that the other creatures were well provided for but found man "naked, unshod, unbedded, and unarmed." Prometheus stole from Hephaestus (Vulcan) and Athena the "gift of skill in the arts, together with fire and bestowed it on man; without fire it was impossible for anyone to possess or use this skill. In this way man acquired sufficient resources to keep himself alive, but had no political wisdom" (321D).

The question in the *Protagoras,* left unsettled at its end, is whether virtue can be taught. Castiglione in the *Book of the*

Courtier retells the *Protagoras* fable of Prometheus, saying that Jove took "pity on the wretchedness of mankind" and sent Mercury down to earth "bearing justice and self-respect to adorn their cities and unite the citizens." Mankind was wretched because of the lack of civic virtue. Jove ordained civic virtue should be instilled in every person and that "all those who were unjust and shameless should be exterminated and put to death as public menaces." Castiglione concludes that civic virtues are "granted to men by God, and cannot be learned since they come from Nature."[6] Giulio Camillo relates the story in the same way in his *L'idea del theatro*, adding to Prometheus's gift the arts of political wisdom, given by Jove. Camillo attributes to Prometheus "all the arts, both noble and vile."[7] He does not make Prometheus simply a friend of mankind.

Boccaccio, in his *Genealogia deorum gentilium*, distinguishes three categories of men: *homo naturalis*, *homo civilis*, and *homo doctus*. Prometheus for Boccaccio is *homo doctus*, who educates *homo naturalis* in both science and virtue in order to transform him fully into *homo civilis*.[8] To do this the sage must command the spark of the divine wisdom that only God himself has. God, or what Castiglione calls Nature, is the source of virtue. Prometheus is double. Prometheus is God and the image of himself as *homo sapiens*. Plutarch in *De fortuna* equates Prometheus with human reason (*Moralia* II. 3.98C).

Ficino identifies the fire of Prometheus with human reason. For Ficino, the gnawing by the eagle on Prometheus's liver symbolizes the constant torment of inquiry that is required for the practice of human reason. This torment of inquiry can be relieved and the human unchained from inquiry only when terrestrial reason is joined back to the light of celestial reason, and Prometheus, or man, "will then be entirely filled with the whole light."[9] Ficino held that "the law of living well and happily was granted by Jove, that is by divine providence, through Mercury, which is angelic inspiration."[10]

In *De sapientia veterum,* in his description of Prometheus, Bacon says, "The chief aim of the parable appears to be, that Man, if we look to final causes, may be regarded as the centre of the world."[11] Rousseau's use of the frontispiece follows Bacon's understanding, in *De augmentis scientiarum,* that an emblem is a concept made as an image ("Emblema vero deducit intellectuale ad sensibile").[12] Man is in the center of the engraving and is flanked by his two doubles, the god Prometheus, *homo doctus,* and the satyr, *homo naturalis,* the vulgar seeker of the brilliance of doctrine. Prometheus, the citizen of Geneva, imparts civil wisdom to the nude young man, but indirectly, for he speaks directly only to the satyr. The man only overhears the god-citizen give his warning. In his footnote to the text Rousseau gives the further meaning: fire not only burns but is the source of warmth and light and is the instrument of all crafts, providing one knows how to use it well.

Rousseau's listener, who moves from the emblem to the footnote, still has only part of the meaning. He must listen even further. We must go to the sentence in Plutarch that follows the one paraphrased by Rousseau. Plutarch's tract, in which the warning occurs, is "How to Profit by One's Enemies." In the sentence following the one Rousseau paraphrased, Plutarch says, "So look at your enemy, and see whether, in spite of his being in most respects harmful and difficult to manage, he does not in some way or other afford you means of getting hold of him and of using him as you can use no one else, and so can be of profit to you" (*Moralia* II. 2).

We must look back to Aeschylus, to his now lost satyr play, the theme of which is *Prometheus Pyrkaeus,* in which the Titan warns the satyr and men in the use of fire, the art of the forge and the smith. In the lost satyr play Prometheus is the revered kindler of fire. In the general tradition of the myth, Prometheus is freed from his bonds by Hercules, who kills the eagle with an arrow (see, for example, Apollodorus, *Lib.* II. 5.11), but the conditions of his liberation are set up while he remains bound to the rock in the Caucasus in *Prometheus Desmotes.* He knows from his mother something that Zeus desires greatly to know: Zeus may make a marriage that, unknown to him, will produce a son who will successfully rise up against him. With this foreknowledge Prometheus can turn Zeus's unbridled will into a power against him. Zeus's dedication to power affords Prometheus a means to get a hold on Zeus as his enemy and to use him, as no one else can, to be released from his bondage.

What is to guide the conversion of the power of one's enemy to one's own profit? Prometheus's arts are both "noble and vile." The proper guide of power is virtue, but virtue as described in the *Protagoras* is another gift, one given by Zeus to men out of pity for their failure to overcome the wretchedness of their civil conditions, caused by using, without political wisdom, the arts based in the Promethean fire. At the end of the dialogue Socrates says to Protagoras that he would like to return to the question of whether virtue can be taught, but in so doing to guard against the possibility that Epimetheus might disturb the inquiry with his bungling. Socrates concludes, "I liked Prometheus in the myth better than Epimetheus; so I follow his lead and spend my time on these matters as a means of taking forethought for my whole life" (361D). Socrates prefers Prometheus, or the promise of provision in the sense of prudence, because the very name *Prometheus* means "he who knows in advance, who provides." *Phronēsis,* or *prudentia,* and its synonym *providentia* are the basis of civil wisdom.

Rousseau's frontispiece shows us the original Greek Prometheus as *pyrphoros,* the thief of fire and originator of sacri-

Prometheus among the satyrs. Scene from the Feuardent calyx crater. From Tischbein, *Hamilton Vases*.

fice, joined to the Renaissance humanist and Neoplatonic idea of *sapiens Prometheus,* the allegorical figure of the human soul struggling for wisdom and virtue. Hesiod in the *Theogony* and in *Works and Days* sees Prometheus as introducing work into what had been the paradise of human life (a parallel of the Adamic myth). Rousseau says Prometheus was "hostile to the tranquility of mankind," thus transferring to Prometheus what was traditionally attributed to Zeus. Work makes man responsible for his own condition. Work requires forethought, provision. The arts and sciences, for which fire is necessary, provide man with a means of anticipating his needs in changing conditions.

Hesiod also presents Prometheus as the originator of sacrifice. He tells a story of Prometheus tricking Zeus, not only in the theft of fire but also in offering to Zeus an ox he had killed, having given the meat and entrails of the ox to man for his enjoyment. Prometheus filled the spaces between the bones with white fat and covered the ox with its hide. Zeus accepted the altered carcass and for the moment withheld his anger at this impiety. Pliny says, "Hyperbius son of Mars first killed an animal, Prometheus an ox" (*Nat. Hist.* VII. 209).

Why is the liver the organ of Prometheus's torment? Freud asks this question and concludes that it is because the liver is the seat of the passions and desires: "Hence a punishment like that of Prometheus was the right one for a criminal driven by instinct, who had committed an offense at the prompting of evil desires."[13] Besides the fact that for the ancients the liver was an especially sacred vital organ, I would add that Prometheus's trick with the ox may have been the basis for Zeus's choice to have the eagle gnaw on Prometheus's liver rather than another organ.

Aristotle says, "The liver of a man is round-shaped, and resembles that of the ox. This occurs in the case of sacrificial animals too" (*Hist. of Animals* 496b, 22-24). Aristotle regards the liver of other creatures as irregularly shaped and unlike the human liver. He also says that "no one could ever deem the liver to be the primary organ either of the whole body or of the blood" (*Parts of Animals* 666a, 25-26). The heart is more vital than the liver, but the liver is the organ used for divination—hence its power to symbolize the essence of Prometheus, "provision."

Hegel comments that Prometheus taught man not only the art of sacrifice but also to eat meat: "So it was Prometheus who taught the human race to eat meat, as well as endowing it with other arts."[14] But Hegel remarks, with Plato, that Prometheus taught no laws or ethical norms. The theft by Prometheus makes man like a god. With fire and the arts and sciences man can manipulate the elements and bring new objects into being, and with fire he can sacrifice creatures to the gods. This gives him the special power of foresight, to take the auguries and to influence the patterns of events. But more than this, man can sacrifice animals for his own use. He can even outwit the gods by offering them the bones and eating the meat himself, in imitation of Prometheus. By receiving as a gift the stolen property of Zeus, man can act like a god.

Hesiod reports that Zeus had withheld fire from the human race because of his anger concerning the trick of the sacrificed ox. After Prometheus stole the fire and gave it to the human race, Zeus ordered Hephaestus to shape clay into the form of a young woman and ordered Athena to dress her in wonderful clothes. Then various of the gods placed plagues on mankind into a container that Zeus gave to the young woman, Pandora ("all gifts"). She was received by Epimetheus, who had forgotten his brother Prometheus's warning not to accept gifts from Zeus. Pandora opened the box, releasing all the evils, but one: *Elpis* (Hope) remained within the box (*Works and Days*, 60–105). Pandora's box becomes the constant reminder to men that they are not gods, because it sets forth the conditions of their own mortality, such as sickness, to which no god is subject.

In the episode with Pandora Epimetheus acts out the meaning of his own name: "he who learns only from the event, the heedless." He is unable to heed the foresight of Prometheus's warning not to receive a gift from Zeus, and only after the release of the evils can he realize the significance of the warning. Hope remains the possession of the gods. The only thing that can offset these calamities is the skill man may have in his pursuit of the arts and sciences. There is no reason to believe that there is any counterforce released in nature to work against these things. Man is left with only his intellect and cunning. Plotinus claims the point in the myth at which Epimetheus should reject the gift of Pandora signifies that a life lived in the intelligible world is the better one. Since Epimetheus is not the maker of Pandora, his relations to her would always be external, and his soul would not be free. The error is in accepting Pandora herself; the evils she bears are only consequences (*Ennead* IV. 3.14).

Once Plato's view is introduced into the Prometheus tradition—that virtue and wisdom are needed to guide the pursuit of the arts and sciences—the humanist conception of the *sapiens Prometheus* is given a basis. In this view, which is glossed by Rousseau, man has not fully understood what Prometheus has taught. The divine spark that man as *homo naturalis* takes up is not all that is present in Prometheus's gift, for it is still divine and can stand for human reason. Man has the power to think like Ulysses—that is, to apply the mind as an instrument to solve problems as they are put before us. The divine spark of human reason has a second power. It can pursue Socratic-Platonic self-knowledge and seek to achieve divine knowledge. It can pursue a knowledge of virtue and the real. Prometheus then becomes our double so that, as lovers of wisdom, we stand between the human and the divine order.

A part of the Prometheus tradition that was not unknown to the Greeks (it was generally known, at least in Athens, in the fourth century and later) but that did not capture their imagination was the claim that Prometheus was the actual maker of man. The view of Prometheus as *plasticator* was developed by the Romans, particularly the poets of the Augustan age. Ovid in the *Metamorphoses* says Prometheus mixed earth and water to make man (1. 80-85). Horace says that in making man Prometheus was forced to incorporate a portion of every creature (*Odes* I. 16). Propertius says, "The making of man's reason he performed with too little care" (*Eleg.* III. 5.7), meaning that man is not made naturally wise in the conduct of his affairs. Apollodorus says, "Prometheus moulded men out of water and earth and gave them also fire, which unknown to Zeus, he had hidden in a stalk of fennel" (*Lib.* I. 7.1).

The image of Prometheus as *plasticator* is easily merged rhetorically with Prometheus as *Pyrphoros*, for by making man from the elements Prometheus becomes not simply the bringer of the divine spark to man but the demiurge that places the spark within man. This tradition of the myth is employed by Mary Shelley in *Frankenstein, or The Modern Prometheus*.[15] Her work runs significantly counter to the romantic conception of Prometheus as the ideal of the rebellious, suffering artist, as found in the poetry of Byron, Keats, Elizabeth Barrett Browning, Goethe's *Prometheus* fragment, and Percy Bysshe Shelley's *Prometheus Unbound*.[16]

The Sturm und Drang Prometheus gives no answer to the Cartesian world, nor does Nietzsche's philosophical romanticism of the Dionysian Prometheus in the *Birth of Tragedy*, who has the role of the rebellious, striving individual. Nietzsche, quoting from Goethe's early poem *Prometheus*, in which Prometheus is found defiantly making men in his own image, says, "Man, rising to Titanic stature, fights for his own culture and compels allegiance from the gods, because in his very own wisdom he has their existence and their limitations under his command."[17] The rebellious, suffering creator dismisses himself from the realities of science, as does romanticism. The romantic knows that feeling and the passions have been dealt a blow in the formation of the modern world, but instead of seeking to recover the basis of self-knowledge in the humanist modes of thought that have been abandoned, the romantic substitutes self-indulgence, introspection, and a love of nature for the quest to recover civil wisdom. Mary Shelley's "modern Prometheus" challenges this.

The romantics regard Prometheus as an image of creativity that is imaginative and ideal, but Mary Shelley transfers this to science, which is immediate and actual. She thinks the divine spark may be electricity. Man is not simply the receiver of the stolen gift, nor is his nature made by the divine spark having been placed in him by Prometheus. Man is Prometheus. Man himself can steal the divine spark from the heavens. Kant called

Benjamin Franklin the "Prometheus of the modern age."[18] In the Cartesian world Prometheus can only be linked to science. Marx is quick to do this in his economic "science." In *Capital* Marx says that the condition of the laborer grows worse in proportion to the accumulation of capital, and this "rivets the labourer to capital more firmly than the wedges [*die Keile*] of Vulcan did Prometheus to the rock."[19] This leaves no doubt as to the Promethean meaning of the famous line in *The Communist Manifesto:* "The proletarians have nothing to lose but their chains."[20] Marx's attachment to the Promethean image was as romantic as anyone's in his age.

As moderns, our relationship to Zeus can be negotiated. Lucian in his *Prometheus* has shown the way. Prometheus pleads his case to Hermes, who can carry it to Zeus. Referring to the trickery with the ox meat, Lucian's Prometheus says it was more of a practical joke. What would divine lives be without some form of deception to make them more interesting? Zeus seems to have overreacted. Of the accusation that he has made man, Prometheus insists that he has done the gods a favor, for men have built cities, beautifying the earth. Their activity has actually been at the service of the gods.

What would the gods have wanted him to do: make men not in their image, but unintelligent and ugly? Besides, the gods are fond of coming to earth and visiting men. Concerning the theft of fire, in Lucian's work Prometheus asks Hermes, "Have we lost any fire since men have had it too?" (18). Men need it to make sacrifices to the gods, which the gods enjoy, so why should the gods be so concerned? In "The Wager of Prometheus," Leopardi, writing in the manner of Lucian, portrays Prometheus as giving up on man after viewing the effects of civilization and discovering that man is the only animal that will kill himself or be driven by despair to kill his children.[21]

Descartes the Bringer of Method

Descartes is the first man of modernity. He is not the first modern man, because the society in which he lives is not modern. Descartes invents modernity in thought by reflecting on the mathematization of nature. Modernity is the result of modern science, and modern science in Descartes' time exists in the thought of its founders, their assistants, and those conceiving of and building machines, locks, clocks, and devices with lenses. Science invades common life one hundred years later, with the use of machines as a means of production.[22] Nicolas Oresme's studies of movement in the fourteenth century and Jacques de Vaucanson's mechanical figures in the eighteenth century (including his marvelous duck, which amazed *philosophes* such as Denis Diderot and Jean Le Rond d'Alembert by its ability to peck corn, grind it in its internal gears, and defecate while they watched) were projects of intellectual curiosity.[23]

With the coming of the machine as a means for production of goods, all had to be interpreted in terms of the machine. Julien Offray de la Mettrie regarded Vaucanson's mechanical flute player and duck as demonstrating that it would not be impossible to make a talking man. He saw in Vaucanson's work the possibility of "un nouveau Prométhée."[24] La Mettrie's *L'homme machine* (1748) confirmed the transformation of common life, already underway, to make the material world our world and to make ourselves part of it. What Descartes could only imagine—that the hats and cloaks he saw in the street might be automata—we experience as actual in the life of the technological society.

The myth of Prometheus is that he begins civilization with the gift of fire. The myth of Descartes is that he begins civilization as we know it with his gift of method. Descartes, as it is said, is the father of modern science and the father of modern philosophy. Descartes is the symbol of the beginning of modern truth. The roots of modernity as a historical concept go back much further.[25] The scholarship on Descartes' works and thought is as large as one could wish.[26] This began during Descartes' lifetime, with *Objections and Replies*. The critical interpretation of Descartes' ideas in the ordinary sense that professional philosophers pursue it today is not my intention. This body of work has its own validity. I am concerned with Descartes as a symbolic form; my interest is in how his shade is present in modern consciousness and is its beginning. Descartes remains the archetypal modern.

Descartes is the bringer of method. Philosophy has always had an abiding interest in method, whether it be dialectical, demonstrative, mathematical, empirical, transcendental, positivistic, or phenomenological. Method is not precisely philosophy, but it holds out to the philosopher the promise of providing philosophy what it desires—the way to employ reason to discover the truth that it seeks. To integrate within one's mind the method that leads to truth is to discover the philosopher's stone. Method is the inner alchemy of philosophy.

Descartes in his first published work is the inventor, in the sense of the finder, of the method that makes science possible. This occurs just at the point when science, having entered history, is about to claim dominion over the human soul and all the earth. Descartes' title declares: *Discourse on the Method of Rightly Conducting One's Reason and Seeking the Truth in the Sciences*. The real product of this method was not what Descartes could show of its power in treating the problems of the essays on meteorology, optics, and geometry that the *Discourse* introduces. The real product of Descartes' method was the self. He made a new man.

Descartes' claim about the "I" is known to everyone, to

the educated and the uneducated. "I think, therefore I am" is the subject of cartoons in which computers print it out. It is stamped as a motto on T-shirts, with a hundred variations— "I [this or that], therefore I am"—each version correctly presuming for its point that the viewer already has in mind the original. Descartes' method is intellectual simplicity itself. We begin with something that is already true, which means something conceived so clearly and distinctly that it is beyond doubt, divide up the difficulties of the subject into as many parts as possible, and then proceed through the problem step by step, from simple to complex. The final step is to check our work. This is what thinking is for the technical researcher. It is the natural working of the mind in technical and scientific problem-solving.

In the *Meditations on First Philosophy* Descartes offers a confirmation of what the reader believes at the beginning: that the I exists, that God exists, and that the world exists. These beliefs, carried by the reader to the text, are brought into doubt and then, by its end, stamped with certainty. The reader feels better about these beliefs; he feels relief. What Descartes offers us in the *Meditations* is the Good Housekeeping seal of approval, the Underwriters Laboratories warranty on electrical appliances, the Monsanto Wear-Dated label guaranteeing the length of carpet life, in full rationalist dress.

As we end the *Meditations* we have not attained any knowledge *per causas* of these three existences, but we are now certain of what we believed. It is what the researchers at Good Housekeeping, Underwriters Laboratories, and Monsanto strive for: to remove what Descartes would call "any occasion of doubt" in the areas of our existence over which they exert control. The ideal of modernity is life stamped with certainty, gone over part by part, and carefully checked. In modernity we experience the reliability of the part and presume, although with some anxiety, that the whole is somehow like that. Descartes' promise of provision is the spread of certainty throughout life. The certainty that can be attached to the existence of the self in thought can now be attached to everything in fact. This is Descartes' gift.

Descartes presents his proof of the "I" as something entirely new. In a letter he wrote at Leiden in November 1640 to Colvius, a clergyman at Dordrecht, Descartes says: "I am obliged to you for calling to my attention the passage of St. Augustine to which my *I think, therefore I am* has some relation. I have been to read it today in the town library, and I find he does truly use it to prove the certainty of our existence."[27] Descartes says he is happy to be in such good company.

Vico, in his work *The Most Ancient Wisdom of the Italians*, finds in the *Amphitryo* of Plautus a less dignified precedent for Descartes' first truth.[28] In Plautus's play (441-47), while Amphitryon, the commander in chief of the Theban army, is away at war, he is cuckolded by Jupiter, who assumes Amphitryon's guise. The guise is so perfect that Alcmena, the wife of Amphitryon, innocently presumes the disguised Jupiter to be her husband. In this comedy of errors, Mercury assumes the guise of Sosia, the slave of Amphitryon. After the prologue, Sosia, now returned with his master from war, discovers his double and begins to doubt his own existence when Mercury, still in his guise as Sosia, tells Sosia that he is mistaken about his identity and that in fact he, Mercury, is Sosia: "Oh, you can have the name when I don't want it; *I'm* Sosia and you're nameless. Now get out!" Sosia then looks into the mirror and develops his "Cartesian" proof, concluding, "But, when I think, indeed I am certain of this, that I am and have always been" (*Sed quom cogito, equidem certo sum ac semper fui*).

If Sosia can do it, anyone can do it. But then that is Descartes' point: *le bon sens* is the most equally distributed com-

Drawing of René Descartes from Lavater's *Essays on Physiognomy*

modity in the world. Everyone is provided with it, and Descartes has provided us with the possession that is written deep within this possession: the proof by perfect good sense of our own existence. We are all Sosia, bumbling and stupid, beset by the doubt that in the total scheme of things there may be an "evil spirit" that determines our reality, that makes us truly nameless. But when we look in the mirror, we in our good sense can say back to ourselves that we know one thing: we are. We can in that moment usurp the claim of Exodus 3:14: "I AM THAT I AM." The human way to say it is "I think, therefore I am." And when I say it, I am Leviathan.

Johann Caspar Lavater, the inventor of physiognomy, regards Descartes as the ideal of the great thinker: "See how the soul of *Descartes* is painted in his physiognomy! It would be impossible to analyze each of the features which compose it, but everyone must feel the beautiful and the great in the whole. What can be more animated than these eyes, or more expressive than this nose? The interval between the eyebrows, indicates a genius accustomed to soar, and who does not stop to dig his subject to the bottom. It is impossible for this man to remain tranquil and solitary."[29] On Descartes' face are literally the contours of truth. His face is the face of truth. Descartes' writing follows the same contours. Lavater says: "The pen of *Descartes* will follow the daring flights of his genius; his style will be all fire and intrepidity."[30] Descartes carries fire in his pen. He is fearless. Hegel reminds us that although "we see from a man's face whether he is in earnest about what he is saying or doing," this is only a sign.[31] The physiognomist overlooks that a face is also a mask.

Descartes' body was a symbol. Elizabeth Haldane remarks that his "head is said to have been large in proportion to his body."[32] When his body was exhumed in 1666 to be returned from Sweden to France, his head was stolen. Descartes' head was sold several times before being rescued and placed in the Musée de l'Homme in Paris. His body is buried with another head in the church of St. Germain-des-Prés. At the exhumation in Sweden, the French ambassador was allowed to cut off the forefinger of Descartes' right hand, and it remains lost, unlike the middle finger of Galileo, which is on display in Florence, greeting the visitor to the Istituto e Museo di Storia della Scienza. These are relics of the saints of modern science.

Descartes says in his private notebooks (1619), "Just as comedians are warned not to allow shame to appear on their brows, and thus put on a mask: so I, about to step upon the theatre of the world, where I have so far been a spectator, come forward in a mask."[33] In the third part of the *Discourse* Descartes says that in the period of nine years he spent roaming the world, he attempted "to be a spectator rather than an actor in all the comedies that are played out there."[34] Descartes' notebook entry fits with his motto, *Bene qui Latuit, bene Vixit*—"He who is well hidden, lives well."

Descartes is the trickster, using the art of the mask in the *theatrum mundi* to pass back and forth from the persona of the actor to the spectator. With his pen of fire he is fearless as the provider of the *mathesis universalis* and the certainty of the *cogito*. He is *Pyrphoros,* and as such he is *plasticator.* From the very elements of thought, *clarté* and *doute,* he makes the first principle of the "I." He is the modern man himself, full of action toward truth. But in the same moment he can pass into the spectator, the ancient role of the philosopher. In the *Discourse,* dedicated to divorcing truth from all forms of history, fable, poetry, and rhetoric, he says that the reader may regard his work "only as a history [*histoire*], or, if you prefer, a fable."[35] In the preface to the *Principles* he tells the reader that his philosophy may be regarded as a *roman*.[36] Descartes, the aggressive bringer of the gift of the right conduct of reason, which eliminates the *ars topica* in favor of exclusive concentration on *ars critica,* quickly dons the mask of the man of humane letters and speaks of his work in terms of the forms of thought he has excluded, which portray it as a spectacle.

At almost every turn in the *Discourse* Descartes passes from asserting the absolute truth and the reasonableness of his claims to saying that these are only his reflections, that each person must decide for himself. He is the actor with the script, and then suddenly he is the spectator with the audience, trying to puzzle things out.[37] The powerful image of his tableau of himself alone, forging out his discovery of the method, is a trick, a mask for the process of thought by which he actually arrived at his conclusions over time, under the influence of the Dutch physician Isaac Beeckman. Descartes' scene of discovery is entirely his own invention, but it becomes the archetype of the modern thinker alone in his study. Descartes joins us as the spectator in his own play as he convinces us of the irrelevance of humane learning to the progress of the sciences and the need for philosophical reasoning performed as a pure act of reason.

Descartes describes his discovery of the method as taking place "dans un poêle." He was in Germany in a house near Ulm, where he had complete leisure to occupy himself with his own thoughts. At the center of the myth of Descartes is the scene where he sits "in a *poêle*." The nature of a *poêle* is never explained well in editions of Descartes. A *poêle* as such is a large, old-fashioned stove of clay bricks and tiles which emits radiant heat from the fire within and which sometimes has an adjoining bench or seat. The French term *poêle* is a synecdoche, used both for the room heated by such a stove and for the stove itself; "pour un Descartes le mot *poêle* 'chambre chauffée' était un mot des patois français de l'Est, qu'il employait, logiquement, de la même 'chose' allemande."[38]

Such a heating device was a German marvel. Fernand Braudel says: "In Germany from the fourteenth century the furnace was built in a lighter material—potters' clay (*Töpferthon*). The earthenware tiles covering it were often decorated. A bench stood in front for sitting or sleeping upon. Erasmus explained (1527): 'In the poêle [that is, in the room it heated] you take off your boots, you put on your shoes, you change your shirt, if you wish; you hang up your clothes, damp from the rain, near the fire and you draw near to dry yourself.'"[39] This is what is depicted in Rembrandt's seventeenth-century etching *La femme devant le poêle*.[40] The woman is seated next to the *poêle*, nude from the waist up and barefoot. Cast-iron stoves appeared in Europe only toward the end of the eighteenth century.

The French were impressed with the *poêle*'s mastery over fire and its excellent heat distribution, which surpassed that of the open fireplaces on which they depended. Descartes wrote a letter to Mersenne on October 20, 1642, discussing in detail his views on the problem of smoking fireplaces, complete with a diagram showing a channel at the rear of the chimney for conducting air down and under the fire to create a draw upward, preventing smoke from spreading into the room. This, Descartes points out, would eliminate the need to open a door or window to get the fire to draw.[41] Montaigne, in his famous essay "Of Experience" (1587–88), writes that he had an argument with a German at Augsburg about the healthiness and comfort of "our fires" (*noz fouyers*) versus "their stoves" (*leurs poyles*).[42] In Montaigne's *Journal de voyage*, it is reported that in Switzerland "Monsieur de Montaigne, who slept in a room with a stove in it [*couchoit dans un poesle*], was very pleased with it and with feeling all night a pleasant and moderate warmth of air. At least you do not burn either your face or your boots, and you are free from the smoke you get in France."[43]

In Ulm, Descartes was probably in a room with such a fire, but his decision to portray the *poêle* as the scene of his discovery is not an accident of his lodgings. He deliberately makes it the central element of his highly drawn fable of himself, and this Prometheus image remains as part of his persona. Descartes achieves the divine spark of right reason seated at the forge of the *poêle*. It is Descartes' version of the *furtum Lemnium*, "the theft of Lemnos" (the island of Lemnos in the Thracian Sea, Vulcan's island).

In Descartes' famous three-dream sequence, which he describes in the *Olympica*, he is awakened within the second dream by a clap of thunder. He opens his eyes to find the room full of sparks, which he gets rid of by blinking several times; then he falls immediately back to sleep. Thunder is always the sign of Zeus. In his fire-dream, at the sign of Zeus, Descartes enters Vulcan's workshop. In psycho-mythological terms, in the crucible of the bedchamber, at the forge of the *poêle*, Descartes is a Master of Fire.[44] He is the alchemist of reason, the *sapiens*

Prometheus who can supply to the sciences the universal element of method that is their inner core and who can supply to metaphysics the perfect certainty of the first principle of the "I think" from which our fundamental beliefs can be proved certain, including those traditionally in the province of theology.

Prometheus steals the fire of the gods and tricks Zeus in the sacrifice of the ox. The trickster is a universal figure in human consciousness, found among the Winnebago Indians as well as the ancient Greeks and in Far Eastern and Semitic cultures.[45] Paul Radin says, "Trickster is at one and the same time creator and destroyer, giver and negator, he who dupes others and who is always duped himself." Radin adds that "trickster possesses no values, moral or social," but that values come into being as a consequence of his actions.[46] Descartes the trickster, the Titan of pure thought, steals the basis of theology and turns it over to the possessors of reason and good sense.

In his letter "to those most learned and distinguished men, the Dean and Doctors of the sacred Faculty of Theology at Paris," Descartes changes the relation between theology and philosophy by which thought had lived throughout the Middle Ages: that "philosophy is the handmaiden of theology." He says, "I have always thought that two topics—namely God and the soul—are prime examples of subjects where demonstrative proofs ought to be given with the aid of philosophy rather than theology."[47] In one sentence Descartes converts the fundamental proposition of the Middle Ages to its opposite. In Descartes' forge theology is the handmaiden of philosophy. Philosophy can now demonstrate by reason what theology can offer only as an interpretation of faith.

Theology is Descartes' enemy, but he turns the power of this enemy to his own advantage, offering to secure the matters of God and the soul for the dean and doctors while carefully replacing their power of theological faith with his rational philosophy. His mastery is stated in an ironic and clever way: "It is of course quite true that we must believe in the existence of God because it is a doctrine of Holy Scripture, and conversely, that we must believe Holy Scripture because it comes from God; for since faith is the gift of God, he who gives us grace to believe other things can also give us grace to believe that he exists. But this argument cannot be put to unbelievers because they would judge it to be circular."[48]

In stealing the power of theology to answer the unbeliever, Descartes draws close to the dean and doctors of the faculty of theology and whispers in their ears, "You know and I know that theological thought is more than logic." At the same time he says to the world, through reference to the unbeliever, that all theology has ever produced is a fallacy to be learned in the first lesson of the study of logic: *petitio principii*, an example of which is that we know God exists because it says so in the Bible; we know what the Bible says is true because it is the word of God. Faith is the gift of God. Rational *clarté* is the gift of Descartes. Descartes is the bringer of light. The master metaphor of light, illumination, dominates modernity and its epistemologies. The *lumière naturelle*, the light of nature, is that by which fundamental and certain truths can be seen. Reason loves light; it is the divine spark within the soul. The biblical God releases light upon the world. Reason now can perform this task.

We do not know from Descartes how he comes to his great discovery, only that it was forged in the crucible of the stove-heated room. Miguel de Unamuno regards Descartes as the stove-philosopher and calls his discourse a "stove-discourse" (*discurso de estufa*).[49] But we know that the discourse of the stove-man is potentially divine because it can handle the divine questions and it can defeat the possibility of an anti-God, the evil genius that we could imagine as "not God, who is supremely good and the source of truth, but rather some malicious demon of the utmost power and cunning."[50] Descartes' philosophy can banish such a possible being; it can perform the divine work of providing us with the promise of banning all error and evil from our experience, and can satisfy the desire for certainty that Descartes has induced.

Descartes' gift of a universal method for the sciences faces the difficulty stated in the myth of Prometheus in Plato's *Protagoras:* whether Descartes, like Prometheus, has failed to supply the modern age with civil wisdom. In the preface to the *Principles,* Descartes describes his conception of philosophy as a tree: the roots are metaphysics; the trunk, physics; and the branches, all the other sciences, of which medicine, mechanics, and morals are the three principal branches. Of the third principal branch he says, "By 'morals' I understand the highest and most perfect moral system, which presupposes a complete knowledge of the other sciences and is the ultimate level of wisdom."[51]

Descartes' tree is his torch to light up all branches of knowledge. Prometheus's fennel stalk is "fennel giant" (*ferula communis*). It is assigned by Pliny to the "genus" tree. Such a plant, Pliny says, grows in two forms, the largest being the Greek narthex, which "grows to some height" (*Nat. Hist.* XIII. 122-23). The torch of Prometheus is a symbol for the tree of the knowledge of good and evil (Genesis 2:9). In the *Timaeus* Plato says that man is a tree upside down (90A). The tree, or the torch as a flaming tree, is symbolically an intermediate form of man.

Morals is the last degree of wisdom toward which all of Descartes' philosophy is directed. Yet Descartes the actor, pushing forward the play of right reason, never produced such wisdom. The trickster never does. In the *Discourse* he follows his four-step method with four maxims that he says would provide a code of morals for the time being.[52] His method offers the promise of provision in the sense of allowing us to be certain about the basic truths that shape the future. His moral maxims offer provision in the sense of what can serve for the time being.

The other source of morals in Descartes' writings is his letters, principally his correspondence with Princess Elizabeth. Descartes is the stoic *gentilhomme*. He is the perfect thinker of the "Age of the Gentleman."[53] When his various remarks on morals are added up, Descartes has done no more than provide us the views on morals that would be held by the *gentilhomme* of his age. He offers no civil wisdom or profound conception of *moeurs*. He does offer good advice, brilliantly stated. Because he is a great mind, whatever he turns his mind and his pen to is usually stated with insight and style. But Descartes produces no work to equal Hobbes's, Locke's, or Spinoza's writings on citizenship, politics, government, or ethics.

Descartes relies on his brilliance of discovering the right course for the sciences and promises that, if this is fully pursued, morals and civil wisdom will at some point issue forth. In the meantime, Descartes plays the spectator and holds to a fashionable stoical position in the society of his age. In taking this stand Descartes invents what Jacques Ellul will later call the "technological bluff," which is to ask the individual to trust in the ongoing course of the sciences as applied to life and to believe that, in time, human problems will fall into line.[54] An example of this is Descartes' interest in the power of medicine to prolong life, to confront human mortality effectively. Descartes is thoroughly modern in his belief in medicine as a means to diminish the fear of death.

Descartes wrote to Christian Huygens on December 4, 1637, that he was busy composing *Summary of Medicine,* partly from books and partly from his own theories, which he hoped to use to prolong his own life. He says, "I used to think that death might rob me of thirty or forty years at most, it could not now surprise me unless it threatened my hope of living for more than a hundred years."[55] On January 9, 1639, he wrote to Mersenne, "One of the principles of my moral philosophy is to love life without fearing death."[56] If the very method of truth itself has been discovered, why could the body's propensity toward death not be mastered? Descartes, to his own surprise, died at age fifty-four, of pneumonia, at the court of Queen Christina in Sweden. The French abbé Picot, who once lived with Descartes for three months in Holland, wrote "that he would have sworn that it would have been impossible for Descartes to die at the age of fifty-four, as he did; and that, without an external (*étrangère*) and violent cause as that which deranged his 'machine' in Sweden, he would have lived five hundred years!"[57]

Modern man does not have to undertake the Promethean effort of the mastery of medicine that Descartes attempts; the modern can assume medicine and its ability to keep him alive. The modern has a minimal relationship to mortality. Method masters mortality. Method tends to make us fearless, because once we have the instrument to solve all problems by right reason, life can come under an order of certainty, and mortality and the fear of death can be pushed further and further into our future. The problem of our mortality can be given over to the command of medicine.

Cassirer says: "In Goethe's *Prometheus* fragment, Prometheus, as the symbol of mankind, replies to the question, 'How much then is yours?' by answering: 'Whatever space my energies can fill, Nothing more or less!' The circle of human activity appears to be defined in fact by the two opposing poles of 'I' and 'World' and exhausted by the space between them." Man is the owner of what is, and all thought and activity are man's reflection, either on himself or on the world. The transcendent or the beyond plays no role. Cassirer continues: "Mankind cannot be productive except by dividing the whole of being into partial unities, by separating it into thing-configurations and Iconfigurations. As with man's productive efforts, so too his entire concrete, perceptual grasp of the world is bound to these two basic forms and constantly harnessed to them."[58] Modern life is a two-termed relationship. It is a scene of the dominance of the I over itself and over the world, accomplished by right reasoning and right acting.

Bacon speaks of Epimetheus and Prometheus as "pictures or models of human life," of the School of Epimetheus and the School of Prometheus.[59] The followers of the School of Prometheus are "the wise and fore-thoughtful class of men." Bacon says they avoid many evils and misfortunes, but in their efforts of forethought they "wear themselves away with cares and solicitude and inward fears. For being bound to the column of Necessity, they are troubled with innumerable thoughts (which because of their flightiness are represented by the eagle), thoughts which prick and gnaw and corrode the liver: and if at intervals, as in the night, they obtain some little relaxation and quiet of mind, yet new fears and anxieties return presently with the morning."[60] Hobbes would second this, saying that Prometheus is the man who is overcome with prudence: "So that man, which looks too far before him, in the care of future time, hath his heart all the day long, gnawed on by feare of death, poverty, or other calamity; and has no repose, nor pause of his anxiety, but in sleep."[61]

Descartes the prudent man bequeaths his prudence in the rules for the *Direction of the Mind*. These rules are much more than the four-step method of the *Discourse;* they are a full plan for the modern use of the mind and for technological life. In rule 12 he states, "Finally we must make use of all the aids which intellect, imagination, sense-perception, and memory afford in order, firstly, to intuit simple propositions distinctly; secondly, to combine correctly the matters under investigation with what we already know, so that they too may be known; and thirdly, to find out what things should be compared with each other so that we make the most thorough use of all our human powers."[62] This is modern prudence, the faculties all pulling together to solve a problem. But the perfection of it creates anxiety. It is the anxiety that the true is the whole. Everything is determined in its specifics, but what is the truth of the process itself? Modernity is a science of prudent work to control the factors of human existence, coupled with the anxiety as to whether it is enough. Along the way some pleasures are enjoyed.

Hand in hand with this is the School of Epimetheus, the school of afterthought that can proceed only from the event. Bacon says, "The followers of Epimetheus are improvident, who take no care for the future but think only of what is pleasant at the time."[63] He says because of their ignorance of the future they engage in many empty hopes, and they experience a perpetual struggle with things they do not understand. In the meantime they indulge their genius and take as much delight in life as possible. Epimetheus is heedless because he does not remember Prometheus's warning not to accept a gift from Zeus, so he accepts Pandora and releases from her box all the calamities and miseries now known to man. Carl Kerényi says: "The profound affinity between these two figures is expressed in the fact that they are brothers. One might almost say that in them a single primitive being, sly and stupid at once, has been split into a duality."[64]

Method Versus Memory

The children of Descartes, the moderns, the residents of the technological society, are followers of both the School of Prometheus and the School of Epimetheus at once. In the technological society everyone is an anxious optimist. Pessimism is shunned. The technological resident is always striving to release the one last element captured within Pandora's box: hope. All criticism of technique is expected to end in a plan of hope, of what may be done. Even if the hopes are as empty as those engendered by the School of Epimetheus, they must be expressed. Among the children of Descartes optimism reigns, but it is an anxious optimism, an age of anxiety, even of dread. It is anxious because the fire is a theft. Its origin is not whole. It is a fake gift. We have been given something that is not ours, from one who did not own it. We know the thief was punished, but we appear to be free to act the innocent, knowing the true status of the gift to be that it is not a gift but stolen property.

To understand the status of the gift would be to have civil wisdom, the wisdom that Rousseau is trying to put in the warning to the satyr so that it may be overheard by man and may set him on the way to becoming *homo civilis*. Has Rousseau, the citizen of Geneva who has donned the guise of Prometheus, delivered the torch of civil wisdom in his discourse? Has Rousseau taken pity on man's wretched condition? The Promethean picture of human existence is carried into the beginning of the *Social Contract*, in the famous claim that "man is born free and everywhere he is in chains." Born in a paradise state, man offends Zeus, and, by accepting the gift of Prometheus, he finds himself in the Promethean state.

For Rousseau, civil wisdom does not follow directly from the exercise of reason. It rests on the passions and on a grasp of the origins of man's condition in the history of culture. The philosopher who attempts to impart this wisdom is involved with a theft of the gods. Zeus does not give political wisdom freely, and many tricks must be played on language in order for us to kindle the live spark and see clearly to the heavens. The Promethean *homo doctus* is a threat to the polis that has simply accepted the gift of fire and made it the technique of its existence. The philosopher is "hostile to the tranquility of mankind."

The acquisition of fire was a crime. In this crime the gods were defrauded of a power that only they should have. Man must renounce the satisfaction of desires that the gods need not renounce. The human world of culture is made of the arts and sciences, but the basis of this making is not simply an imitation of the power of the gods. It is based in control of what only the gods rightfully control. Modern man cannot accept that there is no way to undo this theft or to produce civil wisdom directly from it. Technique cannot become wisdom. Rousseau is an ironic thinker; he knows that there is no rational method by which we can give ourselves the gift a second time, this time involving ourselves in no offense. The conditions of the origin are never overcome.

Rousseau's warning was given even earlier, by Dio Chrysostum, who claims that Zeus punished Prometheus because the gift of fire was the beginning of man's "softness and love of luxury." Dio says: "Man's ingenuity and his contriving so many helps to life had not been altogether advantageous to later generations, since men do not employ their cleverness to promote courage or justice, but to procure pleasure. And so, as they pursue the agreeable at any cost, their life becomes constantly less agreeable and more burdensome; and while they appear to be attending to their own needs, they perish most miserably, just because of excessive care and attention" (*Discourse* VI. 28-29). The drive to luxury ties man to the Caucasus of technological reason as surely as Zeus tied Prometheus to the rock, and the lack of self-knowledge gnaws our liver like an eagle. The voice of the *homo doctus*, of the *sapiens Prometheus*, goes unheard. Reason is used heedlessly in the pursuit of luxury, and looked on at any given moment, man seems the master of his conditions and needs, but looked on as a whole, the features of modern life are wretched and sad.

The modern is like the Prometheus of André Gide's *Prométhée mal enchainé*. Prometheus, becoming uncomfortable on the rock, stretches and frees himself; he descends, to appear incognito in a Paris café. He takes the eagle as a pet and feeds it from his own liver. At one point he gives a lecture maintaining three points: it is necessary to have an eagle; moreover, we all have one; and he allows passion its full play.[65] The eagle is his raison d'être, from which he must free himself. The eagle becomes the entrée of a dinner Prometheus hosts at the café. Gide's tale is based on the claim that there is no public morality; it is a tale of self and other without the existence of civil wisdom.

The liver of Prometheus that is ever destroyed and ever renewed is the image of man in history. The liver is the sacred organ of divination, tying man to the divine order. The liver as sacrificial organ is the means by which man transcends time and reaches the dimension of the eternal and divine. The gift of Prometheus puts man in a new position. Ernesto Grassi says, "In the light of the daily world within which history takes place, the sacred organ that ties man to god disappears in Prometheus's prevision." We are forced, Grassi claims, to answer continually the call of the next thing that presents itself as the future. Man's attempt to reach the eternal over and above history becomes futile. Grassi says, "In contrast to the Platonic conception, we have here a mythical conception of man who, in his constant building of worlds, continuously destroys those that have been built before him, with all the hopes, disappointments, and suffering implicit in this process."[66] Prometheus becomes the symbol of human existence. The spark of the divine fire takes man out of the condition of nature and the gods and places him in time.

Descartes hands us the method for achieving certainty in the sciences, but this certainty is surrounded by the doubt whether we can attain moral wisdom in the process. Moral wisdom requires that we establish a relation with the divine, with what transcends history. Descartes' bluff makes us anxious. The great uncertainty that surrounds the great certainty of "I think, therefore I am" is whether, from this certainty as a beginning point, I can in some way attain self-knowledge. How can the truth of self-knowledge come from the certainty of the self's existence if those forms of reason typified in the pursuits of humane letters are put aside in favor of reason formed solely as method? The modern self oscillates between the imitation of the provision of Prometheus and the heedlessness of Epimetheus, between the attempt to control the future by perfecting the use of method, in an effort to proceed further inside Descartes, and the tenacious attempt to solve the problem before us without forethought.

Missing in the modern and what causes its anxiety is origin. C. G. Jung points out that there is "always a tendency to prepare fire in a mysterious ceremonial manner on special occasions.... The anamnesis of fire-making is on a level with the recollection of the ancestors among primitives and of the gods at a more civilized stage."[67] In handling fire we are in touch with the power of the origin and with the tension between gods and man. On a social level this tension can be managed by ceremony, and on the spiritual level it can be formed through the image or metaphor.

Missing in modernity is the Muse.[68] Hesiod gives us the story not only of Prometheus but also of other offspring of Zeus. After his nine nights with Mnemosyne, or Memory, she gives birth to her nine daughters, the Muses (*Theog.* 1-115). Through trickery Prometheus is the bringer of fire and sacrifice. The Muses are the bringers of *mousikē*, of song. They have the power, Hesiod says, to sing of what was, is, and is to come. As offspring of a Titan, like Prometheus, they too must be carefully understood, for, as Hesiod adds, they can sing both true and false songs but they can sing true songs when they will. What the moderns lack, what Descartes did not give us, is memory.

Memory is forgotten by the modern world as our attempt to release hope points us toward the future. The future for the modern world is the present become more extreme. There is no basis for the preparations for the future except the perfection of method and the talk of choice. The constant talk of choice becomes applied ethics, which masquerades as civil wisdom in the age of anxiety. The Muses bring the gift of their singing, which is the power of Memory, their mother. The poet Giuseppe Ungaretti tells us, with complete clarity, "Tutto, tutto, tutto è memoria" (Everything, everything, everything is memory).[69]

Memory is forgotten in the rush to provision. Provision promises all and yet is itself heedless, for it leaves memory behind. It leaves memory behind in its drive to be forward-looking. To have only the present and the future is to be improvident. Even if the human adds to the gift of fire the gift of political wisdom, the mind is still only an instrument engaged in taking up this problem or that one. Hesiod says that the prince as well as the poet require the Muses, for the Muses make the prince speak with the eloquence needed to rule (*Theog.* 75–103).

Eloquence is to speak fully on a subject, to bring forth the whole of the subject in words. Thus eloquence requires the *ars topica*, the power to go to the original places in the mind where the subject itself begins and bring forth in words the whole of the subject. Eloquence is connected to the art of memory through the *ars topica*. Memory is at the heart of culture, for in memory are the myths, the fables, the tales that hold the conscience of the race together. Culture is in this sense a complete speech, done both in words and in actions on the nature of the human. The human is connected, on the one hand, to provision, on the other, to memory.

The collective name for the Muses is not only *Mousai;* they also were called *Mneiai,* a plural of Mnemosyne. There is a story that the Muses were originally three in number. The names of these three came not from mythology but from the poet's practice. They were called *Mneme,* "remembering"; *Melete,* "practicing"; and *Aoide,* "singing."[70] The poet remembers, imitates, and sings. Remembering and imitating are the preparation for the poet's own song. They are part of the poet's act of making. The poet's song is his own ingenious transformation of what he remembers and imitates. These three functions follow the nature of Mnemosyne herself. Memory has the inner form of remembering, imagining, and perceiving connections (*ingenium*).

The harmonious voice attributed to the later nine Muses must come from this inner harmony of memory, which is the inner harmony required for the poet's making. Over and against the Promethean bringer of method stands the poet, who claims connection to another lineage from Zeus. The art of the poets is there before the art of the philosophers. Both arts have their root in memory. The poets introduce *eikasia*. The philosophers introduce *noēsis*. The mother of both is Mnemosyne. The poet and the philosopher are twins from the beginning.

Memory is the mother of philosophy because the philosopher as well as the prince requires eloquence to govern. The philosopher governs not political actions but thoughts. To govern thoughts the philosopher must speak in a harmonious voice, a voice that only the Muses can inspire and teach. The philosopher does not direct efforts toward the release of hope from the box of Pandora. The philosopher acts against forgetting, against the erosion the present and the future enact on the past.

Time always threatens to take us across the river Lethe. If we think only of the present we reside in the house of Lethe, in the underworld of the here and now. To think we must first remember, because language is not simply an instrument of rational thought but a theater of memory, in which all the human world has been and where it continues to reside.

Language is a harmonious voice, a golden bough that allows us to enter and exit the underworld of the here and now. Like the poet, the philosopher needs the Muses to make language speak. In perfecting method, the Promethean philosopher looks only to the future and attempts to ignore the meanings already present in the memory of language. He is both sly and stupid at once: sly because he tries to act as if words had literal meanings (the meaning he would desire any word to have), stupid because he ignores the fact that each word has a history. For the Promethean, language is an empty stage awaiting logical arrangement. Hope is empty if it is just the speech of the future, a speech that merely clarifies and lays plans.

Memory is not the thought of the past but thought that can connect what was, is, and is to come, that can allow us to be Masters of Time. The modern has fragmented time and can only heed the present and project the future. Claude Lévi-Strauss says that "myth and music are instruments for the obliteration of time."[71] At the basis of the humane studies are both *mythos* and *mousikē*. The followers of the schools of Prometheus and Epimetheus are Masters of Fire. Those who follow the school of the Muses are Masters of Time.

The Muses do not bring hope with them, for it remains forever within Pandora's box, just below the lid. The Muses bring relief from care. They bring the relief of song. When the song of the Muses is taken up into the love of wisdom, it becomes the relief of thought, the peace of the soul that vision provides. Hesiod says: "Fortunate is the man whom the Muses love: sweet words flow from his lips" (*Theog.* 96–97). When the Muses are present, "the gifts of these goddesses instantly direct the mind" (103).

How can philosophy reestablish its relationship to memory and find a place from which to counter its current Promethean-Cartesian form? In the chapters that follow I wish to consider the ways in which commitment to method, reflection, and the Understanding has caused us to forget the powers of speculation, dialectic, and reason, which have a natural bond with memory and with the ancient commitment to self-knowledge. Memory and the power of the Muses to modify the modern dominance of method are the subjects of the final chapter. There I wish to return to another version of the Promethean commonplace, one that generates civil wisdom rather than omits it.

Part I
The Historical

I

Barbarism of Reflection

> Finally, they chased the gods out in order to live in
> the temples themselves.
> —Rousseau

In the conclusion to his *Principles of New Science Concerning the Common Nature of the Nations* (1730, 1744), Giambattista Vico says, "If the peoples are rotting in that ultimate civil disease and cannot agree on a monarch from within, and are not conquered and preserved by better nations from without, then providence for their extreme ill has its extreme remedy at hand."[1] A nation may correct itself or it may be corrected by a better nation. If these remedies do not occur, providence, the eternal order of history itself, will bring the cycle of the nation's life to an end.

"For such peoples," Vico continues, "like so many beasts, have fallen into the custom of each man thinking only of his own private interests and have reached the extreme of delicacy, or better of pride, in which like wild animals they bristle and lash out at the slightest displeasure." They have reached this state of ultimate civil disease through unrestrained passions and become slaves to luxury, effeminacy, envy, pride, and vanity. They are unable to withstand any adversity or displeasure. Each individual is easily offended by anything he does not wish to see or hear.

"Thus no matter how great the throng and press of their bodies, they live like wild beasts in a deep solitude of spirit and will, scarcely any two being able to agree since each follows his own pleasure or caprice." In order for each to follow his own caprice, they have become liars, tricksters, calumniators, thieves, cowards, and pretenders. Assemblies are not societies, and when many bodies come together the solitude of the individual is often the greatest. Cicero says, "Who does not believe that those are more alone who, though in the crowded forum, have no one with whom they care to talk" (*De re pub.* I. 18.28). Spirit and will go to sleep in the crowd, and all that is left is desire and gain.

"By reason of all this, providence decrees that, through obstinate factions and desperate civil wars, they shall turn their cities into forests and the forests into dens and lairs of men." The throngs, driven by their desires and masquerading as society, are human forests, placeless and without virtues or purpose. All nations arise from the forest, and they return to the forest in an eternal cycle of history governed by providence.[2] Providence is just this cycle of rise, maturity, decline, and fall that we find in the life of any nation. When a people declines there is an overgrowth of the self by the passions. The individual becomes a lair of the passions, rather than a force of character directing them.

"In this way, through long centuries of barbarism, rust will consume the misbegotten subtleties of malicious wits [*degl'ingegno maliziosi*] that have turned them into beasts made more inhuman by the barbarism of reflection [*la barbarie della riflessione*] than the first men had been made by the barbarism of sense [*la barbarie del senso*]." The return to barbarism is not simply yielding to the baser passions. It involves a corruption of the highest faculties of the soul—*memoria, fantasia* (imagination), and *ingegno* (wit, ingenuity).[3] In the barbarism of reflection we become beasts of the intellect formed as an instrument of desire. The powers of the mind are put in the service of the passions in order to lie, trick, misrepresent, steal, hide, and deceive. All life becomes politics.

"The barbarism of sense displayed a generous savagery,

against which one could defend oneself or take flight or be on one's guard; but the barbarism of reflection, with a vile savagery, under soft words and embraces, plots against the life and fortune of friends and intimates." The first men are all body and think with their senses. They are motivated by their passions both good and bad, without subtlety. Their savagery is generous because it is evident, and ordinary prudence is what is required to protect oneself from it.

The barbarism of reflection that is typical of the end of a nation's life is like that at the lowest level of Dante's *Inferno* (cantos 30–34). Those who have committed sins of the body or sins of violent greed are not at this level; at this lowest level are those who have violated humanity itself by poisoning the common confidences necessary to human society. They turn their *ingegno* into *insidia*. They live like the *lonza* ("leopard"), the third of the three beasts that impede Dante's way at the beginning of the *Divina commedia*. They are the falsifiers in words and deeds, the corrupters of the social fabric. At this level the social nature of humanity is eroded by fraud, by treacheries against guests and hosts, friends and intimates, and relatives. The barbarians of reflection are the last men, who have turned the intellect into an insidious instrument; they are devoid of virtue and full of desire.

"Peoples who have reached this point of reflective malice [*riflessiva malizia*], when they receive this last remedy of providence and are thereby stunned and brutalized, are sensible no longer of comforts, delicacies, pleasures, and pomp, but only of the sheer necessities of life." Providence or history is the great judge. When a society is infected with reflective malice it cannot sustain itself, and the communal sense that holds a true society together comes apart. It comes as a surprise to the barbarians of reflection to discover they are not the owners of history. Things fall apart quickly. The social fabric unravels rapidly because the weave disintegrated long ago. Social life was a sham held together only by the weakest of conventions which covered the corruption of the times. Suddenly history shows its power to bring this form of society to an end, and the last men are stunned to see their lack of mastery of events.

"The few survivors in the midst of an abundance of the things necessary for life naturally become sociable and, returning to the primitive simplicity of the first world of peoples, are again religious, truthful, and faithful." The primitive simplicity of the return to the first world, the conditions of the nation's birth, jars the soul back toward its natural state of justice. Necessity, as the Spanish humanist Juan Luis Vives emphasizes, is the mother of invention, and life governed by necessity directs *ingenium* toward what is natural to the soul: "The first invention of things comes to the aid of necessity; for necessity wonderfully sharpens ingenuity."[4] The new first men, having been brought to their natural sense of virtue, can begin once again to exercise rightly their faculty of ingenuity. For the last men, ingenuity is a power in itself, directed by nothing and bent simply on furthering its own power to combine and manipulate events. In this way wit becomes malicious.

"Thus," Vico concludes, "providence brings back among them the piety, faith, and truth which are the natural foundations of justice as well as the graces and beauties of the eternal order of God." The reduction to nature makes these last men into first men by reestablishing their own human nature. The absence of pleasure and luxury brings humanity back to a concern with the relation between things human and divine, which is the essence of wisdom. Providence begins to teach its lesson all over again in the form of a *ricorso* of the nation. The nation is now reborn into another cycle.

Machiavelli says in the *Discourses* that all republics are destined to run through such a cycle if they are not conquered from without, although he does not speak of a necessary stage of feral wandering.[5] Such a cycle is in Plato's *Republic* (books 8–9) and in the stages of the development of the state in the *Laws* (book 3, 676A–682E). To know the truth about the human condition we must grasp the connection between decline and rebirth. The perfect motion of the circle is the general motion of human affairs. The civil world is forever round.

The sentences upon which I have commented are Vico's condensed portrait of modern life. I wish to consider how the barbarism of reflection develops within modern thought from the Promethean nature of Descartes' method, that is, the pursuit of method that brings with it control of the object but does not bring with it civil wisdom. *Reflection* is not a term that develops on its own within modern thought but is taken over from the development of modern optics. The barbarism of reflection is not simply a form of modern thought; it is also a life-form involving a conception of the human self and its action in society.

Vico organizes his conclusion to the *New Science*, from which the above sentences are taken, in four paragraphs. These paragraphs follow the division of legal forensics in book 4 of Quintilian's *Institutio oratoria*. In most modern editions of the *New Science* this order is blurred by Fausto Nicolini's division of Vico's conclusion into sixteen numbered paragraphs. Vico's original four paragraphs approximate the four-part structure of an address to the judges of a legal case, who in this instance are his readers: *exordium, statement of facts, proofs*, and *peroration*. The sentences quoted above describing the decline of society are the final sentences of Vico's statement of facts. They are the turning point in his argument before he enters his proofs and peroration; they describe the current state of history in which we moderns find ourselves. We share with Vico a life in corrupt times.

Vico looks at history and never smiles. There is no progress in history.[6] A "nation" is a "birth" (*nazione*, "nation"; *nascere*, "to be born"). Each nation has a beginning, middle, and end; a rise, maturity, and fall. As youth, adulthood, and old age are the universal stages of an individual human life lived through its natural course, so each nation in the world of nations moves through the stages of its life in its own way. Vico calls this life cycle of nations "ideal eternal history" (*storia ideale eterna*). Because each human life and each nation enacts this common pattern of stages in a particular way, the pattern itself is "ideal." The particular history of any human life and the particular history of any nation is never exactly the same as any other. What makes it a human life or a nation's life are the features it holds in common with all other lives or nations. The principles of these commonalities of the world of nations are the subject matter of the philosophical science of history. To discover these principles requires the eye of providence.

The Florentine historian Francesco Guicciardini says in his *Ricordi:* "All that which has been in the past and is at present will be again in the future. But both the names and the appearances of things change, so that he who does not have a good eye will not recognize them. Nor will he know how to grasp a norm of conduct or make a judgment by means of observation."[7] Guicciardini's "good eye," his *buono occhio,* is the key to understanding particular human affairs and to understanding human history. It is the ability to see the commonalities in human events over time. Vico's "new science concerning the common nature of nations" is based on this ability to see the repetition in human events and to formulate their principles.

Vichian history is Stephen's nightmare in *Ulysses,* from which he is trying to awake.[8] In Vico's view, men do not literally make history. Men make history only within the providential order of history, which is given as the cycle of ideal eternal history.[9] The life cycle of any nation passes through an age of gods, in which the world is ordered in terms of gods; an age of heroes, in which virtues necessary to conduct and society are personified; and an age of humans, in which experience is ordered by logical concepts and society is based on written laws.

Ideal eternal history is a divine order, and providence is in this respect the demiurge of the forms of those ages. Providence is the divine cyclical order of history, but the divine itself transcends history and has its own reality beyond the human. History is a melancholic process, and the knowledge of its cycle is a melancholic wisdom. The nightmare of history is to think it could be otherwise, to think that history could progress without end. To live this illusion is as false to real conditions as it is to believe that a human life could continue without end. To believe that a nation is eternal is as monstrous as to believe that all men are not necessarily mortal. The providential cycle is given as a certainty. The Vichian scientist of history sets about discovering the presence of this cycle in the commonalities of those things present in the "languages, customs, and deeds of peoples in war and peace."[10]

In writing to Abbé Esperti in Rome in 1726, regarding the limited reception given to the first version of his *New Science* (1725), Vico says a work such as this cannot expect universal applause because it goes against the corrupt spirit of the times.[11] He plays on a line in which Tacitus criticizes the customs of the Romans in contraposition to those of the barbaric but virtuous Germans (*Germania,* 19). Vico glosses this sentiment of Tacitus in the 1730 and 1744 editions of the *New Science*. He says that Roman emperors, when they wished to give reasons for the ordinances they issued, claimed to have been guided by the "sect of their times" (*setta de' loro tempi*).

Vico says: "The customs of the age are the school of princes, to use the term applied by Tacitus to the decayed sect of his own times, where, he says, *Corrumpere et corrumpi seculum vocatur*—

'They call it the spirit of the age to seduce and be seduced'— or, as we would now say, the fashion."[12] When the intellectual virtues are corrupted into the fashion of witticism and falsity in thought, there is a parallel corruption in social life in which the moral virtues are corrupted into flattery, soft embraces, and plots against intimates and friends. Man as rational animal and man as social animal are corrupted together.

In the 1730 edition of the *New Science*, the following statement appears in the middle of the passage quoted above from Vico's conclusion to the 1744 edition: "Because, unlike in the time of the barbarism of sense, the barbarism of reflection pays attention only to the words and not to the spirit of the laws and regulations; even worse, whatever might have been claimed in these empty sounds of words is believed to be just. In this way the barbarism of reflection claims to recognize and know the just, what the regulations and laws intend, and endeavors to defraud them through the superstition of words."[13] In the 1744 edition this statement is replaced by the observation, quoted above, comparing the generous savagery of the barbarism of sense with the vile savagery of the barbarism of reflection.

In the age of ultimate civil disease, the law, which makes man a social animal, is corrupted into a "superstition of words." The law unconnected to justice becomes a repository of wit. The law can be whatever anyone clever enough with words can convince us it is. This is a world without reason or shame. In his revision of this original statement for the 1744 edition of the *New Science*, Vico moves from simply making a point about the corruption of the law and the willful defrauding of its meaning to a characterization of the corruption of the soul that would be necessary for such fraud.

In the decline of society depicted in both editions, Vico presents modernity in uncompromising terms. Modern life is injustice. Modernity is a state in which the soul has lost the internal proportion of its faculties. The intellect and wit walk the world without natural connections to images formed by the imagination, the passions arising in the body, and the turns of events caused by the gods. The senses and the spirit are indulged but are not involved in life as sources that guide it. The intellect has become perverse, living off its own reality of facts and thoughts, seeing only itself in the world. In society this becomes a quest for certainty and luxury, for strategies of the ego, careers, and means of control and accomplishment. The barbarian within is released through the circuits of critical reflection that run through all forms of thought and evaluate all forms of conduct. It is a joyless business. It is a shallow heart.

How did this barbarism of reflection come about in our time? How is it that the mind's relation to itself came to be understood as "reflection"? How is this characterization of thought connected to the ultimate civil disease, in which the social fabric of laws and language are turned into mere instruments of intellect that upset and defraud the natural order of the soul?

Descartes is the first philosopher of reflection. His *Discourse on Method* (1637) is the historical source in French for the philosophical meaning of *réflexion*.[14] In part 5 of the *Discourse* Descartes uses the phrase "après y avoir fait assez de réflexion" in claiming that certain laws that God has established in nature have also been implanted in our minds: "After adequate reflection we cannot doubt that they are exactly observed in everything which exists or occurs in the world."[15] In his proof for the existence of God in part 4, Descartes employs the term *reflection* in arguing from doubt as part of the proof of his own existence to the existence of God: "reflecting upon the fact that I was doubting" (*faisant réflexion sur ce que je doutais*).[16] Descartes proceeds to present his *Dubito, ergo Deus est*.

In a letter written to Arnauld on July 29, 1648, answering objections raised to some of his views in the *Principles*, Descartes

René Magritte, *L'empire de la réflexion* or *L'empire des miroirs*
(oil on canvas, 1938)

writes: "We make a distinction between direct and reflective thoughts corresponding to the distinction we make between direct and reflective vision, one depending on the first impact of the rays and the other on the second." Descartes says the simple thoughts of infants are direct and not reflective, such as when they have feelings of pain or pleasure originating in the body. Reflection can occur in adults. "But when an adult feels something, and simultaneously perceives that he has not felt it before, I call this second perception *reflection* [*hanc secundam perceptionem reflexionem appello*], and attribute it to the intellect alone, in spite of its being so linked to sensation that the two occur together and appear to be indistinguishable from each other."[17] In this passage Descartes draws the analogy that is the basis of the modern conception of reflection. He compares the reflection of light in perception, the subject of optics, with reflection in the intellect, the subject of mental philosophy.

Reflection is a modern term. There is no cognate term in ancient Greek for the modern sense of *reflection* as a philosophical and psychological term.[18] Image in the sense of *eidolon* or *eikon* and *phantasia*, as a power associated with images, is the subject of discussion in Greek philosophy, as are the physical phenomena of mirrors, the reflection of light, and the visual perception of objects.[19] The Atomists regard visual perception as the reception in the pores of the viewer of an image emitted by the object and having its same shape; the Epicureans regard such shapes as entering into the senses whether a person is awake or asleep.

The figure who leaves Plato's cave for the sun first looks on the world above as shadows, phantoms, and reflections of things in water (*Rep.* 509E). On the divided line the lowest segment is *eikasia*, the perceiving of images and reflections (*Rep.* 509E). In the *Sophist* Plato divides *eidolon* into "likeness" (*eikon*) and "semblance" (*phantasma*) (236A-236B). For Aristotle *phantasia* (imagination) is between *aisthesis* (perceiving) and *noēsis* (thinking). *Phantasia* is a motion of the soul originated by sensation that forms and can retain an image after the dispersal of the sensing (*De an.* 427b-429a). Knowledge involves sight, images, *nous*, the metaphor of light, but there is no term in Greek philosophy for the self-optics of the intellect designated by the modern term *reflection*.

In Latin, *reflectere* occurs as a term among classical authors, carrying meanings of "to bend back" (for example, parts of the body), "to turn around" (for example, to retrace one's steps), "to turn away" (for example, the face or gaze), and "to turn back or reverse" (such as a person, or a person's mind) from a course of action.[20] Cicero in *De oratore* speaks of the need for the orator to develop insight into human nature and motives, "whereby our souls are spurred on or turned back [*quibus mentes aut incitantur, aut reflectuntur*]" (*De orat.* I. 53). In the tenth book of Vergil's *Aeneid*, when Juno is appealing to Jupiter concerning the fate of Turnus, Jupiter suspects that she hopes the whole course of the war may also be altered. He informs her that her hope is idle. Juno departs straightaway, saying, "Thou, who canst, wouldst bend thy purposes to a better end! [*In melius tua, qui potes, orsa reflectas!*]" (X. 632). As a classical Latin term, *reflectere* carries no meaning of the mind thinking itself.

The philosophical meaning of *reflection* enters modern languages from late Latin. *Reflexio* is not used in the sense of "self-knowledge" prior to the thirteenth century.[21] In his psychology Roger Bacon refers to the power of the intellect to reflect on the contents of consciousness.[22] In his optics, the fifth part of his *Opus majus*, Bacon describes the effects of the reflection and refraction of light and of color on vision. He considers the phenomena of direct perceptions and the similitude perceived between present and past sensations. Then he says: "But there is still a third perception, which cannot take place by the sense alone, and does not depend on a comparison with previous vision, but without limitation considers the thing present. For its perceptions several things are required, and the process is like a kind of reasoning."[23]

This kind of reasoning, Bacon says, goes on so instantaneously that we are normally not aware of it. The optical process is described as a kind of reasoning. It is a short step for us to entertain the converse of this proposition: that reasoning is like an optical process carried on internally. In the conclusion of his optics Bacon employs *reflection* as a key to the state of the soul: "Man has a three-fold vision: one perfect, which will come in a state of glory after the resurrection; the second in the soul separated from the body in heaven until the resurrection, which is weaker; the third in this life, which is the weakest, and this is correctly said to be by reflection." Bacon reminds us that "the apostle says, 'We now see by means of a glass darkly, but in glory face to face'" (1 Corinthians 13.12). Bacon says that God judges by reflection, for the apostle James says this judgment is like "a man beholding his natural face in a glass."[24]

Thomas Aquinas in the *Summa theologica* employs *reflexio* in reference to the specific operation of the intellect in our knowledge of material things. He says: "That by which the sight sees is the likeness of the visible thing; and the likeness of the thing understood, that is, the intelligible species, is the form by which the intellect understands. But since the intellect reflects upon itself, by such reflection it understands both its own act of understanding and the species by which it understands."[25] He also describes the intellect itself in reflective terms, basing his comments on Augustine's "I understand that I understand" (*De Trin.* X. 11).

Thomas says that the first thing for the intellect to understand is its own act of understanding. He says that this occurs differently in different intellects; the divine and the angelic differ from the human. In the divine intellect essence and act are one, and in the angelic the first object of the act is the angelic essence. In the human intellect the first object of the intellect is the nature of the material thing: "That which is first known by the human intellect is an object of this kind [a material object], and that which is known secondarily is the act by which that object is known; and through the act the intellect itself is known, whose perfection is the act itself of understanding."[26] Although *reflection* occurs in Thomas's texts, it is a term of limited use in them, and in Scholasticism generally.

The source of *reflection* as the key term of modern philosophical thought is Locke's *An Essay Concerning Human Understanding* (1690).[27] Although the term *reflection* exists as such in English before Locke, his *Essay* is the historical source for the use of *reflection* as a philosophical term.²⁸ In describing the origin of our ideas, Locke distinguishes between those from external, sensible objects and those from the internal operations of our minds. He says, "These two are the fountains of knowledge, from whence all the ideas we have, or can naturally have, do spring."²⁹ Locke says that one source of what is in the mind is what the senses convey to it from external objects (for example, yellow, white, hot, cold, soft, hard, bitter, sweet): "This great source of most of the ideas we have, depending wholly upon our senses, and derived by them to the understanding, I call SENSATION."³⁰

The other source of ideas is the experience our own mind has of its operations, which cannot be had from without (for example, perception, thinking, doubting, believing, reasoning, knowing, willing). Locke says: "This source of ideas every man has wholly in himself; and though it be not sense, as having nothing to do with external objects, yet it is very like it, and might properly enough be called *internal sense*. But as I call the other Sensation, so I call this REFLECTION, the ideas it affords being such only as the mind gets by reflecting on its own operations within itself."³¹

In French the step beyond Descartes' use of *reflection* is Condillac's reworking of Locke's views in his *Essai sur l'origine des connaissances humaines* (1746)³² and Leibniz's criticism of Locke in his *Nouveaux essais* (1765). Leibniz says, "Reflection is nothing but attention to what is within us, and the senses do not give us what we carry with us already."³³ *Riflessione* as a philosophical term enters Italian from Locke.³⁴ Its general use in Italian in various senses parallels that of English and French and is derived from the Latin original. The case is much the same in Spanish.³⁵

Locke's *Essay* was translated into Latin in 1701 and into French in 1735. The Latin edition, *De intellectu humano*, was widely employed.³⁶ Locke's conception of reflection, and Descartes' for that matter, is anticipated by the Venetian Paolo Sarpi (1551–1623), who observes that no one can be acquainted with the knowing of knowing without engaging in reflection ("niun conoscente conosce di conoscere se non facendovi riflessioni").³⁷ In *L'arte di ben pensare* (The art of thinking well), the original of which is lost, Sarpi appears to have developed views very like Locke's concerning the distinction between sensation and reflection, the use of words, and so on—all about one hundred years before Locke's *Essay* appeared.³⁸

Kant's critique is the successor to Descartes' methodological use of reflection as a means to certainty and Locke's opposition of *reflection* to *sensation* as one of the two terms that exhaust the nature of human understanding. Descartes from his rationalist position employs reflection; Locke through his psychological approach gives it an identity; Kant equates philosophy itself with it. Kant establishes the firm connection between reflection and the nature of the Understanding (*Verstand*).

In the *Critique of Pure Reason*, Kant criticizes both Locke and Leibniz on the basis of "transcendental reflection." Kant states: "The act by which I confront the comparison of representations with the cognitive faculty to which it belongs, and by means of which I distinguish whether it is as belonging to the pure understanding or to sensible intuition that they are to be compared with each other, I call *transcendental reflection*."³⁹ In the "Amphiboly of the Concepts of Reflection" (*Amphibolie der Reflexionsbegriffe*), Kant claims that both Locke and Leibniz lack a transcendental conception of reflection by which they would be able to distinguish what belongs rightfully to the pure Understanding and what is given in appearance by sensibility. Locke would reduce all objects to what appears in sensibility, and Leibniz would attempt to obtain the inner nature of things by comparing all objects to the Understanding.

Transcendental reflection is the proper operation of the Understanding, of the knowing subject delineating the conditions of its own knowing so that its powers to sense the object are held in proper relation to its powers to form logically what is sensed. The knowing subject reflects on its own operations both sensible and conceptual and grasps the conditions under which it has an object that it knows. Reflection becomes the form of the Understanding. Transcendental reflection is a synonym for critique. Critique or criticism is the reflection of the knower on the conditions of the possibility of the object known. The project of philosophy is defined as the encounter of the mind with its own operations, as the ability to say with certainty how the phenomenal object can be known by the knower: "Thoughts without content are empty, intuitions without concepts are blind."[40]

In the one passage in the first *Critique* in which Kant becomes poetic, he extols the merit of the pure Understanding. He says that he has considered everything in the territory of the pure Understanding and assigned everything to its rightful place. He says: "This domain [the pure Understanding] is an island, enclosed by nature itself within unalterable limits. It is the land of truth—enchanting name!—surrounded by a wide and stormy ocean, the native home of illusion, where many a fog bank and many a swiftly melting iceberg give the deceptive appearance of farther shores, deluding the adventurous seafarer ever anew with empty hopes, and engaging him in enterprises which he never can abandon and yet is unable to carry to completion."[41] Kant's "land of truth" is the kingdom of Prester John in epistemological form.

What we might have thought a fiction is alleged by critique to be not fiction but a land of truth. The fictitious is what beckons out beyond it; it may delude us with empty prospects and projects that we can never complete ("niemals zu Ende bringen kann"). Kant's last sentence is Descartes' warning to those who would listen to fictitious narratives. Those who would allow themselves to be influenced by such stories, Descartes says, "are liable to fall into the excesses of the knights-errant in our tales of chivalry, and to conceive plans beyond their powers."[42] To seek the realm of Ideas is to seek the *Abenteur* of deluded seafarers or the *extravagance* of paladins tilting at windmills, engaging in fictions as if they were real life.

Critique supplies an absolute standard for human action arrived at by the agent's reflection on the necessary presupposition of the agent's own moral action. In practical reason, the categorical imperative expresses as a certainty the one presupposition of any moral act, but it leaves in doubt whether the act has truly lived up to its absolute presupposition. Whether the moral has been done is never fully known. The engine that drives the categorical imperative in human affairs is guilt, or *Schuld*. The agent is uncertain that the presupposition of the act has been perfectly aligned with the act itself, thus guaranteeing its morality. In Kant's ethics we always fall short, so we resolve to step up our will to perfection the next time we act.

Kant says: "For men and all rational creatures, the moral necessity is a constraint, an obligation. Every action based on it is to be considered as duty, not as a manner of acting which we naturally favor or which we sometime might so favor." Our duty is not a pleasant thing. It is a crucible of the will and of the human spirit. Kant continues: "This would be tantamount to believing we could finally bring it about that, without respect for the law (which is always connected with fear or at least apprehension that we might transgress it) we, like the independent deity, might come into possession of holiness of will through irrefragable agreement of the will with the pure moral law becoming, as it were, our very nature. This pure law, if we could never be tempted to be untrue to it, would finally cease altogether to be a command for us."[43] Kant's conception of duty has taken Descartes' conception of the will one step further. In *The Passions of the Soul* Descartes says of the free will: "It renders us in a certain way like God by making us masters of ourselves, provided we do not lose the rights it gives us through timidity."[44]

Critical reflection can never generate virtue. It can judge actions in regard to virtue, but it cannot arrive at virtues themselves through its criticism. Virtues originate in myths that present their embodiments in heroes. Valor is first known through the actions of Achilles, wisdom through the powers of Ulysses as presented by Homer, and the same kinds of heroic embodiments can be said to take place in all cultures. Virtues and what they are ultimately about, the Good, are human realities that lie beyond the island of the Understanding. They lie in Kant's fog banks of illusion.

Virtues can be understood and enacted within experience, but they do not wholly reside within it. The best life attempts to bring virtues into human actions and into civic affairs. Virtues are always something speculative, something to be seen with the soul and to be brought forth with reason into the human world. Virtues do not exist in a realm beyond the critical reflections of understanding as an order of hypotheticals. When we seek justice we do not act "as if" there were justice; we seek justice as a reality to be found in the order of things by our highest human powers.

In contrast to Kant, Hume in *A Treatise of Human Nature* understands well that justice is not created through an act of reflective thought: "No principle of the human mind is more natural than a sense of virtue; so no virtue is more natural than justice. Mankind is an inventive species; and where an invention is obvious and absolutely necessary, it may as properly be said to be natural as any thing that proceeds immediately from original principles, without the intervention of thought or reflexion."[45] To raise a child on the basis of virtues learned as habits of conduct is to produce an adult with character, a citizen. To raise a child as a seeker of rights, based on powers of critical reflection, is to produce a monster, an adult without a center, an individual ridden by guilt, argument, and contentiousness in human affairs.

Kant does not see virtue or the good as first in morals. Kant says it is "not that the concept of good as an object of the moral law determines the latter and makes it possible but rather the reverse, i.e., that the moral law is that which first defines the concept of the good—so far as it absolutely deserves this name—and makes it possible." Kant says the supporters of virtue have inverted the real order of morals. He continues: "This remark, which refers only to the method of the deepest moral investigations, is important. It explains once and for all the reasons which occasion all the confusions of philosophers concerning the supreme principle of morals. For they sought an object of the will in order to make it into the material and the foundation of a law (which would then be not the directly determining ground of the will, but only by means of that object referred to the feeling of pleasure or displeasure); instead, they should have looked for a law which directly determined the will a priori and only then sought the object suitable to it."[46] It is Kant who has it backward. It is because he has dismissed rhetoric.

Intellectually, morals require training in *ars topica:* in metaphor, memory, and commonplaces. Kant says the *ars oratoria* (which depends upon the *ars topica*) deserves no respect whatsoever ("ist gar keiner Achtung würdig").[47] "Topics," which Aristotle as well as the Renaissance humanists saw as part of the organon of thought, is necessary for the self to form images of itself and to recall the great truths of conduct achieved in culture. Our access to virtue is our power to draw forth the outlines of virtue and virtuous action in speech built upon the commonplaces we share with others.

Only when these parts of the communal sense of humanity are produced before us as models of conduct can the *ars critica* of reflection be set in motion. Otherwise, the *ars critica* has no subject matter on which to do its work of understanding and evaluating. Reflection reflects; it has no power to set its own starting points. Modern philosophy has bound itself to the Caucasus of reflection. Reflection, reflective thinking, approaching a question reflectively, is regarded as a good in itself. The dictum to think reflectively, which means to think critically, replaces the dictum to know thyself. It appears to make this ancient dictum unnecessary.

In the third *Critique* Kant attempts to complete his conception of reflection by delineating a second kind of judgment that is not analyzed in the earlier parts of his philosophy. He makes it clear that the faculty of judgment in a system of pure philosophy built on critique would not be a separate kind of knowing, residing between the theoretical and the practical, "but can be annexed when needful to one or both as occasion requires."[48] Judgment in general, for Kant, is thinking the particular under the universal, and this, he says in the third *Critique*, can occur in two ways: as determinant or as reflective judgment: "If the universal (the rule, the principle, the law) be given, the judgment which subsumes the particular under it (even if, as transcendental judgment, it furnishes, *a priori*, the conditions in conformity with which subsumption under that universal is alone possible) is *determinant*." The determinant judgment is what science excels in and is what is desired in ethics. Kant continues, "But if only the particular be given for which the universal has to be found, the judgment is merely *reflective*."[49]

Cassirer, in the best discussion to date on the meaning of the third *Critique*, shows how Kant's conception of the *reflek-*

tierende Urteilskraft, the "reflective power of judgment," embodies a conception of form that is to be found in both the aesthetic and the organic, thus tying the two halves of the third *Critique* together.[50] The reflective judgment is the notion of how to think something as a whole, for example, something that is not an instance of a law but is a law of itself. Such form requires the notion of *Zweckmässigkeit* ("purposiveness"). The elements of an artwork are specific moments in its particular totality.

Susanne Langer points out that one cannot assign individual meanings to the elements of a work of art and translate one work into another, as can be done with languages.[51] There are not "parts" of a work of art that have status apart from their function in the whole, yet the whole as a whole has a universal meaning. An organic natural form, an organism, has parts, that is, appendages and organs, that can to an extent be subtracted from the organism, but the organism is an order of these parts, which do not have meaning independent from this order. Such order is unique to the inner form of the particular organism.

In the third *Critique* Kant comes close to passing beyond the bounds of the critical philosophy. Kant does this by means of his conception of taste as the "subjective principle of judgment in general" in his discussion of the *sensus communis* and in his analysis of the sublime.[52] But he falls victim to his commitment to the Understanding as the standard for discovering the basis of experience. "Taste, then," Kant says, "as subjective judgment, contains a principle of subsumption, not of intuitions under concepts, but of the *faculty* of intuitions or presentations (i.e., imagination [*Einbildungskraft*]), so far as the former *in its freedom* harmonizes with the latter *in its conformity to law*."[53] Kant sees taste to rest on our release of the cognitive faculty into its "free play" (*freie Spiel*). The "freedom of the imagination consists in the fact that it schematizes without any concept," and the judgment of taste depends upon a reciprocal activity between the freedom of the imagination and the law-bound nature of the Understanding.[54]

Kant can orchestrate the dance of the faculties, but that is all. He cannot allow the imagination full access to the object. In the schematism of the first *Critique* the imagination (*Einbildungskraft*) is the source of the schema, but here the imagination is bound within the determinant judgment, as its faithful servant. In the third *Critique* the imagination is released into its own sphere, but it is not put on its own recognizance. It is tied to a new sense of reflection that requires it to be in harmony with the Understanding. Its freedom has a stoogelike quality, ready to be the shill for the "I think" of the categories of the Understanding as it works the crowd.

Kant was unable to see what Vico saw: the origin of all knowledge and experience is in the myth. Because of his commitment to the categories of the Understanding, Kant could not allow the "concepts" of fortune and fate that govern the world of myth to have a rightful place in thought. In his explanation of the categories, Kant says: "But there are also usurpatory concepts such as *fortune, fate*, which, though allowed to circulate by almost universal indulgence, are yet from time to time challenged by the question: *quid juris*."[55] Kant asks these travelers in the world, fortune and fate (*Glück* and *Schicksal*), for their papers, and discovers that they have not been issued papers by any known authority, especially not by the intellect. He finds them wanting in regard to a legal "deduction" and declares that they have no right to be abroad.

Myth is the origin of both the aesthetic and the organic formations of experience. Myth is the product of what Vico calls *fantasia*, or the "making imagination." Through *fantasia*, as a primordial power, the world is formed in terms of gods and heroes, and these are, in Vico's term, "imaginative universals" (*universali fantastici*).⁵⁶ Imaginative universals are the primal thought-form of what Vico regards as *il senso comune* (*sensus communis*). *Sensus communis*, for Vico, as for Shaftesbury, is communal sense, the sense that is made by man as a knowing, social, and image-making animal, acting in the world.⁵⁷ It is the result of human beings making sense together. The first form that this sense takes is the metaphor or imaginative universal.

Before the world is reflected upon, before it is understood, it is narrated in the myth. The world is populated with benign and malignant forces that create orders of sacred and profane. Kant's attention to the *sensus communis* in his doctrine of taste is very close to what is needed, but it misses the mark. To miss the mark here is the same as to hit nothing. Vico says that *sensus communis* is "judgment without reflection" (*giudizio senz'alcuna riflessione*).⁵⁸ This is decisive. Kant has the wrong metaphor. When this occurs in philosophy, thought never recovers, or recovers only by doing what Kant himself advises when things have gone wrong: it is never too late to raze the building.⁵⁹ Kant has the wrong sense of light. He understands this nondeterminant form of judgment, that is not made directly by the Understanding but in harmony with it, to be like *reflected light*, which is light received at a distance by the knower, giving the knower contact with the object known. The object is indirectly seen.

Vico's *universale fantastico* is also based on the metaphor of light. Imagination is itself light. As Aristotle says, "The name *phantasia* (imagination) has been formed from *phaos* (light)" (*De an.* 429a). Literally *phantasia* is "a making visible." Vico's *fantasia* is not reflected light, it is illumination in which the knower and the known are not differentiated as subject-object. The mind is in the world, not simply in the knower. The world is actually made through *fantasia;* it is not simply understood. *Fantasia* is judgment without reflection. The object is not reflected upon by the mind but is felt as a thou and acted on bodily.⁶⁰ Feeling here is not Kant's aesthetic or sublime sense of feeling. The first humans, Vico says, thought and spoke with their bodies. Thus when the protohumans, the *giganti*, experience thunder for the first time, they shake in fear and run into caves, and they feel ashamed to copulate out in the open.

The first humans' experience of Jove is sublime, but not Kant's sublime. It is not Kant's looking on a scene of which no concept can be completely formed. As Vico says, it is a fear, "not a fear awakened in men by other men, but fear awakened in men by themselves."⁶¹ This is not Kant's fear that we might transgress the pure moral law. Fear is the generation of *fantasia*. Through fear, the first men form the thunderous sky as the body of Jove and bring about the distinction between the human and the divine that is the beginning of wisdom. In East Prussia, the light is thin; the world is seen in *Abglanz*. In Naples, *c'è sempre il sole* (there is always the sun).

On his thirty-first birthday, August 27, 1801, Hegel publicly defended twelve theses at the University of Jena as part of his qualification for the license to teach. The seventh of these theses was "Critical philosophy lacks Ideas; it is an imperfect form of Scepticism."⁶² Critical philosophy, or critique, as Kant calls it, is a philosophy committed to the Understanding (*Verstand*). Commitment to philosophy as criticism is commitment to that power of mind that has its seat in the Understanding: reflection. The two terms can be joined: critical reflection.

The Understanding (reflective thinking) approaches the world and the self in terms of theories and facts, concepts and perceptions. Ideas, as Hegel notes, are lacking in the Understanding. Ideas can exist for the Understanding only as hypotheticals, potential sources of hypotheses or viable presuppositions. Ideas can be employed reflectively as centers of "as if" thinking. They cannot be apprehended as genuine realities. This is the teaching of Kantianism both in epistemology and in ethics. Critical philosophy is an imperfect skepticism because it excludes speculation.

Speculation is not a form of reflection. It is the opposite of reflection. At times *reflection* is used in ordinary intellectual speech and in philosophy to mean speculation. Rightly conceived, speculation is a philosophical power of mind having its seat in Reason (*Vernunft*), as Hegel claims. Reflection reveals to us only the surface of things, including the surface of ourselves, what in ordinary terms is called psychology. Speculation is a process that is both inner and outer at once; it takes us both within ourselves and without ourselves. It takes us to the "inner form" of the object of thought.

Kant's philosophy is an encyclopedia of distinctions with a term for each. The essence of Kant's philosophy is making distinctions. In the first *Critique* Kant simply begins by making distinctions and never stops, continuing the process through the next two *Critique*s. There is no greater set of distinctions purporting to be systematic in the history of philosophy. Kant begins the system by simply asserting that there are four kinds of judgments. When Kant faces a problem, he makes several more distinctions and then proceeds to relate them to others. Critical philosophy is imperfect skepticism because it is architectonic. In architectonic something is always left out. The ultimate thing left out in Kant's architectonic is the "thing-in-itself," and it becomes a ghost that Kant cannot keep out of his machine.

The concern of critique is to delineate the principles by which truth can be distinguished from error. The concern of speculation is to find the realities from which all else can be thought and the True itself can be found. A true philosophy of experience would claim to answer the skepticism of Sextus Empiricus or the "historical Pyrrhonism" of Pierre Bayle. But a philosophy dedicated only to the Understanding leaves us as knowers on the terra firma of its island and as skeptics about all else that we see in the distance. Starting from a doctrine of judgment derived from the sciences, we can never get to Ideas except in the negative sense of thought projecting its own limits.

Kant has no sense of what Hegel, in his preface to the *Phenomenology of Spirit*, calls the speculative sentence (*der spekulative Satz*) or the philosophical sentence (*der philosophische Satz*).[63] Hegel uses both names for the same process of interrelationship of subject and predicate. When Kant moves from General Logic to Transcendental Logic he connects logic to experience, but he fails to discover a way to think the presence of Ideas in the world.[64] They remain the shapes in the fog banks surrounding the blessed isle of the Understanding. Through the reflective powers of the Understanding Kant can illuminate the object in experience, but he cannot reach the actual presence of Reason (*Vernunft*) in the world.

Kant is hoisted on his own petard of transcendental certainty. He cannot conceive of a way to think directly the "inner form" of the object. In Kant's reflective sentence the subject remains externally connected to the predicate, and he offers us only a table of contents of experience. Kant suffers from the fact that his thought is not musical. Hegel's *Begriff* (Concept, Notion) destroys the distinction of subject and predicate, thought that critical reflection thinks to be permanent. Hegel says the "conflict between the general form of a proposition and the unity of the *Begriff* which destroys it is similar to the conflict that occurs in rhythm between metre and accent. Rhythm results from the floating centre and the unification of the two."[65] The speculative sentence is musical.

Hegel offers the example "God is being." He points out that being is meant to be not a predicate but the essence of God. God ceases to be a fixed subject in this case and is what is expressed in the predicate. Instead of making progress in thought from subject to predicate, we are thrown back on the subject as what is expressed in the predicate. Hegel concludes, "Thinking therefore loses the firm objective basis it had in the subject when, in the predicate, it is thrown back on to the subject, and when, in the predicate, it does not return into itself, but to the subject of the content."[66] The world has a rhythm that can be captured in the philosophical sentence that stems from thinking the inner motion of the object. The inner motion of the object is governed by an Idea or form of its reality.

Reflection requires the metaphor of the mirror. In transcendental reflection the mind can mirror to itself its own operations that are at the basis of understanding. These are the conditions necessary for the formulation of propositions and syllogisms about what is in experience. Speculation calls up the notion of the mirror (*speculum*), but it also calls up *specere,* to observe, to look, to spy out. Speculation couples the sight of the object with insight into what it is itself. The speculator is a spectator, in the sense of one who can see into the movements of opposites residing in the objects that make up its life. The speculator is not an intellectual optician who orders the categorical lenses through which the object is formed in reflective judgment. The speculative thinker can present these dialectical movements in speech, having seen how in the logical order of the sentence the subject and predicate cannot be kept from moving from their places when an Idea is involved.

Dante, in canto 1 of the *Paradiso,* describes seeing *per speculum:* "The lamp of the world rises to mortals through different passages" (lines 37–38).[67] Beatrice turns to her left and looks at the sun. Dante also is able to see its light: "Thus of her action, infused through the eyes into my imagination, mine was made, and I fixed my eyes on the sun beyond our wont. Much is granted to our faculties there that is not granted here, by virtue of the place made for humankind as its proper abode" (lines 52-57). Having seen that the sun is there, Dante turns his gaze from the sun to its light reflected in Beatrice: "Beatrice was standing with her eyes all fixed upon the eternal wheels, and I fixed mine on her, withdrawn from there above" (lines 64-66). In this second light one sees *per speculum.* In the first light, as mentioned above in connection with Roger Bacon, one sees *facie ad faciem.* Beatrice is the intermediary of the divine light. Dante sees by means of the second light as it is exchanged between himself and Beatrice. Beatrice is his guide.

The speculative act is not separate from reflection in the two senses just described. Speculation involves the presence of the absolute for its act of thought to take place. The speculative act sees in reflected light, but the source of the reflection is not the phenomena of the world or the cognitive relation of the mind to itself. Speculation requires the notion of "seeing beyond," of a divine or noetic vision that first begins and then informs its reasonings. Seeing *per speculum* stands in a dialectical relationship to seeing *facie ad faciem*. One accompanies and presupposes the other.

Vico said of Descartes, and could have said of transcendental philosophy, that to approach the object only in cognitive terms is to see as if at night by lamplight; the object can be seen, but its background is cut off. That is the problem with seeing in terms of clear and distinct ideas. The speculative metaphysician attempts to see the daylight of the divine through the opacity of the bodies of the world. Vico says: "Metaphysical truths are illuminating because they cannot be bounded by any limit and distinguished by any formed body."[68] Speculative reason begins with the attempt by the metaphysician to see the world by the sun and connect it to the second light of the mind's eye of reason. This is to see with the divine eye of providence.

In the *Science of Logic,* Hegel says that ancient metaphysics believed thought could achieve a true knowledge of things, "but *reflective* understanding took possession of philosophy" (*aber der* reflektierende *Verstand bemächtigte sich der Philosophie*).[69] He says the view that philosophy is essentially reflective has become a slogan (*Schlagwort*). What Hegel identifies as a slogan in his day has become the dominant concern of philosophy as practiced in ours by thinkers from Husserl to Gadamer. Husserl places reflection at the center of phenomenology. He says: "The phenomenological method operates exclusively in acts of reflection."[70] Gadamer identifies all philosophy with "hermeneutic reflection," to which, in a wider vision than Husserl, he hopes to connect rhetoric, tradition, and practice. Gadamer says: "What role does reason play in the context of human practice? In every case it takes the general form of reflection."[71]

Merleau-Ponty attempts to get beyond both the impregnable *cogito* of Cartesian thought and the emptiness of the transcendental ego of Kantian philosophy by a more vital or radical pursuit of reflection in which individual life constitutes itself. To this end he says: "Reflection is truly reflection only if it is not carried outside itself, only if it knows itself as reflection-on-an-unreflective-experience, and consequently as a change in structure of our existence."[72] Marvin Farber, in an article, "Modes of Reflection," says: "Every philosophy that is concerned with experience is reflective, more or less. A thoroughly reflective philosophy is an ideal. That would mean the complete examination of the contents, grounds, motives, and aims of experience."[73] Farber needs no justification for this, as he is easily stating the obvious. Hegel's notice that reflection has become a slogan was prophetic.

The source of the turn to the idea of reflection in modern philosophy lies in modern optics. Modern optics is the analogue for the modern conception of the intellect as a source of "reflective" knowledge. Thought is connected with light. The eye is the organ of sight. The mind's eye is that by which we see a truth. Because it makes the object visible, reflection is the key property of light, followed by refraction and color—mirrors, lenses, and prisms. For the Greeks, the meaning of the word *optics* was limited to questions concerning vision and the nature of light. Greek optics concentrated on reflection; the basic phenomena of refraction were known, but the quantitative law of refraction was not known until the beginning of the seventeenth century. The Greeks devoted their energies to questions concerning the philosophical significance of light itself, to how an object was seen and to what its color was due. The ancients were generally concerned with reflection as it plays a role in sensation and in the emission and reception of the image.

In modern optics the philosophical questions concerning light, reflection, and perception have remained, but light has become the subject of experimental science: Newton's study of white light and the spectrum of colors, for example, and the invention of the Dutch or Galilean telescope, the microscope, and binoculars. Most important philosophically is the modern study of dioptrics. That one of the three essays Descartes attaches to the *Discours* is "Dioptrique" is not only significant in the history of the science of light, but is philosophically symbolic. Descartes begins this essay with the assertion that the "conduct of our life depends entirely on our senses" and that "sight is the noblest and most comprehensive" of them.[74]

Dioptrics, the study of refraction, and the discovery of laws of such phenomena change the understanding of the object. Huygens greatly improved the grinding of spherical lenses. Lenses were known to the ancients, and spectacles were probably in use as early as the thirteenth century. Hobbes wrote a treatise on optics published by Mersenne in 1644.[75] The laws of reflection and refraction, which merely described the observed effects of light on surfaces, were combined in a general law announced in about 1665 by the French philosopher Pierre de Fermat: the actual path pursued by light in going from one point to another is the route that, under the given conditions, requires the least time.[76] Light is a phenomenon of pure efficiency, and sight can be manipulated so that the object can be apprehended in any way we wish.

In the letter that Descartes wrote to Arnauld in 1648, which I mentioned earlier, we find Descartes drawing an analogy between the reflection of light and the intellect's reflection of itself. The intellect receives a sensation and then perceives that it has a sensation. This second perception is a reflection of the first, which occurs wholly within the intellect. This is an internal optics. Locke speaks of reflection as an *"internal sense."*[77] A. C. Fraser notes in his edition of the *Essay* that it is left to Locke's interpreter to consider whether reflection should be interpreted empirically or intellectually. Fraser says that the answer depends upon whether this operation of the mind "includes *reflex consciousness of reason proper.*"[78] Reflection is a kind of internal sight, but it remains ambiguous as to whether it is an empirical or wholly intellectual operation of the mind.

Berkeley's *New Theory of Vision* is not an optics but a philosophy of vision that generates a metaphysics of the perceived object.[79] Berkeley brings the implications of modern optics fully into philosophy. Because of telescopic and microscopic lenses, refractions, and prisms, the object can be seen in an indefinite number of ways. With the invention of modern lenses, the object can be perceptually changed in any way we wish. The eye itself is understood to be a lens. What Berkeley explores of the perception of objects of sense is even more true of the second perception or internal sense: reflection as the operation of the intellect on itself.

The modern lens lets us see the object in any way we wish. Once the mind is conceived in terms of a specific function—

reflection—the mind can reflect and refract itself as an object in an infinite number of ways. The mind is whatever it can reflect itself to be. It is not accidental that Roger Bacon is a source in his psychology for the first use of the term *reflection* in the sense of "self-knowledge" and that he is also the author of the most important treatise on optics in the Middle Ages. But Bacon, unlike the moderns, does not regard the intellect as purely functional. Although the intellect can take itself as its object, it does so in order to grasp its essence as the reflection of the divine.

The power of the lens to let us see the object in any way we wish is parallel to the power of the mind to construct the appearance of the object and the object's relation to the mind. Phenomenology, or the science of appearance, has its origin in this functional power of the mind to form itself and the object together. In 1764 Johann Heinrich Lambert published a work entitled *Neues Organon oder Gedanken über die Erforschung und Bezeichnung des Wahren und dessen Unterscheidung von Irrtum und Schein* (New organon, or thoughts on the investigation and indication of truth and the distinction between error and appearance).[80] Lambert was influenced by Francis Bacon's doctrine of the idols and Locke's conception of human understanding wherein the "mind can learn various truths." Lambert called the fourth part of his treatise "Phänomenologie oder Lehre von dem Schein" (Phenomenology, or the doctrine of appearance). He called his phenomenology a "transzendente Optik" (transcendent optics).[81] This optics allows us to see through the forms of appearance, avoid error, and employ human understanding.

Kant was greatly interested in Lambert's conception. On September 2, 1770, Kant wrote to Lambert: "A quite special, though purely negative science, general phenomenology (*phaenomenologia generalis*), seems to be presupposed by metaphysics. In it the principles of sensibility, their validity and their limitations, would be determined, so that these principles could not be confusedly applied to objects of pure reason, as heretofore almost always has happened."[82] In a letter to Marcus Herz dated February 21, 1772, Kant wrote that he planned to produce such a general phenomenology as the first part of a metaphysics.[83] Kant did not carry through this plan as such, but the sense of optics is carried on into critique as a doctrine of "transcendental reflection." Hegel retrieves the term *phenomenology* and uses it in his announcement of lectures for the winter semester at Jena in 1806. Hegel connects this term not with critique but with speculative thinking and his "System der Wissenschaft."[84]

From the reflection of Narcissus to the reflections seen outside Plato's cave to the analogue of the Sun and the Good, light is the medium of knowledge, our primary access to the objects of the world. The eye, being the organ of sight, is the primary sense for knowing. The ancient notion of the inner and the outer eye is tied to the phenomenon of light. The mind, the *mens*, is most like the eye. Like the divine *mens*, it can see ideas. The divine *mens* is omniscient, and it is all-seeing. The human *mens* depends upon the object as conveyed by light. Light transports the image. The power of light is to reflect and refract what is there. Light reflects and makes the unseen seen. It is epistemic and metaphysical power. For the modern, to produce mirrors, prisms, and lenses and, through them, to describe light and formulate its laws is to be at the basis of knowledge and reality itself.

This is the modern project of the new Narcissus. Our knowledge of the physical object is dependent upon light and how the object's presence is reflected to the senses. With the modern production and experimental use of mirrors, lenses, and prisms, the object can be manipulated in an indefinite number of ways. Narcissus now does not simply see his reflection, he can see it as he wishes. Reflection is not determined by the object. Reflection is now a process between the knower and the object. This freedom in relation to the object is analogous to the power attributed to reflection as a faculty of human understanding. When thought takes its own activity as its object, it has the power to reflect or refract its activity in an indefinite number of ways. In modern optics nothing of the object is closed to sight. In modern critics nothing of the mind is closed to itself.

Collingwood has stated this modern sense of reflection as:

"I.72. Any form of consciousness may be reflected upon; that is, it may become the object of another form of consciousness.

"I.73. Let a man have a certain form of consciousness, C_1. Let him reflect on this; let him, that is to say, call into being in himself another form of consciousness, C_2, the consciousness of C_1.

"I.74. Whatever a science of mind can tell him about C_1 is something of which he was already conscious in the state of C_2."

Collingwood continues, using the metaphor of the eye:

"I.76. But when it has been thus worked up every element in the resulting product is derived from the original raw material; for every question has been asked and answered 'with your eye on the object,' where the object is C_1 and the eye C_2."

Collingwood concludes that what a man is in respect to his "capacity of mind" need not be answered by specialists:

"I.88. The general form of answer to many such questions is: *In teipsum redi*. You have the makings of the answer in your own consciousness. Reflect, and you will find what it is."[85]

Collingwood's formulation of reflection shows how far *Verstand* is from *nous* and how much the doctrine of reflective self-consciousness has become the replacement for the ancient doctrine of self-knowledge: *In teipsum redi* instead of *Temet nosce*. Reflection makes thought a circle of itself, an eye that sees itself through its own light. Thought becomes transcendental optics. The ancient definition of wisdom is replaced by this perfect optics.

In the *Charmides,* Socrates speaks with Critias about self-knowledge. Socrates agrees with Critias that wisdom is the science of man's self. Critias understands this self-knowledge to be the knowledge of knowledge or the science of science. Socrates says: "I will admit that there is a science of science. Can this do more than determine that of two things one is and the other is not science or knowledge?" (170A). Socrates is concerned to know what art or subject matter the possessor of self-knowledge, understood as a knowledge of knowledge, would command. Would it be to command, for example, the art of medicine, or the art of music, or the art of building? No, a knowledge of knowledge would not offer us a knowledge of such subjects. We might have knowledge of such subjects or others like them, but we would not require a knowledge of knowledge to possess such specific knowledge.

Socrates says, "Then wisdom or being wise appears to be not the knowledge of the things which we do or do not know, but only the knowledge that we know or do not know" (170D). Critias agrees that this is the inference to be drawn, and Socrates concludes: "Then he who has this knowledge will not be able to establish whether a claimant knows or does not know that which he says that he knows; he will only know that he has a knowledge of some kind, but wisdom will not show him of what the knowledge is" (ibid.). This is, in effect, a refutation of critique or transcendental reflection as a doctrine of self-knowledge. To establish the necessary conditions for the possibility of knowledge is to learn nothing of the most important aim of philosophy: the Delphic inscription "know thyself."

"Know thyself" is unintelligible apart from the second Delphic inscription: "nothing too much." Self-knowledge is tied to *sophrosynē*, which is the opposite of arrogance, that vice of character so detested by the Greeks. We have lost the meaning of *sophrosynē*, perhaps because we have also lost the fundamental sense of self-knowledge that is at the center of Socratic philosophy. *Sophrosynē* means the acceptance of the limits of excellence that are present in human nature and requires control of the impulse to unrestricted freedom and excess. *Sophrosynē* thus goes against the impulse that dominates modernity; it requires the individual to obey the inner laws of harmony and proportion in the human.[86]

Sophrosynē is not a right derived by reflection; it is a virtue grasped by a metaphysical account of human nature and insight into how to obey the inner laws of harmony and proportion. *Sophrosynē* requires a knowledge of the polis and the gods, the order of things human and divine. Socrates concludes in the *Charmides* that we cannot at the moment say what *sophrosynē* is. He suggests that Charmides may have such in himself, as a gift. There is a dialectic between the two Delphic sayings. "Know thyself" suggests the need for a meditative wisdom that can, in Socratic manner, be sought through discussion among friends, and the other, "nothing too much," refers to what may guide our actions in the world of the city.

In the *Phaedrus* Socrates says that he has no time for clever theories concerning the truth of various common views or for the critical evaluation of such theories. Socrates says: "I myself have certainly no time for the business, and I'll tell you why, my friend. I can't as yet 'know myself,' as the inscription at Delphi enjoins, and so long as that ignorance remains it seems to me ridiculous to inquire into extraneous matters. Consequently I don't bother about such things, but accept the current beliefs about them, and direct my inquiries, as I have just said, rather to myself, to discover whether I really am a more complex creature and more puffed up with pride than Typhon, or a simpler, gentler being whom heaven has blessed with a quiet un-Typhonic nature" (229E–230A).

Critique or transcendental reflection goes hand in hand with the conception of knowledge as theory making and theory testing. This is true in modern ethics, in which theories of justice, right, contract, and moral decision are pursued and evaluated. Critical philosophy that pursues the knowledge of knowledge can offer only the Kantian "I think," the "transcendental unity of apperception,"[87] to stand in the place of the Pythia's "know thyself." Kant says: "The principle of apperception is the highest principle in the whole sphere of human knowledge."[88] Kant's "I think" is Descartes' *cogito* in a new suit, but it cannot help us with the problem of the examined life.

Self-knowledge pursues the question of what a human being is, and the answer entails the metaphysical grasp of the interrelation of the human and the divine. This knowledge is the basis for conduct in the world of civil things. Self-reflection masquerades as this, and becomes its modern substitute. Self-reflection simulates self-knowledge because the knower takes knowledge itself as his object. This internal relationship, as Socrates suggests, is empty. It never offers more than the necessary condition of the "I think." Even though the "I think" may be dressed up in various theoretical clothes, it is still empty in itself.

One honest answer to the barbarism of the replacement of self-knowledge with self-reflection appears in Gilbert Ryle's *Concept of Mind*. In a chapter entitled "Self-Knowledge," Ryle abandons all pretense to the ancient pursuit of self-knowledge and reduces the quest to the proper use of the pronoun *I*. Ryle says: "When a person utters an 'I' sentence, his utterance of it may be part of a higher order performance, namely one, perhaps of self-reporting, self-exhortation or self-commiseration, and this performance itself is not dealt with in the operation which it itself is."[89] Ryle concludes: "'I' is like my own shadow; I can never get away from it, as I can get away from your shadow. There is no mystery about this constancy, but I mention it because it seems to endow 'I' with a mystifying uniqueness and adhesiveness."[90] William James points out in *The Principles of Psychology* that the "I" of Kant can never have any content: "To sum up, then, my own opinion of the transcendentalist school, it is . . . a school in which psychology at least has naught to learn, and whose deliverances about the Ego in particular in no wise oblige us to revise our own formulation of the Stream of Thought."[91]

Vico's "barbarism of reflection" is not only a barbarism of mind and reason but also a barbarism of practice and society. Success in life in corrupt times depends not on virtue, piety, faith, and truth but on the simulation of these attributes by wit. The self, unable to know the nature of its own humanity by its powers of reflection, develops patterns of action and ways of using language that simulate a social animal. Modern peoples live, not through an ingenuity that responds to necessities forced upon them by nature, but through an ingenuity in social relations that aids in their quest for luxury. In *Momus*, Leon Battista Alberti offers a picture of the humanist turned vagabond that is an archetype for Vico's last men.[92]

The vagabond is the modern barbarian, who has given up on any sense of the ancient pursuit of self-knowledge. He has discovered that what is required is not virtue in human affairs, or the just order of the soul, but the power to reflect critically on the dynamics of any situation and to simulate what is required in order to satisfy his desires or to gain from it. The vagabond is a man without qualities who is engaged in the art of appearing to have them, transforming himself into whatever persona will work. He is the artful pragmatist. He has learned from the humanist the art of wit or *ingenium* as the key to human affairs, but he puts this power into effect without any concern for moral principles except to simulate them if the occasion requires.

Since critical reflection, the Understanding, cannot give us wisdom or self-knowledge, we are left with a world of rights, decision procedures, and positive law unsupported by custom or character. Society is a throng of individuals out for what each may get by his wits from the others, each, as Vico says, "thinking only of his own private interests" and capable of lashing out "at the slightest displeasure." Alberti's conception of the god Momus and its connection to his unique version of the tale of Prometheus illuminates Vico's state of "ultimate civil disease."

Hesiod classifies Momus among the children of Night; Momus is the personification of "blame" or "censure" μῶμος (*Theog.* 214). Homer seems not to have known of Momus. He is scarcely referred to in Greek literature until he appears in the work of Lucian. *Momus* was a satyr play by Sophocles, of which little is known.[93] Momus is alluded to by Plato (*Rep.* 487A) and Aristotle (*Parts of Animals* III. 2). In Lucian's *Hermotimus*, Lycinus and Hermotimus discuss the marks by which the true philosopher might be distinguished from the false. Lycinus recalls the story of the faults Momus found with Hephaestus: "The story goes that Athena, Poseidon, and Hephaestus were quarrelling over which of them was the best artist. Poseidon modelled a bull. Athena designed a house, while Hephaestus, it seems, put together a man. When they came to Momus, whom they had appointed judge, he examined the work of each" (*Herm.* 20).

Lucian does not relate here the faults that Momus finds with the first two, but according to the general tradition of the story Momus criticizes Poseidon for not putting the horns of the bull beneath its eyes so that it could better see where it struck (see also *Nigr.* 32, *True Hist.* II. 3), and he criticizes Athena for not putting iron wheels on the house so it could be moved with the owners when they went out of town. Momus, Lucian continues, criticizes Hephaestus's creation of a man because "he had not made windows in his chest which could be opened to let everyone see his desires and thoughts and if he were lying or telling the truth" (*Herm.* 20). Lycinus says he believes that, even without such windows, Hermotimus has the ability to see through the chest of each man and know what each man wants or thinks, and whether he is better or worse in character.

Lucian is the source for Alberti's *Momus*. The story as told by Lucian of the three creations, bull, house, and man, is also told with variations by Babrius and Aesop. In Babrius's fable "Momus the Fault-Finder," it is Zeus, not Hephaestus, who is the maker of man, and Zeus is criticized by Momus for a lack of windows in man's chest (*Fab.* 59). In the *Aesopica* are two tales of Momus, one in which he has difficulty finding fault with any aspect of Aphrodite's beauty and finally makes fun of her sandal (455), and another which tells the tale of the bull, house, and man (100). In this version Zeus creates the bull and Athena the house, but it is Prometheus who creates the man, and Prometheus is criticized by Momus for not making man so we can see immediately what he has in his mind. Zeus, vexed by the fault-finding, banishes Momus from Olympus.[94]

In some accounts Prometheus steals fire from Olympus, in others Prometheus steals it from the forge of Hephaestus, and in still others Prometheus, not Zeus, is the maker of man. These aspects of the Prometheus myth are played upon loosely in the telling of the Momus fable. In all versions of the fable, Momus emerges as the critic who with his comments can limit the power of the gods. Whether they devise something natural (the bull), artificial (the house), or human (the man), Momus can find its imperfection. He has a power of insight the other gods do not possess. In his ability to limit the power of the gods he is like Prometheus, who angers Zeus and limits his power by giving fire to man.

Lucian's telling of the fable glosses Plato's *Republic* VI, in which the question of who the philosophers are and who they are not is summed up (484A). Plato is engaged in the Promethean task of making the true philosopher's nature through his system of education. Having delineated the properties of the soul necessary to such a person, Plato says, "Momus himself could not find fault with such a combination" (48A). Plato seems to be aware of the principle of Momus's criticism: the need to see into the soul to know what man truly is. Plato has taken on the task to employ his own art of seeing in order to show what the window would have shown were man so created. For those with an eye to see, Plato has offered the window that Momus requires. In Lucian's account, Hermotimus is credited with this power of the philosophical eye, the ability to distinguish the true philosopher from the false and the good and the just nature from the unjust, the crucial ability for ruling the state or the conduct of human affairs in general.

Alberti's *Momus* opens with the creation of the world. Jove expects to relax, to observe and enjoy the order of gods and the obedience of man to him. Instead, Prometheus steals the sacred fire, and the potentially peaceful order of creation is disrupted. Before relating the theft by Prometheus, Alberti relates the tale of the creation of the bull, house, and man. In Alberti's telling, Prometheus is the creator of man, and Momus advances his criticisms of each, noting that man is an image of the gods.[95] Alberti's version of the Prometheus story differs from other versions, and it forges a new key to the nature of modern society and the modern individual.

In Alberti's version of the Prometheus story, the sacred fire was eternal; it had the extraordinary property to reignite itself without the addition of any liquid or other substance. The sacred fire was held among the threads of a material made by the goddess Virtue. These threads were on top of the forehead of all the gods holding within them this sacred fire; those who have the element of the fire have the power to transform themselves into any form they wish.[96] In Alberti's version, what is stolen from the gods and given to man is not the power of fire to dominate the physical world and the other creatures that walk the earth, but a power whereby the individual can move through human society like a god, assuming any shape he wishes. The version of the Prometheus myth found in Plato's *Protagoras* (320D–322A) and other places contains the warning that the gift of Prometheus does not bring with it civil wisdom.

Alberti's version of the Prometheus myth is the imparting to man of a false civil wisdom. The power that Prometheus takes from the gods and gives to man is the power of simulation (*simulatio, simulare*). Not only does man have the image of god, but he can act as a god to transform himself into whatever sort of person a situation might require. Human beings quickly abuse this new power, even going so far as to simulate the gods themselves. For his theft Prometheus is chained to the Caucasus. For his criticism of Jupiter's rule of the celestial order Momus is expelled from the gods and forced to live among mortals, who now possess the power of simulation.[97]

In Alberti's fable Momus is not simply the critic of man, as Plato refers to him; he is a manipulator of man and a model of deception among mortals. In the theft of the sacred fire of simulation, the connection of the fire with Virtue is severed, so this power can be used for whatever the individual desires. As the modern individual can reflect the object of perception in any way he wishes through the power of the lens, so he can reflect himself as an "I think" into any persona he desires, once he receives Prometheus's stolen gift.

Not only is Momus the embodiment of Promethean simulation, but he is also like Narcissus, the god of reflection, whom Alberti regards in the *De pictura* as the inventor of painting.[98] Narcissus can only admire his image, but Momus, because of his powers of critical insight, can transform his image and make himself appear as he wishes. In Alberti's tale Momus goes about among mortals showing them arts of deception, even offering instruction in the art of cosmetics. Alberti likely has in mind the myth of the ring of Gyges, as Plato relates it in *Republic* II. When turned, the ring makes its wearer invisible, able to move about the world filling his every desire without consequences. Plato asks, Would not even the just man, if given the ring of Gyges, help himself to anything he might choose, sleep with whomever he chose, and kill or release from prison whomever he wished? Plato asks, Would not the possessor of such a ring "in a word go about among men with the powers of a god?" (360C).

Momus is the master purveyor of the ultimate art form of *savoir vivre*, the ability to simulate whatever sort of persona is required to succeed in a situation. Alberti creates what he calls the vagabond (*erro*). Modern man is the practitioner of vagabondism. The vagabond is the humanist without virtue. The vagabond is an aesthetic lifestyle, one practiced by all modern individuals. It is a life of spiritual homelessness that depends upon the practice of pure wit or *ingenium* directed by no goals except the satisfaction of desire. Momus explains that vagabondism is not an art like geometry or other arts that require a period of formal study, in which rules and their applications are learned. The vagabond need only act at his own convenience: "This art stands on the ground of complete indifference to all those things that are held indispensable in other arts."[99]

Momus says: "Feign and yet do not [appear to be feigning]. . . . The essential principle is this one only; namely, that there is no feeling that one cannot cover with perfection under the appearance of honesty and innocence." The simulation of virtue can be the ring of Gyges if this power is taken up without any reservation or shame. Momus continues: "Adapting our words, we will brilliantly attain our image, and whatever particular externality of our persona, in a manner that seems to be similar to those who are believed to be beautiful and moderate." The vagabond is engaged in an ultimate aesthetic in which appearance is all that is ever needed in human affairs. He needs only to speak and act well as required by the moment, not as required by virtue. Momus concludes: "What a splendid thing it is to know how to hide the more secret thoughts with the wise artifice of colorful and deceptive fiction."[100]

In his autobiography, Vico says he "will not here feign [*fingere*] what René Descartes craftily feigned as to the method of his studies simply in order to exalt his own philosophy and mathematics and degrade all other studies included in divine and human erudition."[101] Vico says he will relate his studies plainly, step-by-step, as a historian. We are reminded of Descartes' claim, in his *Cogitationes privatae*, that he steps upon the theater of the world in a mask.[102] Descartes' mask is language. He must practice a "many-tonguedness" (*versipellem*) because he must employ rhetoric, topics, memory, metaphor—erudition of all kinds—to accomplish his point while at the same time degrading such studies as practiced by the humanist and historian.[103] Vico conveys his largest truths in the form of the fable, but unlike Descartes, he does not falsely claim that what he says could just as easily be spoken in *bas breton*. Vico always strove for the humanist ideal of wise, eloquent, and prudent speech.[104]

In a world governed by critical reflection as the standard for thought, where eloquence and wisdom have no place, language, the medium that holds society together, dissolves into flattery and witticism. The law becomes a superstition of words; jurisprudence becomes whatever the words of the law can cleverly be made out to mean. In the age of the barbarism of reflection, Vico says, we are left with "soft words" and "malicious wits." This is a world without fear and without shame. It is without fear because no starting points are required.

Critical reflective thought begins with a given and proceeds methodologically to understand and to sort out truth from error. For Vico the starting points in human thought and life require the recapitulation of the original moment of fear, in which the first humans flee from the thunderous sky, which they form as Jove. The aesthetic existence of the vagabond is fearless, without starting point or shame, because all that is needed is the ingenious response to the given moment. For Vico shame is a civilizing passion; it causes us to orient ourselves to a standard of virtue. The success of the fiction prevents shame from ever arising for the vagabond.

The vagabond as a figure of modern life is not Odysseus, using his wit to master any situation and move closer to Ithaca, his home. Odysseus is on a journey; the vagabond is just traveling. The vagabond is only seeking a comfortable spot. He does not know that he is a vagabond. Odysseus feels the adversity of his situation. He is cut off from himself because he is cut off from his home. The vagabond moves with the sense of the times, which is to seduce and to be seduced, and proceeds to feign whatever is needed. In a world governed by civil wisdom, the individual can move about on the basis of character. In a world governed by procedures and situations, the individual can move about by means of flattery. Flattery is shameless speech, language put wholly at the service of the ego in its career of self-movement.

Modern life is essentially aesthetic. In modern life, all forms of life can be indulged. The individual who is not simply submerged in the mass is free to cultivate all sorts of aims; one is as good as another, for there is no traditional order present in society that sets a standard of the good citizen. In place of character the individual may develop the appearance of character, for what is character anyway? It is not known. Aesthetic in this respect is not true aesthetic, for the truly aesthetic in human experience requires that a sense of absolute beauty be revealed in the aesthetic. Aesthetic in this respect is the aesthetic of the anarchist and of Felix Krull, confidence man.

Hegel speaks of a world of "pure culture" (*die reine Bildung*) in which all is inverted and alienated from the actual world and from thought. It is the world of Enlightenment speech. In this *Verkehrung,* anything is possible. The thoughts of good and bad are inverted: "What is characterized as good is bad, and vice versa, . . . the consciousness judged as noble and ignoble, are rather in their truth just as much the reverse of what these characterizations are supposed to be."[105] Hegel says that in this kind of world everything the mind says about itself is a perversion and a deception. Its language is clever and witty (*geistreich*).

Parallel with Alberti's vagabond, Hegel speaks of a spirit whose existence is all talk and devastating judgment which appears as truth because everything else is overwhelmed by it. He speaks of the "shamelessness [*die Shamlosigkeit*] which gives utterance to this deception."[106] Quoting Diderot's *Rameau's Nephew,* Hegel says: "This kind of talk is the madness of the musician 'who heaped up and mixed together thirty arias, Italian, French, tragic, comic, of every sort; now with a deep bass he descended into hell, then, contracting his throat, he rent the vaults of heaven with a falsetto tone, frantic and soothed, imperious and mocking, by turns.' "[107] Hegel says that to the tranquil and honest consciousness, "this talk appears as a 'rigamarole of wisdom and folly.' " The *Bildung* of the vagabond is many-tongued; his ability to change form is his stock-in-trade.

In the state of the thirty arias, we cannot tell the difference between true and false philosophy. The humanist ideal has no center and is out of control. The moving image becomes reality. We are in the reflected light of the fire in Plato's cave, without the promise of the sun. We are in Vico's cycles of history, without the eye of providence. All is simulation, taught by the mocker. Carl Sandburg says:

> I wonder, Momus,
> Whether shadows of the dead sit somewhere and look
>   with deep laughter
> On men who play in terrible earnest the old, known,
>   solemn repetitions of history.[108]

Life lived within a world of simulation is a life of technological desire. Here I have only suggested the elements of desire unconnected to virtue or to the pursuit of self-knowledge in the figure of the modern Momus. The technological world is a world of "terrible earnest" in which technology advances itself by repeating itself in all areas of human life.

What can affect this process and allow consciousness to open itself to itself? Is it possible to see beyond the object formed by reflection and the life formed by simulation? For this something radical is required that cannot come directly from thought itself. It can come from a phenomenon that is directly human and in which the human is uniquely in touch with itself and its own spirit. For this we must understand folly.

2

Metaphysics of Folly

> First Clown: "I'm the father of seven sons!"
> Second Clown: "I'm the son of seven fathers!"
> —Circus-clown joke

In 1568 in Poland there was a society of fools called the Babinian Republic. It was a shadow government that adopted a duplicate of the Polish constitution, with a complete set of governmental offices occupied by fools. If a person did something sufficiently foolish, he was invited to join. If reluctant, he was hounded until he accepted. "He was then given a license with a large seal and an office appropriate to his folly. If, for example, he had talked knowingly of things he did not understand, he was made an archbishop. The society grew so large that there was hardly an important person in any branch of church or government who did not hold an office in it. Finally the King of Poland, Sigismund August II, asked whether the Babinian Republic also had a king and was told that as long as he lived the society would not dream of electing another."[1]

Erasmus calls attention to Horace's report of a Greek who sat alone in an empty theater for days on end, "laughing, applauding, enjoying himself, because he thought that wonderful tragedies were being acted there, whereas nothing at all was being performed." In other areas of his life he comported himself well, being a worthy neighbor, a good host, agreeable with his wife, and generous with his servants, even if they secretly took some wine from his storage casks. Out of their concern for his behavior in the empty theater, his friends convinced him to take some medicine (hellebore), which cured him of his disease. Having been cured, he said: "Damn it all! you have killed me, my friends, not cured me, by thus wresting my enjoyment from me and forcibly depriving me of a most pleasant delusion." Erasmus comments that it was indeed the friends who were deluded and needed medicine for thinking that such "gratifying madness was some kind of evil."[2]

Rabelais describes an academic debate in which "Panurge nonplused the Englishman who argued by signs." The Englishman, Thaumaste, conducts the debate in terms of obscure bodily motions, before a rapt audience. Prior to the debate, Pantagruel, whom Thaumaste had challenged to the debate, is up all night studying ancient works on numbers and signs, on unnarratables, and on things that cannot be uttered. Panurge, Pantagruel's pupil, tells him not to worry and spends the night playing dice. Panurge's own preparation is to affix to his codpiece a lock of silk, colored red, white, green, and blue, and to place an orange inside the codpiece.

At the moment of the debate Panurge comes forward and asks to debate Thaumaste as a pupil representing his master, with Pantagruel to serve as the official for the debate. Thaumaste accepts this and begins the debate with a series of complicated hand signs, placing his fingers in various positions. Panurge counters these, and the tempo increases. In the penultimate moment, Panurge took out his codpiece, drawing it out for a full cubit and a half (about the length of his arm). He took out the orange and tossed it up and down in the air; "then he began to shake his fine codpiece, showing it to Thaumaste." Thaumaste replied by puffing out his cheeks and "breathing as if he were blowing up a pig's bladder." Panurge then "put one finger of his left hand in his asshole, and with his mouth sucked in air as when we eat oysters in the shell or sip up our broth."

In desperation, Thaumaste took out a dagger, holding the

point down. "Whereat Panurge took his long codpiece and kept shaking it as hard as he could against his thighs; then he put both hands, linked in the shape of a comb, on his head, sticking out his tongue as far as he could and rolling his eyes around in his head like a she-goat ready to die. 'Ah, I understand!' said Thaumaste, 'but then what?'" Further small signs are exchanged. In the final moment, Thaumaste put the thumb of his left hand on the tip of his nose, holding the rest of his hand closed. "Then Panurge put his two forefingers in each side of his mouth, pulling it open all he could and showing all his teeth, and with his two thumbs he pulled his eyelids way down deep, making a pretty ugly grimace, so it seemed to the spectators." Thaumaste has now been put to a nonplus, and he pronounces to the audience and to Pantagruel that they have in Panurge a great treasure.[3]

Thaumaste has confronted Panurge in the debate with a series of what may be called cognitive bodily signs, none of which have clearly identifiable meanings but which appear abstractly profound. These are ultimately met by Panurge with his fool signs, as he had planned from the start by decorating his codpiece in motley and inserting the orange. He shows Thaumaste his fool's bauble, or "lady's playfellow," and swings it about. The only phallus Thaumaste can offer is a dagger. Panurge couples his bauble with the comb made with his fingers on top of his head. This is the sign of the cock, the enduring sign of the fool.

The fool (folly, *folie*) is associated with the Latin word *follis* ("a leather bag, bellows, windbag," also "puffed-out cheeks"). When Panurge takes an orange from his fool's bag, his scrotum, Thaumaste breaks out of his abstract hand signs in an attempt at his own fool sign. Thaumaste puffs up his cheeks as if blowing up a pig's bladder, but he loses the battle of puffing and blowing when Panurge turns his whole self into an inverted bellows, sucking in air. In a last glimmer of understanding, Thaumaste makes a beak by extending his nose with his thumb and fist (the rooster's beak). Panurge acknowledges this and tops it by turning his face into the spread-out lips of the exaggerated smile of the clown with the drooping eyelids. Folly has won. No greater pupil could a master have. No greater master could a pupil have.

These are three examples of folly at work in the premodern world. Each involves the central principle of the art of folly—the inversion of the ordinary. I wish to consider folly as a human phenomenon that lies at the root of the impulse to speculative thought. Speculation is not simply a decision taken in thought as an opposition to reflection; it is based in a deeper level of consciousness that emerges in the activity of the fool. The fool is dialectic in action. He forces us to see through an order of things to an equally plausible order that is their opposite. Speculation is this same process done in thought. It finishes what the fool can only begin. The fool can direct vision to the inverse, but he cannot develop this as a form of metaphysical comprehension. Reflection, in contrast to folly and to speculation, never looks to the other side of things; it sets forth to verify and make certain for thought what it finds before it. In this sense it always promotes a one-sided view of the object.

The fool not only provides a key to the speculative impulse; he also provides an insight into the human condition. The fool's art is essentially a way of acting in relation to the world; there is implicit in the act of the fool a doctrine of prudence. The fool is not in possession of an ethic in the sense of either a knowledge of virtue or a principle on which to base deliberate choice, but the fool accomplishes something in his folly. The fool has something to teach concerning acting in the world as well as indicating for thought possibilities of the dialectics of the real. If we wish to think beyond reflection, we must recover those insights that were present in the world before the dominance of reflection and the objectifying impulse. How does the figure of the fool teach these things?

In the modern world there is no place for the fool. The fool has disintegrated into the professional comedian, the clown, and the mental patient. Folly exists as fragments of entertainment in the comedian's jokes and the clown's burlesque (the circus clown, or the clown for hire for children's birthday parties), or it exists as a symptom of mental illness (the incomprehensible phrases or the repetitive motions of those wandering the mental wards of hospitals or the city streets). In such phenomena only glimpses of the fool can be had. The modern eye looks quickly away. Folly is no longer a corrective of government, a source of the self, or a guide to wisdom. The fool and the trickster often associated with him are human types found in all cultures, ancient and modern, and folly is a theme in all mythologies and literatures.[4] The fool as a continuous tradition in Western society originates in the thirteenth century,[5] the same century in which *reflection* becomes a term for the mind's apprehension of itself.

Reflection goes on to shape the modern self; folly reaches its peak in the sixteenth century, and then declines.[6] Although the fool tradition is a late medieval and Renaissance phenomenon, the fool and folly were present in the world of the ancient Greeks and Romans. To verify this we have only to look to the works of Lucian, the plays of Plautus, the Greek satyr plays (the fool shares with the satyr the symbol of the goat and, like the satyr, is a figure half-animal and half-human), and the parasites and laughter-makers that abounded at the courts of Philip and Alexander, who were known by such names as Lark, Pod, the Ham-Cleaver, and Mackerel.[7]

Early in the fool tradition, the natural or innocent fool, the fool by birth, is distinguished from the "artificial" fool, the fool

The fool as clown (Alberto Fratellini)

by profession, the king's fool, the court jester, the buffoon. The true fool may be a combination of both, neither simply a mental defective who does amusing or even profound things nor the fully competent person who has mastered the art of acting foolish. Folly as an instrument of moral instruction, portraying the ways in which one may stray from the path of Christian virtue, is presented in Sebastian Brant's panorama of more than a hundred types of fools in his famous *Narrenschiff*, published in 1494.[8] The medieval world of the morally deficient fool gives way to the Wise Fool, or folly as a kind of wisdom, in Erasmus's *Moriae encomium* (The praise of folly), which he formulated during his journey from Rome to England in 1509 in order to avoid wasting the whole time, as he says, in "crude and illiterate talk."[9]

There are the wise fools of Shakespeare, especially Falstaff and Lear's Fool, the adventures of Gargantua and Pantagruel, and the antics of Don Quixote.[10] In *Candide* Voltaire uses themes and devices of folly and the figure of Doctor Pangloss to refute the Leibnizian doctrine that "everything is for the best in this world."[11] Swift's description of the Laputian professors in *Gulliver's Travels* has a place in the study of folly. He spoofs theory of knowledge by having the thinkers carry with them huge bundles of the actual objects that are known to them.[12] But in the eighteenth century the devices of folly have become a deliberate form of criticism.

By the beginning of the nineteenth century the fool is exhausted, a casualty of natural selection. A work of the period states that the fool's "exercises are commonly divided into four parts, eating and drinking, sleeping and laughing: for these are his chief loves; a bauble, and a bell, coxcomb, and a pied coat: he was begotten in unhappiness, born to no goodness, lives but in beastliness, and dies but in forgetfulness. In sum, he is the shame of nature, the trouble of wit, the charge of charity, and the loss of liberality."[13] In the late 1960s Vancouver, British Columbia, employed a town fool, supported by a grant from Canada Council. He roamed the streets "like a living fossil, looked at with amusement or anger but devoid of any sociocultural and metaphysical function."[14] The fool's life had been over for a long time.

From the perspective of social history, folly exists on a continuum from innocent behavior to dangerous and psychotic behavior that threatens the life of the person involved as well as the lives of others around him. Anton C. Zijderveld points out that when the behavior of the fool became physically violent and dangerous, medieval men and women were quite helpless. For the medieval the fool was a varied phenomenon. The fool was understood as *deviatus*, but he was also called *ignarus, ineptus, stultus* (the term used in the Latin title of Brant's work, *Stultifera navis*, and also used by Erasmus), *fatuus, stolidus, exensis, demens, insensatus, insapiens, garrulus, baburrus, idiotus, rabiaticus, maniacus, furiosus, demoniacus, lunaticus,* and *melancholicus* (a term also applied to the philosophical temperament). Zijderveld says that the fool "could not be denominated by one single epithet, as Rational Man would do: 'mental patient.' It is also obvious that all these colourful names were but variations of one theme: the fool as a looking-glass image of the 'normal' human being."[15]

In a rational world supported by critical reflection and dedicated to progress there is no place for the fool, especially as a potential source of civil wisdom or self-knowledge. With the rise of the bourgeois class the fool has no value.[16] In the modern world *deviatus* has no value in itself; it is a condition to be cured or controlled. Folly is dismissed from the definition of the human itself only to reassert itself in dark ways, as a form of mental illness. Having no positive way to understand folly except as the subject of comic entertainment, the modern is as oddly helpless in coping mentally with folly as part of the human condition as the medieval was in coping physically with the violence of psychosis.

Can something still be learned from the late medieval and Renaissance phenomenon of the fool and folly? Does folly offer a source of knowledge that stands opposed to the barbarism of reflection? Erasmus says that the fool, unlike the scholar, practices "true prudence": "The wise man [*sapiens*] retreats to the books of the ancients, and there learns mere verbal trifles. The fool plunges into the thick of things, staring danger in the face, and in this way (unless I am badly mistaken) he acquires true prudence."[17] The humanist ideal connects wisdom, eloquence, and prudence. The fool has a natural eloquence that never fails to obtain our attention.

Does the fool's *prudentia* have a metaphysical wisdom on which it depends and which acts as its guide? The fool does in fact possess such wisdom, which can be summed up in the idea of *inversion*. The fool's metaphysics is his power to invert the apparently real. This metaphysical talent of world inversion is the fool's guide to morals, and morals is grounded in the sense of prudence that the fool teaches. To learn the secret of the fool is to observe speculative philosophy in action and from this perspective to perceive the basis of virtue.

Speculation and self-knowledge depend upon inversion: the passing of one thing into its opposite. Reflection inverts nothing. Reflective understanding constructs sensation into an object for cognition through the power of judgment. Determinant judgment aims at a categoreal formation of the world. Such judgment gives us a single understanding of the object. It is monotone thinking. If the understanding gives us two equally credible judgments, it has failed in its power and can even go into a swoon. Speculative reason can pass back and forth between opposite forms of comprehension. Irony is the trope of inversion and dialectical reversal.

Hegel exploits irony, humor, and the inversion of opposites in his confrontation of the Understanding with speculative Reason in his *Phenomenology of Spirit*. Hans-Georg Gadamer says: "Hegel is a Swabian and shocking people is his passion, as it is the passion of all Swabians."[18] Bertolt Brecht writes: "I have never met a person without a sense of humor who has understood Hegel's dialectic."[19] Hegel's principle that philosophy makes common sense stand on its head is the same as that attributed to folly. Hegel disrupts the Understanding from inside and establishes the self-knowing *I* of his philosophy of *Bildung*.[20] Hegel does this by placing the inverted world (*die verkehrte Welt*) within the Understanding as a stage of consciousness. His metaphor of the *verkehrte Welt* appears in the chapter "Force and Understanding" in the *Phenomenology of Spirit*. In the *Science of Logic* Hegel refers back to the *verkehrte Welt*, using the same examples that he uses in the *Phenomenology*.[21]

Hegel takes the term *die verkehrte Welt* (the inverted or topsyturvy world) from the title of the play by Ludwig Tieck, who is better known for *Der gestiefelte Kater* (Puss in boots). Tieck's play, *Die verkehrte Welt*, published in 1799, was not performed in his lifetime and has rarely been performed since.[22] Tieck gave it the ironic subtitle *A Historical Drama in Five Acts*. The play begins with an epilogue and ends with a prologue. It is to be staged such that "a fictive audience is shown on stage, watching a play on a fictive stage, this play being visible to both the fictive and real audiences."[23] Characters are allowed to determine their own distinctions between appearance and reality. At one point, one of the actors decides to exchange roles with one of the members of the fictive audience.

In the last act the fictive audience rises up to order the action according to its own tastes. "In the play the fictive audience is watching, the personages at one point sit down to watch a play, in which the personages once again gather to watch a play. The fictive audience is now in a whirl; the walls of reality seem to buckle; reality threatens to dissolve in a dream; and one of the fictive spectators suddenly cries out 'What if *we* were fiction too?'"[24] At the end of the "prologue," that is, the end of the play, one of the chief personages comes out to address the audience, saying that the whole prologue has been directed to him, yet he has been unaware of it, and he is the only person here. He concludes: "This is a marvel that deserves to be investigated by the philosophers."[25] Tieck's play is like a work of Pirandello. It is remarkable that it exists at the beginning of the nineteenth century.

Hegel's inverted world comes just at the moment when the stage of "Consciousness" in the *Phenomenology* collapses in on itself and gives way to the stage of "Self-consciousness." Consciousness has moved from apprehending the object as a here-and-now of sensation to the perception of the object as a thing, to the construction of the object as a force subject to the principles of the Understanding. Hegel's presentation of the stage of "Force and Understanding" is the most difficult to grasp in the *Phenomenology*. John Findlay, the one commentator in our time who has captured Hegel's spirit in his own thought,[26] regards this section of Hegel's work as the primary example of a place where the reader is "only sure that he is saying something immeasurably profound and important, but [is not sure] exactly what it is."[27]

In a work that is not easy to read, this section of Hegel's *Phenomenology* is especially difficult. I think that the sense of impenetrability lies not so much in the quality or details of the exposition as in our feeling that we can never fully reach what inversion means, that we can never quite get to its vanishing inner point. We see two lines opposite each other receding infinitely into the distance to form an apex, but we are never able to see the exact point of the apex where one receding line turns into the other and comes back to us in the foreground. The fool can get to this deep point of vision and make the turn from one to the other. The turn may also be made by those who have mastered dialectic.

Generally speaking, consciousness arrives on the threshold of the inverted world when it realizes that the object of knowledge it seeks is not a substance in which perceivable qualities inhere. It realizes that a thing can be understood as a force that exists among these qualities or properties, a kind of particular massing of them that follows certain laws which express the actions of one entity on another. These laws are not perceivable and in this sense exist in a "supersensible" realm. The thing itself, the ground of the internal order of the object's properties, what the object is, is supersensible and cannot be the object of perception. The world loses its footing.

The object is there only as the Understanding understands it. The critical understanding constructs the object. To avoid solipsism, the Understanding reflects on its own operations in making determinant judgments. But the standard of this criticism—the basis for distinguishing what counts as a principle of knowledge and what does not—is given only in logic and science. Why should we believe that logic or science presents to us the true nature of things? The fool's answer, and dialectic's answer, is that we cannot. The sensual and the perceptual sense of the given have been replaced by the cognitive sense of the given. No account of the validity of the given has been produced. In fact, things have grown worse, because the object can be formed for the knower in various ways.

The problem is even worse than the existence of competing ways of knowing. The understanding put purely on its own terms cannot find a solution to justify the given being one thing and not another. Having conceived the world in one way, the Understanding can just as well entertain the thought that the world is in reality exactly the opposite. This is Descartes' "evil genius" formed as a purely epistemological principle of doubt.

Here we need not think of the possibility of an anti-God who bends all his efforts to deceiving us; the Understanding can throw itself into a quandary by realizing that it commands no principle by which it can declare that one term of an opposition refers correctly to the real nature of things rather than the other.

As Hegel puts it: "What tastes sweet is *really*, or *inwardly* in the thing, sour; or what is north pole in the actual magnet in the world of appearance, would be south pole in the *inner* or *essential being*; what presents itself as oxygen pole in the phenomenon of electricity would be hydrogen pole in unmanifested electricity. Or, an action which in the world of *appearance* is a crime would, in the *inner* world, be capable of being really good."[28] Hegel points out that an objectively bad action may be well-intentioned; punishment may only appear to be punishment and actually benefit the criminal. What we know of the discrepancies between inward and outward behavior in human beings gives us reason to think that things can be the exact opposite of what they seem. The human world certainly involves inversion, and the Understanding cannot demonstrate that the world of natural phenomena is any more stable.

The Understanding becomes desperate. Inversion offers two equally plausible answers to the question of what the object is. Suddenly, consciousness realizes that its mistake has been in directing its energies to the objectifying impulse, in directing its reflections to the object and not to itself, the subject. The extremes of inversion vanish. Hegel says, "This curtain [of appearance] hanging before the inner world is therefore drawn away, and we have the inner being [the *I*] gazing into the inner world—the vision of the undifferentiated selfsame being, which repels itself from itself, posits itself as an inner being containing different moments, but for which equally these moments are immediately *not* different—*self-consciousness*."[29] Hegel's term for curtain here is *Vorhang*, or a stage curtain. The curtain of the theater of the world is suddenly raised, and there is the *I* declaring its own reality as self. Like the protagonist of Tieck's "epilogic prologue," the *I* is there as the new subject for the philosophers to investigate. Philosophy begins here with the *I*. Since Socrates, self-knowledge is the aim of philosophy, and it begins here in the sense that inversion of the ordinary world is the principle necessary for philosophy to begin.

Hegel writes to his friend Peter van Ghert on December 18, 1812: "To the uninitiated, speculative philosophy must in any case present itself as the upside-down world [*die verkehrte Welt*], contradicting all their accustomed concepts and whatever else appeared valid to them according to so-called sound common sense [*gesunder Menschenverstand*]."[30] The self emerges within consciousness through the phenomenon of inversion, and at this moment the basis from which speculative thought can develop is born. The life of the self develops slowly through many stages.

The power to invert is the most archaic power of the self. It lies in the depths of its existence. This is the power that the fool touches; his manifestation of it is what attracts us to him. This presence of inversion is also the reason for the natural attraction and repulsion we have when encountering the abnormal person, the person making insane gestures in the street, the mentally defective, the retarded. We encounter the inversion that is ourself. Diane Arbus, with her photographs of the mentally retarded dressed for birthday parties or Halloween, or her unusual photographs of twins, tries to make us see the other of ourselves. It is a sense of the Other that Derridians rarely think of, if at all. For the Modern such an encounter in real life is an experience to be endured. For the Medieval such an encounter was an occasion of instruction arranged by nature.

In such an encounter, the ordinary citizen in the Middle Ages was exposed to a being who had a connection with another form of reality. The purpose of the medieval Feast of Fools was inversion.[31] The Feast or Festival of Fools (*festum stultorum*) was between Christmas and Epiphany, a period when there was an inversion of roles in the clergy and in society. Faces were painted grotesquely; masks and strange costumes were worn. Ordinary religious and social structures were inverted: the Mass was tampered with, and blasphemy, lechery, and debauchery were allowed, as was the eating of such special foods as blood sausages. There are similarities in this with the Roman *Saturnalia* and with the ancient Babylonian *Saccaea*.[32]

In *Geschichte der deutschen Poesie im Mittelalter* (History of German poetry in the Middle Ages), Karl Rosenkranz traces the theme of the *verkehrte Welt* to two phenomena in the Middle Ages: the *Narrenschiff*, or ship of fools, and the *Totentanz*, or dance of death.[33] In the *Deutsches Wörterbuch* the Brothers Grimm cite Brant's *Das Narrenschiff* as a source for the verb *verkehren*.[34] Michel Foucault in *Histoire de la folie* claims that such ships or boatloads of fools did exist and plied the rivers of the Rhineland and the Flemish canals, taking their insane cargo from town to town. The watery soul of the fool had a sympathetic connection to movement on water. Of the fool's situation Foucault says: "He is the Passenger *par excellence:* that is, the prisoner of the passage. And the land he will come to is unknown—as is, once he disembarks, the land from which he comes."[35]

At Hegel's hands we are the prisoner of the phenomenological passage, for the *I* that emerges from the Understanding is not immediately in possession of speculative wisdom. It will forget much and have to start over many times, enter many forms of illusion and foolishness, before reaching the stage of absolute knowing (*absolutes Wissen*) that is the ideal of the philosopher. We become the prisoner of Hegel's "highway of despair" (*der Weg des Zweifels*). Hegel says in the preface to *Phenomenology:* "When natural consciousness entrusts itself straightway to [philosophical] Science, it makes an attempt, induced by it knows not what, to walk on its head too, just this once . . . relatively to immediate self-consciousness it presents itself in an inverted posture [*als ein Verkehrtes*]."[36]

The dance of death involves the *verkehrte Welt* because it places life in the mirror of its opposite. Death dances with each person. It affects equally pope, king, and child. The dance of death inverts our sense of what is real, from what is here to what is beyond, and thus makes uncertain our "sound commonsense" understanding of things. One of the earliest works of Germanic literature contains a discourse with Death. *Der Ackermann aus Böhmen* (The plowman from Bohemia), written by Johannes von Saaz in 1401, says: "The earth and all that therein is are built upon transience. In our day they have become unsettled, for all things have been reversed [*alle ding haben sich verkeret*], the last has become the first, the first has become the last, what was below has risen above and what was above has fallen below. The greater part of people has turned wrong into right."[37] This portrait of *Verkehrung* is not far from Hegel's inversion of north and south polarities and of good and bad. In another place Death says: "Fools call good what is wicked, and wicked what is good."[38]

The relationship of death and the fool is complex. Death can appear as a fool wearing a fool's costume and cap, who drags off the human fool, the lump who once wore them. William Willeford says: "According to a late Medieval conceit, Death, himself a fool, makes fools of us all. . . . The fool survives his own death: abandoning the *prima materia* of the human image, the fool enters the dimension in which Harlequin once led a horde of ghosts. A similar form of immortality is implied when the circus clown jumps to his feet after having been hit over the head with a sledge hammer."[39] The fool survives his inversion of things and, like consciousness at the end of the *verkherte Welt* experience, he survives as an *I* on a different plane.

Rosenkranz says, "The Dance of Death exposes to view the claim the fool's world has on us and inverts the inversion [*verkehrt ihre Verkehrung*]."[40] The dance of death is a *Verkehrung* of the fool in us; it is both a kind of folly—the celebration of death in life—and the element of self-correction in folly that opens to us another plane of existence. Consciousness is thrown back upon itself and the problem of its own reality and truth. "Death," as Hegel says, "is of all things the most dreadful."[41] Rosenkranz says: "Death, that which runs counter to the human being, brings his foolishness into consciousness for him."[42]

Inversion is not itself dialectic because in inversion as present in the Understanding there is no *Aufhebung*, no movement like that found in the "speculative sentence."[43] *Verkehrung* is not simply reversal but a kind of perverse reversal of events. This perversion is the fact that in the inverted world of the Understanding there is only back and forth movement, for example, south to north and back. There is no possibility of a resolution or a new beginning. We are, on the simple level of inversion, a prisoner of the passage that begins nowhere and goes nowhere in principle.

The art of the fool differs from the art of dialectic in that dialectic holds the true to be the whole. The fool has only opposites. Dialectic requires a movement through and beyond both sides of an opposition. All opposites become contraries. The fool can only invert, can only reveal the other half, the other side of whatever is taken to be real. The fool reminds us that dialectic is possible. The fool gives us again and again a beginning point, but he cannot complete what he starts. His actions of inversion point us inward to the *I*, to the fact that our own existence is somehow beyond any given pair of opposites.

Unless the fool's actions remind us of our existence as self, his actions and his existence are merely upsetting. They threaten the order settled on by the Understanding and healthy common sense. True philosophy slips away from us, and we fall into false philosophy, or sound thinking (literal-mindedness), which is the same thing. The origin of dialectic or speculative thinking in the art of the fool produces a new sense of *Aufhebung* (*aufheben*, to cancel and preserve at once) as based in human wit or *ingenium*.

Ingenium is that power, so prized in the Renaissance, to see a connection, to form a hypothesis, to express a metaphor. This is not done by a method of induction. The fool's inversion forces us to see a connection between opposites. *Aufheben* approached in this way is not the stolid mechanism that has been so often attributed to Hegelian dialectic. Hegel's use of *aufheben* has been taken too seriously, and not enough attention has been given to the canceling aspect of the verb. *Aufheben* is rooted in what is accomplished in ordinary speech through the trope of metaphor or that of irony, in which a connection between two things is struck and a new outcome is produced, a new sense of things or a new thought that places us beyond a situation.

Aufheben, being the form of wit itself, or *ingenium* is also the form of the joke. The joke cancels and transcends at once. The joke strikes out against something and then transcends it by placing us in a new, unexpected relationship to the thing joked about. Cicero says, "There are two types of wit, one employed upon facts, the other upon words" (*De orat.* II. 59.239–40). The joke can play upon two senses of a word, which is also the practice of oracles, or upon two perceptions of a situation, which is the practice of the magician. Cicero says that although jokes can be about either words or facts, "people are most particularly amused whenever laughter is excited by the union of the two" (II. 61.248).

The fool can delight by using either manner or by using both. The fool's speech is often accompanied by gestures and actions. In the film *Animal Crackers* (1930) Groucho Marx gets his brother Chico to remark, "He thinks I look alike." Groucho responds, "Well, if you do, it's a tough break for both of you." In another scene Groucho divides himself into two, and the two Grouchos interact.[44] This is the foolishness of the mirror, the child's joke of asking, "Do you want to see a monkey?" and then handing his friend a mirror. This might be called the joke of Narcissus. It upsets the ponderousness of the Narcissus myth.

The fool's stock-in-trade is laughter, the production of it in others. The fool is an agent of memory because folly acts against forgetfulness. When we settle on one version of the world, we are thinking categorically. It is a natural way of thinking that we might call "Kantian" in the sense that it proceeds from the impetus of the Understanding flatly to assert the truth and has no dialectical quality. The impetus to attempt to understand the world in one way, and its accompanying impetus to universalize the meaning of human actions, is to forget that things can just as well be the opposite. We settle on the view that all human beings are the same, only to be confronted by an ethnic joke. The joke reminds us of the particularity of the human condition, which reminds us of the fact that one similarity among humans is that they all respond to ethnic jokes.

Each stage in Hegel's phenomenology of consciousness develops itself to the point of illusion by trying to claim that its grasp of the world is categorically true. Consciousness forgets that it has done this same thing before and that it was freed from the confines of that stage when it "remembered" that things can be understood another way. Consciousness takes itself seriously, only to discover it is closer to the truth when, suddenly, it is able not to take itself seriously and able to grasp another possibility. The new stage, of course, brings with it its own version of forgetting. Memory must always be reestablished; this requires the principle of inversion. Memory itself is constantly forgotten, only to be revived by consciousness's power of folly or power to react to folly.

Rational man, who is essentially a stoic, has difficulty with laughter because in laughter the body overcomes the mind. The mind may enjoy a joke; a joke may be read or it may be run over in the mind, but only the body laughs. Descartes describes laughter in physiological terms: "Laughter results when the blood coming from the right-hand cavity of the heart through the central arterial vein causes the lungs to swell up suddenly and repeatedly, forcing the air they contain to rush out through the windpipe, where it forms an inarticulate, explosive sound." Laughter would seem at most to have an effect on the anima rather than the animus, the heart having an old significance as the organ of the anima. Descartes continues: "As the air is expelled, the lungs are swollen so much that they push against all the muscles of the diaphragm, chest and throat, thus causing movement in the facial muscles with which these organs are connected. And it is just this facial expression together with the inarticulate and explosive sound, that we call 'laughter.' "[45] Descartes' account of the physiology of laughter does not differ greatly from more modern accounts.[46]

Laughing cannot be an act of will; one cannot decide to laugh. By exerting self-control one may suppress or attempt to suppress a laugh. Laughter is not an act of mind as such. Laughter appears in all normal children in all cultures at about the fourth month of life. Spinoza says that laughter is among those things that are "attributable to the body only, without any reference to the mind."[47] Laughter is not a cognitive function. It must be explained as an action of the body and as one of the passions. For the rationalist, laughter can at best be a source of pleasure or at worst a source of disturbance.

Descartes regards laughter as only tangentially connected to joy and says that in laughter "there is always some slight occasion for hatred, or at least for wonder."[48] Bacon sees a connection between laughter and joy, in that they are physiologically similar.[49] Hobbes agrees.[50] They both point out that laughter often involves not only surprise (wonder) but in many cases derision and lack of sympathy for another's infirmities. The German word *Schadenfreude*, which means to take malicious joy in the misfortune of another, expresses this sense of laughter. Thomas Fuller protests against jesting about a person's natural defects and says, "'Tis crueltie to beat a cripple with his own crutches."[51]

In the humanist tradition the relation between laughter and wisdom is problematic. Plato claims it is inappropriate to make the young into lovers of laughter or for noteworthy human beings or gods to be portrayed as overcome by laughter (*Rep.* 388D-389A; compare *Laws* 732C, 935B). Aristotle says some jests are more becoming than others: "Irony better befits a gentleman than buffoonery; the ironical man jokes to amuse himself, the buffoon to amuse other people" (*Rhet.* 1419b. 8-9). The human animal is the animal who truly laughs, although other animals can engage in humorous action. Irony, ridicule, and mockery are as much a feature of the human community as are deductive inference, theories, and verification. Vico claims that because laughter, like reason, is a human prerogative, we feel that by laughing we are experiencing that we are human. But Vico claims that laughter as such does not justify our humanity.

Vico says: "Laughing men (*ridiculi*) are about half way between austere, serious men and the animals. By 'laughing men' (*ridiculi*), I here mean both those who laugh immoderately and without reason (who should be more properly called *risores*) and those who make others laugh (who should be properly called *derisores*)."[52] Vico says that serious men are not easily distracted and aim toward the truth. He says that *risores* are easily distracted, and worse than simple distraction is the deliberate corruption of the truth that characterizes the *derisores*. He says that the poets understood these points by depicting *risores* as satyrs, indicating that they are between men and animals. A *risor* is a laugher. A *derisor* is one who derides and mocks. The laugher finds everything funny and cannot attain the concentration necessary for the search for truth or the achievement of wisdom. The *derisor* is prevented from truth and wisdom because he uses his mental powers not to think but to mock whatever is seriously thought.

The humanist knows that laughter has a day side and a night side. Laughter as a passion is not itself a virtue, and mockery that employs laughter is not a virtue because it is an unproductive guide for civil life. To make the young into lovers of laughter is to produce a race of buffoons, and to teach the young to hold the gods and the noteworthy up for ridicule is to produce a race of mockers. Such is antihuman, for a society of buffoons or a society of mockers has no principle of order; everything for such beings is a distraction. The art of the fool is not simply buffoonery, nor is the art of folly simply mockery. The words or deeds of the fool, the perception of folly within human affairs, or the interruption of the processes of ordinary consciousness by the telling of the joke must have something virtuous about them. The lover of wisdom cannot also be a lover of laughter, for laughter and mockery must be moderated, and they function in harmony with the other passions and parts of the soul. In medieval and Renaissance culture the fool never appears as worthless but as a figure of natural virtue whose actions have a meaning and who is a voice other than our own.

Democritus is the figure of the laughing philosopher. In late antiquity Democritus was identified with laughter, perhaps because of his doctrine of "cheerfulness" εὐθυμίη. Seneca claims it was said that Democritus "never appeared in public without laughing" (*De ira.* 2.10.5). Democritus found all the foibles of human beings to be laughable. Seneca contrasts this with Heraclitus, who is said to have wept in pity for all the wretched conditions of humans that he observed whenever he left his home. Seneca concludes that "everything gives cause for either laughter or crying" (ibid.; compare Juvenal 10.28–30). Laurent Joubert, in *Treatise on Laughter* (written in 1560, published in 1579), takes the side of Democritus: that the wisest approach to the world is laughter, not tears. He says, "Democritus, so perfected in wisdom (as is witnessed by Hippocrates) that he alone was able to make all the men in the world wise and prudent, laughed as a rule."

Joubert says that he does not know why Democritus put out his own eyes, but holds that one explanation might be that "perhaps he was of the opinion that by this he would become more fat which is most helpful in engendering laughter. Whatever the cause, he lived 109 years, being dissatisfied with nothing" (compare Tertullian, *Apol.* 46D; Plutarch, *De curios.* 521D). Of Heraclitus, Joubert says: "Heraclitus the weeper, on the contrary, always sad and upset, frequented the desert, lived on herbs and other foods that only sharpen the appetite, so that finally weakened and undone, he died hectic in the hide of an ox, in which state he was devoured by wolves, and found in the fields not recognizable as a man."[53]

Joubert sees Democritus as wise, not simply as derisive. Laughter is a kind of prudence for life that allows us to maintain ourselves and to hold the world at a distance. In this view Democritus is not simply a laugher; his laughter is a kind of prudence and a means of achieving the moderation necessary for wisdom. In Joubert's account Democritus appears to be a kind of cynic. In *Traite des causes physiques et morales du rire* (1768), Louis Poinsinet de Sivry says that Democritus died with the secret of his *mal* (ailment).[54] We do not know the cause of his laughter.

The fool is not a skeptic. Folly is not the theme of the skeptic. Skepticism is tied to the Understanding; skepticism and doubt are disturbances of the Understanding. Thought must transcend the Understanding and become speculative for folly to be regarded as more than a wrongful or regrettable human act. Critical reflection, the Understanding's stock-in-trade, is seriousness, the attitude of mind that it takes to refute or attempt to refute skepticism. The skeptic puts the workings of the Understanding against themselves, but he does so with logic, showing that the Understanding does not have as firm a grip on knowledge as it claims. When the mind is directed toward wisdom rather than simply knowledge, the fool's activity can be appreciated as a source of insight.

The fool's responses are not those of the skeptic, but they are allied to the types of actions and responses characteristic of the Cynic. This is particularly true of the Cynicism or "dogism" (κύων "dog") of Diogenes of Sinope. The antics of the older Cynicism of Diogenes and his followers are more like the activity of the medieval fool than is the later intellectual and satirical Cynicism of Lucian that influenced Erasmus. Diogenes is a scandal. Augustine, in his discussion on the "utterly absurd indecency of the Cynics" in the *City of God*, comments on the practice of the older Cynics who fornicated on street corners. He says he is relieved that the later Cynics have abandoned the practice of acting like dogs.

Augustine says that he prefers to think that Diogenes and others did not really do such things but more modestly made the motions under a cloak (*De civ. D.* XIV. 20). My own guess is that Augustine is wrong and that the Cynics had the ancient power of the fool's bauble at their disposal and openly used it. Ophelia in *Hamlet* says: "Young men will do't if they come to't, / By cock, they are to blame" (IV.v.57–58). For the Cynics, sex is a natural act not to be covered by convention. Convention cannot justify its own claims to validity.

Diogenes Laertius reports of the Cynic Diogenes: "When someone first shook a beam at him and then shouted: 'Look out,' Diogenes struck the man with his staff and added, 'Look out'" (*Lives* VI. 66). The staff or club carried by the old Cynics was to recall the club of Hercules, who was their model. Once, Diogenes "was asking alms of a bad-tempered man, who said, 'Yes, if you can persuade me.' 'If I could persuade you,' said Diogenes, 'I would persuade you to hang yourself'" (VI. 59). The appeal to the club, *argumentum ad bacculum*, is a sophistry in logic, but in the hands of Diogenes it is an instrument of instruction.

All so-called informal fallacies have legitimate uses in particular contexts, such as the use of *ad hominem* in questioning the character of a witness in a legal proceeding and *ad populum*, the "appeal to the populace," which can establish common opinion on an issue relevant for social policy, although it is not an argument for its correctness. It is not thought that *ad bacculum*, the appeal to force or the threat of force, is ever appropriate, but its valuable use shows itself here in the pursuit of Cynic wisdom by confronting stupidity in a way argument never can. Hegel shows this when, in arguing against the phrenologists in the only violent passage in the *Phenomenology*, he suddenly speaks of beating in the skulls of the skull-doctors.[55]

Diogenes, "found behaving indecently in public [masturbating in the town square], wished, 'It were as easy to banish hunger by rubbing the belly'" (VI. 69). "At a feast certain people kept throwing all the bones to him as they would have done to a dog. Thereupon he played a dog's trick and drenched them [urinated on them]" (VI. 46). Hegel plays a similar trick at the end of his discussion of phrenology, when he says that the phrenological doctrine of mind joins the highest activity of man, knowing (*Wissen*), with the contours of a bone, the skull, as "nature naïvely expresses in linking the organ of its highest perfection, the organ of procreating, with the organ of pissing [*Pissen*]."[56]

Menippus in his *Sale of Diogenes* relates that when Diogenes was captured and put up for sale as a slave, he was asked what he could do. "He replied, 'Govern men.' And he told the crier to give notice in case anyone wanted to purchase a master for himself" (VI. 29). "Asked why people give to beggars but not to philosophers, he said, 'Because they think they may one day be lame or blind but they never expect to become philosophers'" (VI. 56). Our literal-minded philosophers of today have lost the power of such responses. The postmodern philosophical mind, with all its attempts at cleverness, cannot touch the humor of Diogenes or of Hegel.

In the fool-business of Diogenes one is reminded of the exchanges of Zen masters with their pupils: the master pushes the novice off the cliff; the novice climbs back up and pushes the master off. The master may repeat words back to the novice, or strike him from behind, or reply to the question of what Buddha-nature is with "The Buddha is a bucket of shit!" or bark like a dog when asked whether a dog has Buddha-nature. Zen Buddhism is a religion with a sense of humor. Consider Tanzan's version of the last laugh: Tanzan "wrote sixty post cards on the last day of his life, and asked an attendant to mail them. Then he passed away." The cards read:

> I am departing this world.
> This is my last announcement.
> Tanzan.
> July 27, 1892.[57]

The laugh releases energies of consciousness that go back to the origin of consciousness, to its primordial scene of light and darkness. As the cock with its crow breaks the light of day, the laugh is a reaffirmation of beginning. Folly can connect life and death as the cock connects night and morning. At the end of the *Phaedo* (118), as Socrates passes into the silence of death, he uncovers his face and says to Crito: "We ought to offer a cock to Asclepius. See to it and don't forget." Crito replies that it shall be done and asks: "Are you sure that there is nothing else?" Socrates makes no reply.

The traditional interpretation of this passage is that since Asclepius is the god of healing, Socrates may be saying that death is a cure for life. This may be true; but the cock—feathers and beaks—is an archetype of human consciousness and the sign of the fool throughout all literature. Is it a joke? Crito, the decent, good, conventional, well-meaning follower of Socrates, does not get it, and he asks if there is anything else. Socrates, having spent his last hours engaged in arguments, even saying never to be an enemy of argument, offers a final assertion that logic cannot understand. As a master of metaphor and of irony, he offers a joke. Is Socrates the sacrifice, the cock that has the power to open the beginning of the day? Is death just another cure to be overseen by Asclepius? With a wink, Socrates' soul is at peace.

Pico della Mirandola says, in his *Oration on the Dignity of Man:* "Pythagoras will enjoin us to feed the cock, that is, to feast the divine part of our soul on the knowledge of things divine as if on substantial food and heavenly ambrosia. This is the cock at whose sight the lion, that is, all earthly power, trembles and is filled with awe. This is the cock to whom, we read in Job, intelligence was given. When this cock crows, erring man comes to his senses. This cock in the twilight of morning daily sings with the morning stars as they praise God." The cock mediates between heaven and earth, as does the soul of man. Pico continues: "The dying Socrates, when he hoped to join the divinity of his spirit with the divinity of a greater world, said that he owed this cock to Asclepius, that is, to the physician of souls, now that he had passed beyond all danger of illness."[58] Socrates dies at the end of the day, which is the beginning of the new day.

In *Laughter*, Bergson says that "comic absurdity is of the same nature as that of dreams."[59] In the dream the self experiences what logic will not allow. Where do we obtain our notion of the absurd? It comes from the contrast we apprehend between what can occur in our dreams and what is possible in our waking world. The joke, the trick of the fool, the Hodge, the hodgepodge, the tomfool, allows us to introduce absurdity in a structured fashion into the world of healthy common sense. But when this element is introduced we do not have full control of it. It always has something of the power of the dream to transport us into a perspective that is on the other side of things (*Jenseits*). Although jokes and forms of laughter can be analyzed, there is no method for their creation, any more than there is a method for wit itself.

Freud, in *Jokes and Their Relation to the Unconscious*, isolates a special kind of joke that he says is among the most numerous: "They are the kind which are generally known as *'Kalauer'* (*'calembourgs'*) [puns] and which pass as the lowest form of verbal joke, probably because they are the 'cheapest'—can be made with the least trouble."[60] The *Kalauer* (*kalauern*, to make such puns) is a dumb pun as distinguished from a true play on words (*Wortspiel*). It is the lowest common denominator of humor.

The *Kalauer* is the opposite of the type of pun found in literature and philosophy. Consider Hegel's use of *das Meinen* in his discussion of sense-certainty in the *Phenomenology*, in which he plays on the German words *mein* (something that is mine) and *meinen* (to opine); or the plays on meanings in the Platonic *Dialogues*, such as, at the end of the *Republic* (621B-621C), in the tale of Er, the play on being "saved" ἐσώθη; Er is saved by coming back from the underworld, the tale he tells has been saved by being given a deeper meaning than its superficial features, and we can be saved by it); or the puns in Shakespeare's comedies or Joyce's *Finnegans Wake:* "Calling all downs. Calling all downs to dayne. Array! Surrection."[61]

The *Kalauer*, the dumb joke, the dumb pun, keeps consciousness closed. This type of pun allows the punster to confine language within his own limits, thus making himself seem clever. It is very difficult to have a conversation with someone who picks up one's words and puns upon them. Such puns can prevent anything from truly being said and even stifles ordinary conversation. Because *Kalauer* are never really funny, they tend to make the speaker what the Germans call *Mundtot* (literally mouth dead, reduced to silence). University administrators are often among those fond of puns; some have reputations as great punsters. The punster regales those present in a conversation with puns made at the expense of the person speaking or interrupts a conversation by drawing attention to a mispronunciation made by the speaker, forcing the listeners to find it humorous. It is a language of domination while at the same time appearing good-natured and amusing. The *Kalauer*, when it appears, reduces all in its presence to a common denominator: "Hey! We're all bozos on this bus, aren't we?"[62]

Lavater (1741-1801), thought to be one of the greatest scientific minds of his day by such figures as Wieland, Herder, and

Goethe, founded physiognomy, which became the source for Franz Joseph Gall's "phrenology." Lavater presents the modern notion of truth that is based in seriousness and grimness through an analysis of the visage of Democritus that is very different from that of Seneca or Joubert. Below an engraving of Democritus in *Essays on Physiognomy* Lavater says: "No; this is not the Democritus before us: it is the image of Democritus the Laugher, who grinn'd and grinn'd at everyone he met. He who laughs continually, and at every thing, is not only a fool, but a wicked wretch; as he who is always crying, and at every thing, is a child, a changeling, or a hypocrite. The face of the perpetual laugher must be degraded together with his mind, and become at length insupportable."[63] As mentioned in the Introduction, Lavater closes his work with a comment on Descartes' (grim) face as the most rare, perfectly thoughtful, and serious face possible. Both laughing and crying are problems for the modern conception of truth; they call out for a non-Cartesian understanding of our relation to the body.[64] Emotion has no place in the grim approach to truth.

Umberto Eco attacks this grimness as a condition of truth in *The Name of the Rose*, the theme of which concerns the discovery that Jorge has hidden from the world Aristotle's lost treatise on comedy, the second book of the *Poetics*, in the "greatest library of Christendom." At the end of the novel, when the monastery and its library burn to the ground, Jorge is seen eating the pages of the lost text on comedy. He hid the book in hopes of hiding laughter from the world, because laughter transfers to the belly what is proper to the mind. As the library burns, the protagonist William says: "Jorge feared the second book of Aristotle because it perhaps really did teach how to distort the face of every truth, so that we would not become slaves of our ghosts. Perhaps the mission of those who love mankind is to make people laugh at the truth, *to make truth laugh* [*fare ridere la verità*], because the only truth lies in learning to free ourselves from insane passion for the truth."⁶⁵

The modern pursuit of truth, the Promethean art in which the work of the gods has been taken over by the human power to command nature on one's own terms, has not solved the problem of laughter. William says to Jorge: "The Devil is not the Prince of Matter: the Devil is the arrogance of the spirit, faith without smile, truth that is never seized by doubt. The Devil is grim [*cupo*] because he knows where he is going, and, in moving he always returns whence he came."⁶⁶ The devil is a man of method. Method always knows where it is going in principle, and it always returns to itself for its next application and solution.

William says that he would like to lead Jorge downstairs naked before the monastery "with fowl's feathers stuck in your asshole and your face painted like a juggler and a buffoon, so the whole monastery would be afraid no longer. I would like to smear honey all over you and then roll you in feathers, and take you on a leash to fairs, to say to all: he was announcing the truth to you and telling you that the truth has the taste of death, and you believed, not in his words, but in his grimness [*tetraggine*]."⁶⁷ William wishes to dress Jorge in the classic symbols of the fool: feathers and the harlequin suit. As Jorge begins to eat the lost text of Aristotle he laughs for the first time, his mouth stuffed and dripping yellow slime from the dissolving pages.

Truth is the grim face that forbids laughter, the look of rationality that makes us think of "close readings" or arguments, of decision procedures or theories, but all that is really there is Jorge: all that is really there is *grimness*. Laughter is a danger to the grim sense of truth because laughter humanizes the object toward which it is directed. The laughing face shows itself to be human. To make truth laugh is intolerable because it transfers to the belly what is proper to the mind. But what is to stop us? William asks Jorge at an earlier point if he thought he could "eliminate laughter by eliminating the book." Jorge replies, "This book could strike the Luciferine spark that would set a new fire to the whole world, and laughter would be defined as the new art, unknown even to Prometheus, for canceling fear [*la paura*]."[68]

Hegel has his own version of making truth laugh. In a little piece called "Who Thinks Abstractly?" (*Wer denkt abstrakt?*), written about the same time as the *Phenomenology*, Hegel says that common sense thinks abstractly, not philosophy. Common sense would reduce everything to its own abstract terms. It follows its instinct to classify everything into categories without ever seeing into what lies beyond them, what the world is like as a self-movement. Hegel says, "Let those who can, save themselves!" He says that he has no ambition to instruct the world against its will. He intends to make his purpose clear from the beginning. He says that we must unbutton our "metaphysical overcoat" (*metaphysischer Überrock*) and expose the "flashing star of wisdom."[69] Folly is what we require to work the buttons.

When we step upon the stage of the theater of the world, if we cannot unbutton the metaphysical overcoat we are doomed to suffer forever the rational stare and to know little more of human wit and language than is present in the *Kalauer*. But once we have opened the overcoat, how can we learn the element of folly that is needed for self-knowledge and prudence? The fool has his own optics that runs counter to the optics of the barbarism of reflection.

The folly of the Babinian Republic creates a double vision for the king and for all in the ordinary government. Because of the existence of the Babinian Republic, there is a constant mime of what is occurring, a constant reference point of which anyone in any office must be aware. They are being imitated.

This is like the Roman custom of the professional *archimimus* who mimicked the gestures and attitudes of the deceased in the funeral procession in an ancient dance of death.

Horace's Greek man in the empty theater is an individual version of double vision. He can see the world as others see it and demonstrates this in the agreeable way he associates with his friends, his wife, and the members of his household. But he has another reference point, that of his hours in the empty theater. What is he seeing? He has his own theater of the world within the theater of the world that is society. This provides him with a pleasurable corrective to the ordinary single-visioned world.

Rabelais' debate transfers the mind to the body. The debate in signs is a semiotics of folly and a folly of semiotics. We struggle, along with the audience, to grasp the exchange as a process of words and ideas, but we are forced to confront things otherwise. The exchange of Pantagruel and Thaumaste is like the original mute language of humanity, yet it is done with complete sophistication, in fact with ultra-sophistication, taking turns and yielding conclusions that we cannot fathom. We are caught up in its folly, and we must become double-visioned about thought: the universe of learning, in dumb show.

Inversion is not simply to be found in the grand gestures of the fool; it is what the fool brings to every situation and reminds us of the arbitrariness of the order of our everyday world. Zijderveld describes a twentieth-century domestic fool, Peppi, who died in 1978 and who was part of the household of Zijderveld's parents-in-law in Vienna. Peppi, Zijderveld reports, throughout his life would intersperse his sentences and gestures with a repetitive "bitte-danke, danke-bitte" (please-thanks, thanks-please). If asked a question that he did not like, he would rattle this off several times as his answer. He would also interrupt a conversation with guests or visitors to the family with the same series of expressions.[70]

What could be more clever, given the constant polite use of these words in German conversation? Peppi was inverting their order: *bitte* (Please enter, take this seat, and so forth); *danke* (Thank you for the welcome, the seat, and so forth); *danke* (I take the seat); *bitte* (I am pleased you took it). Why say one thing rather than the other? The interruption to the conversation means that what is being said might just as well be said in the opposite. Peppi has mastered Bergsonian "cinematographic time," in which events might equally well be run in reverse. Peppi's words were routinely allowed to go unnoticed, at least at the conscious level, and he was politely dismissed to return to his tasks. Peppi is the digression of nature (and *durée*) into the cultured speech of civilization, which cannot be heard by the ear that has evolved through the Enlightenment.

The fool was known by sure signs, particularly when he flourished in the sixteenth century. The principal sign was his dress. Shakespeare's stage fools were dressed like Elizabethan idiots, in long coats or petticoats made of coarse woolen stuff of mixed color with a dark greenish tinge. This was generally known as motley and was used both to dress fools and to make cheap garments for artisans, barbers' aprons, and cloakbags or pokes. This garb was the standard dress "(a) for 'born fools' or idiots in general, (b) for professional domestic fools (whether real lack-wits or clever 'artificials'), and consequently (c) for their imitators on the stage."[71] When Shakespeare's Jaques meets Touchstone in the forest, he knows immediately by his dress that Touchstone is a fool and says, "Motley's the only wear!" (*As You Like It* II.vii.34).[72] The fool is actually dressed in a cloakbag or poke, which fits with the cry of the audience: "Away with the fool!"[73] In the medieval tradition, the human body is a mere sack that holds the soul. Rather than ordinary clothing the fool wears a sack that is a second body in which he moves about, and that reminds us unconsciously of our own transitoriness: that we mortals are cloakbags of the soul.

The other signs of the fool are his coxcomb and his bauble. King Lear's fool enters the play showing off his coxcomb (*Lear* I.iv.105). The fool is the human rooster who crows. As Willeford says, "The cock could be taken as the emblem or even the genius of that realm of fools, the cock being lecherous, vain, and stupid."[74] The cock is the mime of human reality. Can it be an accident that, when within the Platonic Academy man was defined as a "featherless biped," Diogenes brought a plucked rooster into the lecture hall?

In *All's Well That Ends Well* Lavatch speaks of his bauble as the emblem of the fool (IV.v.31–32). The bauble is sometimes the "lady's playfellow," as mentioned above, but it is also the fool's scepter. The scepter is usually topped by a small head of a fool with belled cap that imitates the fool's own cap. The fool's scepter, by which he reigns, which gives him license to speak as he wishes, is a duplicate of himself. The fool's authority is folly, and folly is part of nature. The fool is part of human nature.

Fools, madmen, and wild men populate the premodern world. The fool in his belled cap, in his feathers, in his rooster suit; the madman with his wild eyes, his nudity, his ability to tolerate extremes of temperature; and the wild man, with his beard and hairy body, sitting in his tree or walking on his hands, peer out at us from their historical place.[75] They greet us around the next corner, at the circus, at the asylum: the insane, giving long lectures to themselves; the wild man of Borneo; the laughing hermit. These are portraits of the human, of its other voices, other rooms. They are here in the walking insane of the cities, in the laughing old coots sitting among their collectibles in a thousand rural landscapes. It is not the hollow wisdom of the mad or the secret knowledge of the wild man that contains instruction of philosophical interest; it is the fool's *folie*.

The urtext in the Western tradition of folly is Sebastian Brant's *Das Narren Schyff,* written in medieval German and published in Basel in 1494. Brant's use of *Narr* as opposed to other terms current at the time (for example, *Tore, Affe, Esel, Gouch*) established it as the primary term for fool.[76] The work contains 112 sections: each, except the last, describes in verse a type of foolishness, and each is prefaced by a woodcut depicting that type of folly. Some of the woodcuts are the work of Albrecht Dürer, who visited Basel between 1492 and 1494.[77] Brant's work was translated into Latin in 1497 by his pupil and protégé Jacob Locher as *Stultifera navis,* which made it available to an international readership. Katherine Anne Porter refers to this translation in her novel *Ship of Fools*.[78]

Brant's work became an immediate best-seller and was translated into Low German, French, Dutch, Flemish, and English. It was also expanded in various ways. The Flemish thinker Badius Ascensius thought that there were an insufficient number of women on board Brant's ship and wrote an enlarged version with six more ships of female fools (1501).[79] Hieronymus Bosch painted the ship of fools. Erasmus met Brant in 1514 in Strasbourg, and they were probably together again in Antwerp in 1520. Erasmus greatly admired Brant. Brant composed a six-line Latin verse on the appearance of Erasmus's *Moriae encomium* (1509). Hans Holbein furnished illustrations for Erasmus's text in 1514. Erasmus was only eight years younger than Brant, and he was familiar with at least the Latin version of Brant's work before 1509, perhaps through his friendship with Badius. Brant is the Scholasticist on the threshold of humanism, and Erasmus is the humanist par excellence.[80]

Brant's metaphor of the ship is not original with his work. The idea of putting those living borderline lives in a ship was widespread from Holland to Austria, and the idea of such a ship was the subject of orations, several works, and a sermon before Brant's time.[81] Brant's work, as he himself says at its end, is *gesammlet,* that is, compiled.[82] The title is not original with him and to a large extent neither is the content. The portraits of fools are likely built on the practice of the Swabian *fliegende Blätter,* in which fly sheets depicting types of fools were circulated with the heading: "Der ist ein Narr" (This is a fool).[83] Brant's work resembles a collection of such sheets. Like Erasmus, he glosses many biblical passages and classical authors, and his favorite book of the Bible is Ecclesiastes.

The powerful image of the ship of fools has stuck in the Western mind. It may be related to the Roman *carrus navalis* of the festivals of Dionysus-Bacchus, from which comes the word *carnival* and which is related to the carnival floats in Europe of the sixteenth and seventeenth centuries.[84] But more important for Brant's work is the Christian tradition of the church as the ship of Saint Peter. Jesus embarks on a ship with his disciples (Matthew 8:23-27, Mark 4:36-41). Jesus preached from Peter's boat (Luke 5:3). The ship of Christianity is carried over rough seas to heaven. Brant's ship of fools is the inverse of this. It is a vessel of those who have been unable to ingest the wisdom of Christian virtue and who have wasted their substance in the various forms of foolishness that Brant describes. They are on a ship without purpose, unless it be to travel to the underworld. In life they move about aimlessly, with watery souls.

Brant's work is an encyclopedia of folly and illusion. In this it is like Hegel's *Phenomenology of Spirit,* in which consciousness finds itself in each of its stages to be short of the stage of absolute knowing. Consciousness in each stage is in a form of illusion, a form of foolishness through which it must persist until it can attain the next stage, in which another more elaborate illusion is developed that must be firmly surmounted. In

Hegel's "ship" there is a dialectical progression of cabins; that is, there is a progression if consciousness does not simply settle into one of the cabins, which happens if we take up some form of wisdom that is less than absolute. Brant's ship is a collection of types of folly with no progressive or dialectical order. Brant's last section is entitled "The Wise Man," and, like Hegel's sage of "absolute knowing," it shows the final answer to the folly of illusion present in the other cabins.

Brant says his work is a mirror: "For fools a mirror shall it be, / Where each his counterfeit may see." The mirror will show the truth: "His proper value each would know, / The glass of fools the truth may show." If the mirror reflects when we look in it, then we who see our reflection know we are not wise: "Who sees his image on the page / May learn to deem himself no sage."[85] The reason for the book is to have "the world's whole course in one brief look."[86] Brant says, "One vessel would be far too small / To carry all the fools I know."[87] There are "fools galore" in the world, and no one, Brant says, is without the fault of folly in some respect: "Both men and women, all mankind / Their image in this glass will find."[88] Brant says, "With caution everyone should look / To see if he's in this my book."[89]

Brant has produced a foolometer by which we can gauge our own and others' folly. It is a *speculum stultorum*. The forms of foolishness Brant describes range from "Of Useless Books" (those who involve themselves with books in order to glorify themselves but who do not understand the books they have) to "Of Useless Studying" (those who have not learned the proper things, "Thus money spent to train and school / Has often gone to rear a fool") to "Taking Offense at Fools" (those who ridicule fools or do not heed them, thus quickly becoming fools themselves) to "Blowing into Ears" (those who pass on what others say).[90] In addition to these are the follies we might commonly expect, follies related to envy and hatred, complacency, anger, pride, adultery, bad manners, ingratitude, gambling, contempt of holy writ, making noise in church, causing discord, blasphemy, and so on, and some esoteric follies, such as "Useless Hunting" (spending too much time at it) and "Experience of All Lands" (being overly interested in other places).

The point of Brant's mirror of folly is the recognition of prudence. "The Wise Man," his conclusion, is based on the pseudo-Vergilian poem "Vir bonus," and his example is Socrates: "A good, wise man of prudence rare, / As one can find scarce anywhere / In all the world, is Socrates."[91] The mirror of folly, unlike the mirror of the Understanding of the barbarism of reflection, reflects not an object but oneself. Recognition of folly is the beginning of self-knowledge. This is the ultimate wisdom. Brant says Apollo gave Socrates this gift of prudence.

The key to Socrates' wisdom, for Brant, is his doctrine of ignorance. Nicholas of Cusa, in *De docta ignorantia* (1440), echoes this in his own way by claiming that ignorance is the greatest learning. Cusanus' advice to the searcher for knowledge is parallel to Brant's advice to the searcher for virtue: to find the particular form of folly appropriate to oneself. "Nothing could be more beneficial for even the most zealous searcher for knowledge than his being in fact most learned in that very ignorance which is peculiarly his own; and the better a man will have known his own ignorance, the greater his learning will be."[92] The "fool" (the foolish person) pretends, to others and to himself, to know how to comport himself—but he does not know.

The key to Socratic wisdom is to know of whatever one knows that there is yet something not known. To be wise in human things is not to be wise in divine things, and human wisdom is above all to know that one is not fully wise in them. A doctrine of ignorance is naturally connected with irony (it is ironic that wisdom requires ignorance) and with dialectic (the other side of anything known must always be seen to complete the knowledge of it). A doctrine of ignorance is the key to prudence, for ultimately prudence requires the realization that we do not know what virtue really is. We must always think of its opposite; corresponding to every act that seems virtuous is a form of folly, of that act wrongly done.

The teaching of virtue requires example, and it may benefit from the use of images. Brant's use of woodcuts coupled with their embodiment in words is like Shaftesbury's "noble virtuoso scheme of morals," in which he uses images coupled with commentary to instruct in morals, as he explains in the unfinished *Second Characters*.[93] Brant's work is less complex than that envisioned by Shaftesbury in that the woodcuts, although quite fine, are not as complex as the emblem of the shield of Hercules or the tablet of Cebes, which Shaftesbury uses and which embody whole fables. The verses that accompany the woodcuts are not extended commentaries, but they combine the image and the word in an allegorical fashion.

The depictions and the verses guide our vision back into the world, to see the folly in human action that otherwise would seem only part of ordinary life. Our vision is heightened in the mirror of Brant's book; we see the world with a new vision, and we see ourselves in it. Like the fool's optics of looking at his scepter, which bears the likeness of a fool, we look and see ourselves in our foolishness. This is the crucial moment for the development of prudence, the sense of things that all virtue requires. Brant intends his book to be a device to affect our vision in the way that the fool actually affects our vision with his mimicking of ordinary actions and words, and although we do not inhabit Brant's world, his forms of folly are mostly still here in our world, if we look.

Erasmus's work is often understood only as satire, as Brant's work is often seen only as a work of Christian moralizing. Erasmus's work is moral satire, but it differs greatly from the satires of manners that appear nearly one hundred years later, such as *A Horseload of Fools*, by Queen Elizabeth's jester, Tarlton, in which fools go through Fleet Street in a pony cart; or *A Nest of Ninnies, Simply of Themselves Without Compound* (1608), by Shakespeare's fool, Robert Armin, in which the World, "wanton sick," is shown by Sotto, "as one besotted," various types of foolishness as illustrated by six characters.[94] These satires of manners mark the end of the philosophical importance of the fool, who dies at the close of the sixteenth century and is slowly buried in the ages of reason and enlightenment. In the world of method and research there is no place for the fool's impromptu art of inversion. The world ceases to be a theater and becomes a laboratory for the rational and empirical researcher that culminates in the use of machines as a means of production in the eighteenth century.[95]

Erasmus thinks differently. His metaphor is the *theatrum mundi*, the theater of the world. It is the stage on which each of us steps to play his role: "What fools these mortals be!" Erasmus says: "Now the whole life of mortal men, what is it but a sort of play, in which various persons make their entrances in various costumes, and each one plays his own part until the director gives him his cue to leave the stage?"[96] He then asks: "What do you think Ecclesiastes meant when he cried out, 'Vanity of vanities, and all is vanity'? No more nor less than this: that all human life is nothing but a stage-play of Folly."[97] The play is at the direction of *Stultitia* or *Moria*, Folly herself, who is the narrator of Erasmus's work. He dedicates his *Moriae encomium* (The praise of folly) to his friend Thomas More, on whose name the title puns; More kept a fool in his household.[98] Since all is folly in Erasmus's account of human affairs, it appears as if the work is a universal satire containing no positive doctrine.[99]

If the human comedy is just a comedy in which folly reigns

supreme, then all is meaningless. Any meaning found in anything is itself, in truth, just another type of folly. Erasmus says that "the human mind is so constituted that it is far more taken with appearances than reality."[100] Comedy becomes not an aspect of life but the order of life itself: "In fact, human life is nothing more than an entertainment staged by Folly."[101] If this is so, then Jorge's fears in Eco's novel are justified, and so is Vico's observation that because laughter is a distinctive capacity of the human, humans think that to be *risores* and *derisores* is sufficient to justify their humanity.

Erasmus speaks of Momus the mocker.[102] The profession of mockery is a hollow life-form because it requires no self-knowledge, no virtue, and can master a situation only by responding to it in a characterless way. A society of mockers is impossible because there is no basis in mockery for any principles of social order. Mockery disturbs folly and its pleasures, Erasmus says. He says that the gods could not tolerate Momus's mockery and threw him out, and "no mortal at all deigns to offer him hospitality in his exile."[103] Mockery of folly gives us no insight into its wisdom or its true role in human affairs.

At the beginning of his work Erasmus speaks of "foolosophers," of "foolers" of wisdom and "fool-sages." *Foolosophers* ($\mu\omega\rho o\sigma\acute{o}\phi o\upsilon\varsigma$) was coined by Sir Thomas Chaloner in the first English translation of Erasmus's work (1549) to play on the Greek word *sophomore* (*sophos*, "wise"; *moros*, "foolish"), but inverted as *morosophos*.[104] What is this wisdom? In Brant's work wisdom is the opposite of folly. Yet as I have described it, folly for Brant is the necessary beginning of wisdom: that is, the recognition of folly points toward the need for Socrates' self-knowledge, the key to wisdom in human things. In Brant's terms, recognition of folly is the essential step toward the path of Christian salvation, a place within the ship of Saint Peter instead of the ship of fools. Erasmus sees wisdom within folly itself, not as a goal external to it. The key passage for this in *The Praise of Folly* is that quoted above, on the fool as the practitioner of "true prudence."[105]

It is not accidental that, in Kant's conception of practical reason, prudence (*Klugheit*) is an imperfect state, an inferior way of human conduct that is to be pursued only if the rationality of the categorical imperative cannot be achieved. In the *Foundations of the Metaphysics of Morals* Kant makes this clear: "The word 'prudence' [*Klugheit*] may be taken in two senses, and it may bear the name of prudence with reference to things of the world and private prudence. The former sense means the skill of a man in having an influence on others so as to use them for his own purposes. The latter is the ability to unite all these purposes to his own lasting advantage. The worth of the first is finally reduced to the latter, and of one who is prudent in the former sense but not in the latter we might better say that he is clever and cunning [*gescheut und verschlagen*] yet, on the whole, imprudent [*unklug*]."[106]

In his attempt to realize the categorical imperative, Kant is on a fool's errand, as are all those since him who have sought ethics in terms of theory and practice. To seek a theoretical principle of ethical behavior that can be applied to particular ethical situations is the great fool's errand of modern morals. In morals all is practice; all ethics is "applied," for there is no true theory.[107] Moral life as it is lived is based on analogy: the actions in one instance are guided by those actions accomplished in another. This is what the fool knows, in Erasmus's account, and this is why the fool does not go to books. The fool accepts the particular conditions of life and acts on them.

Prudentia and *providentia* are synonyms in Latin, as they are more or less in English. The prudential, like the providential, is foresight, the ability to see through the situation. This is the fool's art, his folly of wisdom. He takes the events not as fixed but as subject to inversion, to having another nature than they seem to have. The fool is not afraid to act. The fool acts out of his own innocence and he prevails. He prevails because he is not overcome by events. In this way the fool shows us that it is possible to act in any situation. There is no set of events not subject to interpretation in terms of folly and none on which the fool cannot act. When others stand still before a state of affairs, the fool surprises us by the totally unexpected, and movement is shown to be possible. All this is accomplished without a theory, without a full intellectual understanding.

As ignorance is a necessary presupposition of our pursuit of wisdom, folly is a recurring presupposition of our pursuit of virtue in action. It is not that the fool is in possession of any particular virtues or of the Good that they embody. The practice of particular virtues in the conscious best life requires reason, yet reason unconnected to folly cannot act in a fully human way. But practical wisdom is not a form of folly. If it were, all would truly be comedy, and life would be truly a comedy of errors, a world of mockery and self-mockery. The fool shows us what it means to act directly out of what one is. He acts as a fool, and the virtuous man, as Aristotle says, must act from a consistent character.

The fool commands a special art of inversion, of acting dialectically, with the power to see to the other side of events that is required for prudence. Metaphysics is a guide to morals not because metaphysics offers us experience in theories but because it offers us experience in speculative reason; prudence in this sense is action that allows us to attempt to realize virtue.[108] We discover who we are by seeing ourselves in our actions done in accordance to virtue. Folly, our constant companion, guides us toward happiness, but it is not happiness itself. The positive doctrine of happiness in Erasmus is the happiness of accepting the folly in which we all participate; this requires "decorum," which is crucial to prudence but not equivalent to it.[109] Erasmus's favorite word, *festivus* (festive, cheerful, companionable), describes the quality that characterizes the good life.

The presence of folly in the world counteracts the objectifying impulse. The struggle in modern thought and in modern life is to come to some form of self-knowledge, civil wisdom, and happiness. Vico attempts this in his conception of the "nation" founded on *sensus communis,* Hume attempts it in his conception of "common life,"[110] Hegel attempts it in his conception of a "science of the experience of consciousness," and Cassirer attempts it in his conception of the "crisis of man's knowledge of himself." These are among the heroes of true philosophy in modern times.

Richard Rorty is correct that the conception of the mind as the "mirror of nature" has been the guide for the creation of the modern philosopher.[111] As modern philosophy is built the mind is disconnected from human wisdom, and it is disconnected from the divine in order that it be fully connected to the object. The mind ceases to be *nous* or the soul and becomes the Understanding. The concern of the Understanding is not with itself but with the object. The objectifying impulse makes the mind completely worldly. To think is to be objective.

The objectifying impulse is always there in the ancients, the medievals, and the humanists, but the moderns make it their occupation. Freud's discovery of psychoanalysis was immediately controversial because he discovered the self in a world of objective understanding in which the self is conceived only as a cognitive agent. He discovered that inside the self are all the themes that are outside the self in the world of myth and religion and that run beneath all ancient and humanist speculation. The self becomes the subject of the new science of psychoanalysis.

The modern world finally takes its genuine shape. The modern world is composed of psychoanalysis and its variations joined to the cognition of the object. Humanistic thinking, the self in literate discourse with itself, is forgotten, forgotten in the sense that it no longer determines anything in life, except in some individual lives. Rorty looks into the mirror of nature and sees the disappearance of the humanist and eighteenth-century wit. He proposes "conversation," the humanist stock-in-trade.[112] It is too little too late.

Philosophy is refreshed by conversation (which never occurs among professional philosophers), but philosophy is not sustained by conversation. Philosophy is sustained by wisdom, its true and proper love. Wisdom is a knowledge of things divine and human. Philosophy must see by the eye of metaphysics and the eye of morals. Without the dialectic between these two, philosophy has only an urbane life, a sophistication of talk; it does not have the tension between the divine and the human that takes it continually toward speculation. Rorty rightly sees the limits of the mind as understanding and looks the other way, to conversation, but he is tied to the single vision that scans only the horizon of knowledge for a solution. Reason has been left behind for a more open use of the Understanding—conversation. Reason in a speculative sense is to see the unseen within the seen. It requires the double vision that is only learned by the art of inversion. Folly is the example of this art as found in life. Folly unsettles the settled.

The objectifying impulse leads finally to the barbarism of reflection. Reflection presents the object as a vacuous actuality, that is to say, as a given which has no inner life or significance. Both the phenomenal object and the thing-in-itself are vacuous givens, since their significance lies only in the role they play in the activity of judgment. The self cannot be reached by the employment of concepts unless it is reached simply as another object or given. The self of the behavioral sciences and cognitive psychology or cognitive science is the self as an object investigated by reflective understanding. It is the self as here and now, functioning in the world. This is true even if attention is directed to the self's use of metaphors or tropes of various sorts to define this world. The self of the humanist is not reducible to such study.[113]

The speculative impulse runs counter to the objectifying impulse and upsets the order of the world accessible to the concept joined to the sense perception. The first form in which the self encounters itself as subject rather than as object is the act of inversion. Inversion is rooted in the passion of wonder. The capacity for wonder allows us to experience the object as a marvel, as marvelous. The marvel as something before the mind is never fully seen even by the mind's own eye. The marvel breaks into time and brings with it a glimpse of the beyond. Zijderveld says: "Folly is very much an aboriginal layer of consciousness in the human species, testifying to impulses which lay, as it were, prior to any socializing and civilizing process, piercing through the veneers of culture with an unpredictable, often noisy and irritating force."[114]

The marvel reached by the capacity of wonder appears at the point dividing the human and the divine. What is marvelous is always touched with the miraculous. The fable, *fabula*, is rooted in the power of speech to narrate or form what is seen as a true story. To form the seen as a story is to understand it as having a beginning, middle, and end. The reality grasped in the narration of these three moments, which are identical with the original powers attributed to the Muses (to tell us of what was, is, and is to come), is not vacuous. What is fabulous, the marvelous, has an inner life. The self exists in the process of birth, maturity, and death, and a fable that illuminates these moments in their interconnections offers the self a way to grasp its own being. The world is full of the fable: the stories parents tell to children, the stories families tell to themselves, the life stories of individuals, the histories of nations, the stories of the gods and of the actions of the divine in the world.

At the basis of the speculative, the fabulous, the marvelous, is the phenomenon of inversion. Not all fables or marvels are directly about inversion, although inversion, as the protagonist in Tieck's play says, is a subject always to be investigated by the philosophers. The power to invert the world lets the self know it exists. Inversion is its own unique power that can produce the laugh, that can establish the divine as an order beyond the rational order formed by the Understanding. To invert what is there before us lets us know that we are. The inversion is a wonder; we are stopped before it.

Inversion of events need not be the extreme inversion to the logical opposite, as in Hegel's inversion of North to South Pole. The inversion may be only to point ironically to a different order of meaning, but behind such limited inversion or irony is always the metaphysical possibility of Hegel's "inverted world," the fact that things could be exactly the opposite of what they are—that what seems may be indeed what is, and the reverse. The poet and the true philosopher know this, and their productions are based on the capacity for wonder that the possibility of world-inversion engenders. The poet and philosopher stand common sense on its head and oppose literal-mindedness. Their activity shows this power of the marvelous to the mind in words. In this sense their speech can be thought mad, because it is a speech that is between the purely human and the divine.

The fool differs from the poet and philosopher in that the fool shows such truth directly in the world in actions and in his very presence, in his motley and belled cap. His words and his actions overtly break into consciousness and into the fabric of society. His thoughts are not the same as those of the poet and the philosopher. Yet all three are tied to wisdom, for the poet imitates what the philosopher pursues in reason, and the fool's inversion is a key to prudence. The fool always teaches something; we can never tell quite what.

The poet and the philosopher are followers of the Muses, who are presided over by Mnemosyne, or Memory, the mother of the Muses. The philosopher who has taken Hegel's advice and gone to school with the poets (*die Lehererin der Menscheit*) knows that truth is the bacchanalian revel at which not a member is sober but which, looked at in another way (the way of *absolutes Wissen*), is just as much a scene of transparent, unbroken calm. The fool and those of us who have gone to school with the masters of folly know that the Feast of Fools is a scene of our humanity.

The *sottie,* the Feast of Fools, is presided over by Mère-Folle. She is the mother of this brood of sots, knaves, and ninnies, and she alternately nurtures and mocks them. Mère-Folle is Erasmus's Moria, who specializes in foolosophy and reminds us that the bacchanalian revel constantly inverts itself. Mnemosyne and Mère-Folle are the mothers of us all. The question is how to live with them. In the barbarism of reflection of the technological society, folly remains, but it remains denied and unnoticed. If we can remember even some of what folly is, we may gain a vital standpoint outside the modern order. This memory can allow us to transcend the dominance of the Understanding and grasp the dialectical power of speculative reason and its connection with true prudence.

Speculation and prudence, the topics opened up by the fool, come together through the exercise of philosophical memory. Once the barbarism of reflection takes its full form as technological society, philosophy is left helpless to be more than reflective and ratiocinative; it must limit itself to the powers of the Understanding as opposed to the broader powers of Reason to speak of the whole. Only when philosophy remembers its original connection to memory and to poetic and rhetoric can it project another version of itself in the modern world. Speculative reason becomes the one agency that acts against the destruction of memory in the building of the technological order. Technology and philosophy then find themselves in a dialectical struggle with each other, a struggle that has no immediate resolution. If philosophy engages in this struggle, instead of merging its own form with that of technology, it finds a new place to stand. This new place is the revival of the energies and insights of its origin in self-knowledge.

PART 2

The Human

3

Technological Desire

No one escapes from technique.
—Jacques Ellul

In his famous depiction of master and slave in the *Phenomenology of Spirit,* Hegel says: "Desire has reserved to itself the pure negating of the object and thereby its unalloyed feeling of self." The self gives its being over to desire (*Begierde*) in an effort to deny reality to the object and assert its own unqualified claim to be real. "But that is the reason why this satisfaction is only a fleeting one, for it lacks the side of objectivity and permanence." The self cannot maintain its own reality as something merely in itself. To have experience requires it to stand over and against something other that is truly there and is not simply a projection of its own subjectivity. "Work, on the other hand, is desire held in check, fleetingness staved off; in other words, work forms and shapes the thing." Work (*Arbeit*) is a way for desire to confront the object and experience it. Instead of hectically denying reality to the object, the object's seeming permanence and independence may be mastered and reduced by making it a project of work.

Hegel continues: "The negative relation to the object becomes its *form* and something *permanent,* because it is precisely for the worker that the object has independence." The nature of the object and the nature of its permanence can be affected only through the process of actually working on it. The object cannot simply be negated or conquered by a passion. "This *negative* middle term or the formative *activity* is at the same time the individuality or pure being-for-self of consciousness which now, in the work outside of it, acquires an element of permanence." Without the self's relation to something other, its experience of its own reality is fleeting. It has only the strength of its moment of desire. Through work the self not only defines the form of the object but also defines its own activity and achieves a permanence in this activity.

Hegel concludes: "It is in this way, therefore, that consciousness, *qua* worker, comes to see in the independent being [of the object] its *own* independence." Consciousness now accepts the permanence of the object as a key to its own permanence or independence, and the self realizes that the object can be incorporated into its own existence by transforming the passion of desire into the power of work.[1]

This stage of consciousness is commonly referred to as that of the "Master-Slave," which is a useful rendering of Hegel's title "Herrschaft und Knechtschaft," of the *Herr* (master, mastership) and the *Knecht* (servant, servitude). The *Knecht* is not literally a slave (*Sklave*) but has this meaning in a figurative sense (*knechten*, to enslave). In the struggle of self-consciousness the *Knecht* is bound in his whole existence to the *Herr* and is "enslaved." The *Knecht* is not an employee. The master is his lord to whom he is bound. In Hegel's struggle of selfhood, the slave, the bondsman, comes off the better in the struggle and wins mastery over his own reality. The master is left hollow and defeated. This is because the master's self-identity depends upon his power over the slave. The master's aim is the pleasure or enjoyment (*Genuss*) of the object through the slave's work on it. The slave discovers that although his reality is essential to the master, the master is not essential to the slave's selfhood. The slave's selfhood is realized through his work on the object. The master knows how to direct the work, but the slaves actually know how to do it, and they keep this knowledge to themselves in times of crisis.

Hegel's metaphor of master-slave captures all forms of the struggle of selfhood in the world. It can be filled out in economic, sociological, psychological, historical, and philosophical terms. It has proved to be one of the richest metaphors in Hegel's thought and has been important for Marxian materialism as well as bourgeois social theory. The modern world is not shaped by either Marxian doctrine or capitalist economics. It is shaped by technology and the logic that inheres in technological developments, what Jacques Ellul calls "the technological system" (*le système technicien*).[2] Ellul holds that capitalism and communism fundamentally disagree only on which system most adequately supports technology: "Communism's fundamental criticism of capitalism is that financial capitalism checks technical progress that produces no profits."[3] Events of recent years have shown that the communists were wrong; capitalism is the better doctrinal match for technology. But systems of economics do not determine technological advance. They follow along after it and supply monetary structure to what operates by its own internal forces.

It is not possible to think of a reformulation of philosophical thought on humanist principles apart from an understanding of the actual structure of modern life, which has been produced by a dedication to reflection joined with the desire to control the object and all that is in the world. Technology is the Promethean gift of Descartes realized as a way of life. In it all is method; it is literally a world of means without ends apart from the means. Technological society is not a choice; it develops in history. But it is grounded in a structure of the human self. What in the nature of the human makes technology possible? The immediate answer is that the human is not only *homo sapi-*

ens but also *homo faber*. Distinctive to the human being is tool manufacture and tool use. Tools are the essence of work. Tool-making and use are not engaged in by only the human animal, as was once thought, but are found among nonhuman animals. The Promethean gift, not of fire itself but the tool, is wider than once thought.

Technological society is not merely a vast panorama of tool use, differing in degree of magnitude from primordial and early tool use and traditional mechanical processes. Technological society comes about with the first uses of machines as means of production in Europe in the 1750s. Marx says that John Wyatt began the Industrial Revolution in 1735 with the production of his spinning machine, and that this beginning took place "without a word."[4] To describe this new form of society I will use the terms *technique* and *technology* interchangeably. English does not have an exact counterpart for the German *die Technik*, French *le technique*, and Italian *la tecnica*. Literally, the word *technology* designates only the study of technique, not technique itself.

Technological society, which is modern society, differs in kind, not degree, from traditional forms of human society. Ellul makes an important distinction between the "technical operation" (*l'opération technique*) and the "technical phenomenon" (*le phénomène technique*).[5] Technical operation is what we commonly understand as tool use; it is nothing more than the use of means to accomplish something. Every operation in any traditional society involves technique or the means to accomplish something. Society becomes "technological" when technique becomes an object for "rational judgment," when a concern for the "one best means" is introduced. With the introduction of rational judgment the question immediately is asked, of any means: Is it the best means? Can it be improved? What was a matter of tradition, individual genius, and social evolution is now rationally interrogated as to whether it is the one best means. Everything in the technological society is constantly replaced, improved in a cult of the new.

To the direct application of rational judgment is added the intervention of "consciousness." Not only is any means judged in terms of its possibilities for improvement, but a consciousness of technique is built up so that techniques in one field of endeavor may hold clues to their possible transference into other fields of activity. A second question is added to the question of the one best means: Where else might this means, perhaps with modification, be applied? Everyone becomes involved and concerned with the possibilities of technique. In the technological society everyone is fascinated with performance, whether it be of household appliances, gadgets, computer programs, sound systems, communication, or spacecraft.

The suggestion box is everywhere. The worker is expected not simply to perform his work but to participate in its efficiency. This is true for the consumer, who is constantly polled concerning his satisfaction with a product or service and its possible improvement. Evaluation cards to be filled out by the customer are placed on the tables of chain restaurants and in hotel rooms. Course evaluation forms are filled out at the end of the term by each student in all university courses. The point is twofold: the information gained may be of some actual use, but more important is the continual engagement of the worker and consumer in the process of improvement itself.

Technical consciousness accounts for the rapid and far-flung expansion of technique in all areas of life, including forms of managerial organization, techniques of human relationship and self-improvement, and devices for entertainment and pleasure. No human activity escapes the "technical imperative." Nothing counts in society unless it is subject to technical formation. "The computer is down" is the equivalent of *Geworfen-*

heit ("thrownness"). We are "thrown" into conditions and must wait until the computer "comes up" for any activity to go forward. When it comes up, there is light again.

Technology is rooted in desire, in the primordial struggle of the self to be something. The struggle of self-consciousness that divides itself into master- and slave-selves is a struggle for the self to be real, to emerge in the world as different from the object. The consciousness that has mastered the world of objects attempts to master the new object of the self through force (*Kraft*). This produces the two selves. The self is born through fear (*Furcht*). The master fears that he may be nothing and requires the recognition (*Anerkennen*) of the slave to verify his existence. The slave fears that he may be reduced to an object by the master's domination. The slave, as related above, discovers that he has the unique possibility to realize his self-identity in the activity of work. Through work he comes to be the master of the object; he comes into being as its permanent other.

The struggle between the master and the slave is a life-and-death struggle. When the slave survives by discovering work, he leaves the master with the problem of claiming his own reality. The master knows he is not real and can find no solution. Hegel says that he who does not play out this struggle to the end may simply become a person (*Person*): "The individual who has not risked his life may well be recognized as a *person,* but he has not attained to the truth of this recognition as an independent self-consciousness."[6] Hegel says, "To describe an individual as a 'person' is an expression of contempt."[7]

A person is a failed self. It is someone without character, that is, someone who has not forged the self as an inner form of his being and is a self only on the surface. No matter what happens, anyone can claim personhood; selfhood is another matter. It is not by accident that the idea of "person" claims constant attention in technological life. "Persons" have rights. The tireless claims to the status of victim and to rights of every conceivable sort are based in the person's quest to fill up a reality that is all surface. Technological life's quest for certainty and "fullness" is driven by its *horror vacui.*

Hegel's phenomenology of spirit is not a series of inductive generalizations from history arranged as a progression of stages of consciousness. It is a "science of the experience of consciousness" in which the structure of each form of human consciousness is articulated directly from human experience and in which each form is placed within the dialectical order of the whole of consciousness. The forms of human consciousness that Hegel delineates appear in various periods of human history. In the *Phenomenology* Hegel suggests this by referring to historical periods that illuminate various stages of consciousness. To understand history historically is the task of the historian, who considers events in terms of their ideational, material, social, and political causes. To understand history philosophically requires finding the particular phenomenon of consciousness that underlies any historical period. Any configuration of historical life is a consequence of its ground in the human itself. Human history is always derivative of the human. We may look within Hegel's book to find what fundamental feature of the human underlies our historical condition.

We live in a technological age. The form of modern society is technological. The key is given in Bacon's famous assertion: "Human knowledge and human power meet in one; for where the cause is not known the effect cannot be produced. Nature to be commanded must be obeyed; and that which in contemplation is as the cause is in operation as the rule."[8] Bacon's "new instrument" (*novum organum*) is a means for power over nature, a means for the self as knower to master the object known. The essence of modern thinking is captured in Bacon's statement. The ways of nature are to be understood in order that the knower can have his way with nature. We obey nature in order to command nature: "Natura enim non nisi parendo vincitur." The cause of the instrumentality of knowledge is the passion of desire.

Descartes defines desire as an "agitation of the soul caused by the spirits, which disposes the soul to wish, in the future, for the things it represents to itself as agreeable."[9] We desire to command nature for our needs and, further, to do so for our own enjoyment, which, if pursued, will lead us to the production of luxury. Vico says, "Men first feel necessity, then look for utility, next attend to comfort, still later amuse themselves with pleasure, thence grow dissolute in luxury, and finally go mad and waste their substance."[10] Rousseau says, "Luxury rarely develops without the sciences and arts, and they never develop without it."[11] Desire, if pursued as a pure passion unconnected to eros, ends in the cultivation of luxury. Eros is another matter, for it is classically a drive toward the good and it is properly tempered by piety.

Hegel says that the master's pure pursuit of desire fails to allow him to conquer the independence of the object directly and make it a thing existing solely for his own enjoyment. He says: "Desire failed to do this because of the thing's independence; but the master, who has interposed the slave between it and himself, takes to himself only the dependent aspect of the thing and has the pure enjoyment of it. The aspect of its independence he leaves to the slave, who works on it."[12] Our relationship to technology is a relationship of selves. The technological system is an alter ego. We, the egos of the technological society, occupy the place of the master in Hegel's picture of the primordial struggle of self-consciousness.

Technique, the new instrument, fulfills the function of Hegel's slave, working on the object and confronting its independence. Technique offers up the world to us as a thing for our enjoyment. We believe we control technique and that it controls the world. The new instrument is more than Bacon could ever imagine. It is not simply a new logic of thought; technique is a new way of putting thought into action, so that nature is not only obeyed but is transformed into a thing that willingly fulfills our desire. Through technique the world will become what we wish it to be. It is not an accident that in the early development of household appliances they were advertised as "mechanical servants."[13] The image of the servant persists in the world of the personal computer; a current provider of access to the Internet is called "CompuServe." The computer enters the household as a servant of our personal informational needs. We now have a servant not only of the body but of the brain.

Technique stands in the place of the slave or servant-self, there to do our bidding, and we think technique can be directed according to our choice. "Technology is a means at our disposal and we must decide whether to use it for good or for ill." How often do we hear such nonsense? Every day, in one form or another. It is the "bad faith" (*mauvaise foi*) of ourselves as masters. We lie to ourselves, saying that means are a matter of choice, when in fact in the technological society all choice is made through the alternatives available in the technical system. The master becomes quickly dependent upon the slave.

The enjoyment and in fact the master's own reality is dependent upon the slave who appears to be at his control. But the choices the master may make are dependent upon those made possible by the slave. These are given as a result of the slave's work on the object. The slave defines his own choices in terms of the ongoing process of his work. When the slave discovers the object as work, the life-and-death struggle is over. The master is no longer a threat; the master's ability to fulfill his desire and prove the reality of his masterhood depends upon his uneasy reliance on the slave's work. The problem any administrator has is with his own reality; all other problems are within his power to solve.

When the life-and-death struggle is modified in the above way, the master ceases to be a lord and the slave a bondsman. The master becomes an administrator of the slave's activity, and in so doing the master becomes a *person*, in Hegel's sense of one who has avoided the full risk of being in the struggle, who has not "stared the negative in the face." The technological person feels dehumanized. This common anxiety of feeling dehumanized verifies that technique is our alter ego. The technical is our constant environment; it is the *Umwelt* of the human organism. The question of dehumanization goes deeper. The technological world is dehumanizing because there is no technique of the human, of being human. There is no technique for self-knowledge, the knowledge of the self as self, which is the basis of civil wisdom. Wherever the self looks, it encounters itself only as *homo faber*, the self acting on the thing as object or on itself as object.

What Descartes could only imagine, we encounter as actors in the technological society. Descartes asks, when he looks out a window at men crossing the square, "Do I see any more than hats and coats which could conceal automatons?"[14] Today there is nothing remarkable about the possibility of automatons or of computerized brains. The technological world is full of automation. In Descartes' dialogue *The Search for Truth*, Eudoxus says: "I shall lay before your eyes the works of men involving corporeal things. After causing you to wonder at the most powerful machines, the most unusual automatons, the most impressive illusions and the most subtle tricks that human ingenuity can devise, I shall reveal to you the secrets behind them, which are so simple and straightforward that you will no longer have reason to wonder at anything made by the hands of men."[15] In the technological world everything is possible. Thought reduced to method and applied to the object as instrument, the union of rationalism and empiricism, puts technique into the "hands of men," and technique takes on a life of its own.

The sense in which technique rules the modern age is captured in the original French title of Ellul's major work, *La technique ou l'enjeu du siècle* (1954), known in English as *The Technological Society* (1964).[16] This title is literally "Technique, or the stake of the century." The use of the word *enjeu*—a term associated with gaming tables and meaning a stake, wager, money placed at risk in games of chance—implies that human society has gambled all on one phenomenon: *technique*. The stake for this wager, accumulated over the second half of the eighteenth century and throughout the nineteenth century, has been directly wagered in the twentieth century. The results of the wager will determine what is to come in the future. What we have *en-jeu*, "in-game," is our cultural, economic, political, and personal lives. We have risked them totally on the single factor of technique.

This wager is reminiscent of another French thinker's device: Pascal's famous wager argument concerning the existence of God. Here, the individual in the deep solitude of his spirit and will can know nothing for certain of the existence or nonexistence of the deity. Pascal says: "I am forced to wager, and I am not free" (*On me force à parier, et je ne suis pas en liberté*).[17] The technological citizens are in this position: they must stake all they have as humans without any way to know the actual value of the wager they have made (for they are wagering all that there is) or to predict the outcome (for the odds are beyond calculation). As in Pascal's wager, the technological society always offers a choice without a choice.

Ellul defines technique as the "totality of methods rationally arrived at and having absolute efficiency (for a given stage of development) in every field of human activity. Its characteristics are new; the technique of the present has no common measure with that of the past."[18] Technique is the reduction of all human needs, wishes, and actions to means. All fields of human activity come together in an "ensemble of means." The employment of means is governed by the constant drive for the "one best means." Technique in Ellul's sense is not only the means by which man accomplishes the production of goods and the mastery of the material world, it is also the means whereby man produces forms of social organization of all types and at all levels and whereby the individual seeks to control and improve the forces of his own personality.

A life of means is in principle a life in which the traditional forces of fortune and fate are brought under control or eliminated. The wager of the century offers us the managed world, the managerial life, and for ourselves as individuals, therapy, support groups, and self-help programs. "Technique integrates everything. It avoids shock and sensational events. . . . When technique enters into every area of life, including the human, it ceases to be external to man and becomes his very substance."[19] Technique is the medium of modern existence. "Technique has only one principle: efficient ordering."[20]

The conception of "efficient ordering" is rooted in Descartes' conception of a "method of rightly conducting one's reason and seeking the truth in the sciences." Descartes' conception of truth as method is the technician's circle of efficient ordering. The beginning point for a technique is some result already arrived at, one clearly and distinctly given by an earlier act of technical ordering. From this, by dividing the situation into its parts and proceeding step-by-step to work out what is desired, a new advance in efficient ordering is achieved. The efficiency of the process is guaranteed; the circle is closed by a final act of checking the work and correcting for any loose ends. What I will call the "technical circle" is Cartesianism in action in all areas of life, whether it be in machine production, electronic conveying of information, time-study organization of the motions of prison guards, cafeteria feeding of mental patients, or a step-by-step method for successful human relationships. Inside technology is Descartes' method, the homunculus of rational madness.

No theory is applied in technique; technique recapitulates itself. The quest for the "one best means" in every field of human endeavor produces technical civilization. Such a civilization is governed by a technical imperative, a science of techniques progressively elaborated. "This science extends to greatly diverse areas; it ranges from the act of shaving to the act of organizing the landing in Normandy, or to cremating thousands of deportees."[21] There is no personal choice in the technical world. "There is no personal choice, in respect to magnitude, between, say, 3 and 4; 4 is greater than 3; this is a fact which has no personal reference. No one can change it or assert the contrary or personally escape it. Similarly, there is no choice between two technical methods. One of them asserts itself inescapably: its results are calculated, measured, obvious, and indisputable."[22] Once one is committed to a method for the truth, there is no choice concerning the results. Rightly conducted, reason produces a truth that is the beginning point for the production of another truth. There is no choice between methods when one will yield the truth and the other will not. We are unable to flee from the *huis clos* of technical thought. There is no exit. Every "problematic situation" that occurs within technological life is a new opportunity for a technological solution. In fact, technology requires this.

The self as master is born in the realization that nature can be commanded. Real mastery requires a means. The self develops technique—the idea of work put into the hands of another agency held in bondage to the self. The agency in servitude that will allow the self to be free to enjoy the world is the machine. The machine used as a means of production is the first embodiment of technique involving the principles of rational judgment and consciousness: the technical phenomenon. The machine is a process that, once set in motion, will produce a desired end with only incidental human intervention: the mechanical servant. The self now has, but does not realize that it has, another self. This is the human self that is tied to the machine.

A factory is itself a machine having both human and nonhuman parts. Human operators of the separate machines in a traditional factory are disposable once the principle of the machine is perfected. In the modern factory workers are replaced by automatons, which are more perfect than humans. The entire process is automated by the joining of mechanical systems with systems of electronic control: robotics. The human element is reduced to those who supervise the control panels and perform maintenance, some of which is also automated. The modern factory is its own closed world. The closed system of the factory applies not only to production from inert materials; the same principles apply to the production of chickens and animals as meat. Henry Ford is commonly credited with inventing the assembly line, but its origins go back much earlier, to the Cincinnati slaughterhouses of the 1800s.

The human self that was once physically tied to the machine as its incidental extension is now tied to the productive society in a wider sense. As a technological person moved to the "service industry," the former machine operator continues to require factory-produced goods. Now a producer not of goods but of services, he or she is also a consumer of goods. No one has been set free, no leisure gained. Consumerism is a duty of Kantian proportions, imposed by the very order of things. It is the second role of every producer. Consumerism involves schooling in waste. The fast-food meal bought at the counter is packaged

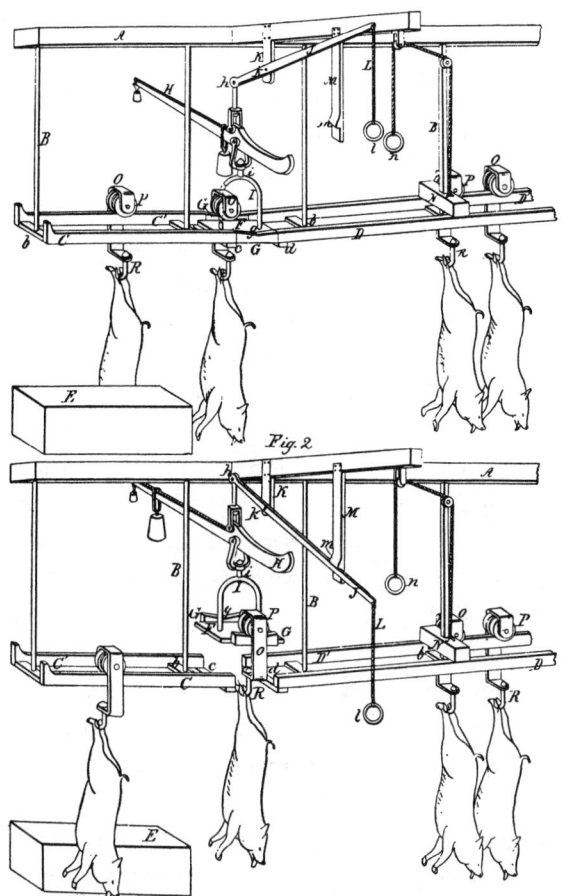

Automatic hog-weighing apparatus for use in packing houses
(Cincinnati, 1869)

as if ready for travel into outer space. It is to be consumed a few feet away and the packaging disposed of on exit in a matter of minutes. In the technological world everything is carefully produced as disposable. Packaging is immediate waste and is recycled, in a microcosm of the technical circle itself.

Once the machine appeared as a means of production of goods in the 1750s, everything had to be understood in terms of the machine. La Mettrie's *L'homme machine* (1748) is the advance statement of the idea of the modern self.[23] Once the computer appears as a means of intellectual order and social organization, a repeat of this process occurs: everything must be understood in terms of the computer. This occurs in the philosophical debates concerning "artificial intelligence."[24]

The fear that he is nothing rides the back of the modern rational man. Karl Jaspers says modern man is haunted by the sense that something is behind him: "A dread of life perhaps unparalleled in its intensity is modern man's sinister companion."[25] It is not a fear of a specific danger. Because of this initial and absolute fear the self feels dehumanized in its work. The Russian philosopher Nicolas Berdyaev says that in the world of technics man "loses his own image and is dissolved into his component elements. Man as a whole being, as a creature centered within himself, disappears. . . . Man has disappeared; there remain only certain of his functions."[26] The fascination with the importance of the individual, coupled with the fascination with the possibility that we are nothing, dominate the modern personality.

A symptom of dread is the constant concern for comfort. No one is to be made uncomfortable in the educational process; no one is to hear unwanted speech or to "feel" that one is working in a "hostile environment." Anyone at any moment may require counseling or therapy or need "quality time." Nothing is to be endured for the sake of learning or wages. Another symptom of dread is the ever-present concern with prediction of the weather. In a society where the uncertainties of the weather are of little consequence for daily life, the weather is predicted over and over; the slightest changes are carefully and relentlessly reported.

Death in the technological society is confronted by life insurance and, if desired, cryonics. After the explosion of the U.S. space shuttle in 1986, the death of the astronauts was described as a "major malfunction." Technological man does not want to encounter his own phantom. In a society based on bringing certainty to the vicissitudes of individual life, death, the uncertain certainty, is an especially difficult presence. The modern funeral is a model of efficiency. The body is embalmed and made lifelike with cosmetics to produce a "memory image" for family and friends at the viewing. Funerals may be prepaid. The ceremony is brief and may be videotaped. There is no dignity for the technological citizen, even in death.

The technical impulse is rooted in Hegel's depiction of desire as the primary passion in the formation of selfhood. This depiction can be connected to his portrait of modernity in the stage entitled "The Spiritual Animal Kingdom and Humbug, or the Matter in Hand Itself" (*Das geistige Tierreich und der Betrug oder die Sache selbst*). The cult of the matter in hand, of self-absorption, that was the particular vice of German romanticism is likely what Hegel had in mind as an immediate historical example of this type of consciousness. John Findlay has pointed out that this goes much further: "The American business executive, the nineteenth-century empire builder, the disinterestedly frightful Nazi, or the pure practitioner of scholarship or research" are also examples.[27] Executives, managers, empire builders, Nazis, professors—all are part of the great *ménagerie* or "spiritual zoo" that makes up technological life, which is dominated at every moment by engagement with the matter in hand.

Hegel says the kind of self involved in the world of the matter in hand is one that "is simply in a reciprocal relation with itself."[28] The spiritual animal kingdom, the *geistige Tierreich*, is a collection of human selves held together by a kind of general spirit or sense of things that is analogous to that which holds the animal kingdom together. Hegel says: "Just as in the case of indeterminate animal life, which breathes the breath of life, let us say, into the element of water, or air or earth, and within these again into more specific principles, steeping its entire nature in them, and yet keeping that nature under its own control, and preserving itself as a unity, in spite of the limitation imposed by the element, and remaining in the form of this particular organization the same general animal life."[29] The animal kingdom does not really mean anything in and of itself. It works toward no particular end, yet each of its forms of life is completely concerned with its own matter in hand—the performance of its own types of activity. There is no overall goal to the animal kingdom except to perpetuate itself. It is just the activity of its own form of activity. It is "a Nothing working towards Nothing."[30]

In this world there are no real goals. There is just the business itself to be attended. There are no ethical or teleological directions. There is nothing beyond the self's reciprocal relationship to itself, a nothing working away at nothing. The self is completely in its own work, its activity. There are no formulated goals toward which the work of all the individual selves point or toward which they are dedicated. What lies beyond their individuality is only the general spirit of things, a kind of medium through which they all relate but which does not function as an end or a goal. It is a system of internal relations.

Each pursues the particular thing of his or her choice and believes it to be his or her unique form of being. Everyone has a career. But all choices are really just variations on the thing at hand, just specific courses of action in a general medium of action. This corresponds to Marshall McLuhan's thesis, in *Understanding Media,* that "in operational and practical fact, the medium is the message."[31] The medium is not a medium of anything; there is no message, no goal or cause outside of it. There is just activity to be enjoyed, a world of luxury as action and the consumption of action.

All that the individual is engaged in are activities of one sort or another. In this field of activity that is modern life the constant talk of individual choice is simply *Betrügerei*, "humbuggery," a deceit of whistles and bells. All this individuality and working together are just deceptions. The individual can never really choose, because he cannot choose to act apart from the thing at hand. He must choose one cause or another as his work. The highest thing to say is "I am just doing my job." Soldiers in the U.S. military do not see themselves as fighters for a cause; they "have a job to do."

An individual heroic act in any sphere of modern life is immediately denied as heroic by the person who did it. Instinctively, the technological person knows that the idea of the hero is anathema to the technological society. There also can never be true working together, because the individual, if he is not to be nothing, must cling to his cause—which is always the particular "mineness" he can work out in relation to the particular thing. In the technological society all persons are potential victims, because the activity of others can at any moment infringe on the egocentric activity of the individual. When individuals are not feeling victimized by others but are busy and active, they find themselves thrown together with strangers in the fields of their activity.

In a traditional society a band of hunters tracking a dangerous animal under dangerous conditions have common values as to the practical and cultural meaning of the animal, their own identity as hunters, and the place of their activity within the total scheme of things. They also must be fully aware of the virtues and weaknesses of each of their companions: who can be relied on to stand firm at a crucial moment of the animal's charge, who is the most skilled, who is the least courageous, whose judgment is the most wise.

In a modern flight crew, complete strangers can be put together to operate an aircraft without any knowledge of each other's virtues or personality traits. All that is necessary is that they are fully trained and certified. If in an emergency the qualities of character or special intelligence of the crew takes over, it is simply a fortunate element. Training provides a certainty of procedure that in principle replaces any need for shared values or self-knowledge. The work is held together by training and technique. Nothing more is needed.

Hegel says, "The distinction between a content, which is explicit *for* consciousness only *within consciousness itself*, and an intrinsic reality outside it, no longer exists."[32] In other words, nature as external to the individual makes no sense. Neither does it make sense for the individual to believe that he has a nature. Human nature makes no sense. Hegel says, "Accordingly, an individual cannot know what he [really] is until he has made himself a reality through action."[33] This is Hegel's statement of the principle of existentialism: existence precedes essence. In the world of the matter in hand, everyone is an existentialist, everyone makes his or her essence through his or her sphere of activity.

Everyone is anxious, experiences dread, because activity is nothing working away at nothing. It is not possible to specify the end or goal of this activity, apart from the specific aim of some individual project. We cannot say what human activity as such means. It is nothing. The individual experiences his being as nothing. He is just his activity, just his project at hand—waiting on tables in the cafe or seducing his companion in off-hours. The deception here is continual self-deception because the self cannot say to itself what it is apart from one of its roles.

The technological human world, like the animal kingdom, is just a general field of activity, with itself as its own end.

The existential doctrine of the self makes sense in the technological form of society and consciousness. The medium of the technological world is *technique*. All activity is held together by technique. Everything is a procedure to be found in manuals, from those instructing restaurant employees ("waitrons") on the procedures for good service to those instructing anyone on methods for successful seduction, for sale in mall bookstores. Neither honest work nor eros is anywhere to be found. In the technological society all individuals are engaged in activity, and this activity is part of the general field of activity that is the technological society itself.

Herbert Marcuse explains his concept of one-dimensional man: "In the medium of technology, culture, politics, and the economy merge into an omnipresent system which swallows up or repulses all alternatives."[34] Ellul says: "It was Lenin who established political technique. He did not succeed in formulating a complete set of principles for it, but from the beginning he attained a twofold result. Even a mediocre politician, by the application of the 'method,' was able to achieve a good average policy, to ward off catastrophes, and to assure a coherent political line."[35]

Contemporary politics is determined solely by the medium, by the newscast "sound bite" and the candidate's television commercials. While the individual is told continually that he should vote on the issues, none of them is ever truly explained, nor could it be. In a world of information and interviews, explanation and interpretation are rendered unnecessary and in fact are meaningless. The deceptions natural to politics in traditional society are transcended by the systematic ambiguities, the "doublespeak" and "bad faith" of politics in the technological society. In technological society, even the most intimate human behavior is understood as politics—sexual politics, the politics of the classroom, the politics of parenthood, or political correctness. Moral philosophy is replaced by ideologies of "social dynamics," justice by "social justice."

In the technological society good and bad judgments make no sense. What makes sense is achievement, which can include the successful acquisition of victimhood in a particular area and the subsequent claim to special rights. Hegel says: "In contrast with this unessential *quantitative* difference [in comparing one individual's work with another], 'good' and 'bad' would express an absolute difference; but here this is not in place. Whether something is held to be good or bad, it is in either case an action and an activity in which an individuality exhibits and expresses itself, and for that reason it is all good; and it would, strictly speaking, be impossible to say what 'badness' was supposed to be."[36] The individual "can experience only joy in himself."[37] He has no basis from which to judge himself in terms of good or bad. He is a performer. As he experiences himself in action he is happy with himself. The technician whistles while he works. He is in the El Dorado of action.

To the self in reciprocal relationship to itself, moral judgments make no sense. In the technological universe, which stands only in relationship to its own activity, moral judgments cannot make sense. To be a victim is not to achieve a moral standpoint; it is to attain an advantageous position from which claims on others can be made. The victim replaces the citizen. Ellul says, "Technique never observes the distinction between moral and immoral use. It tends on the contrary, to create a completely independent technical morality. . . . Not even the moral conversion of the technicians could make a difference. At best, they would cease to be good technicians. This attitude [that technique could be used for good or ill purposes] supposes further that technique evolves with some end in view, and that this end is human good. Technique is totally irrelevant to this notion and pursues no end, professed or unprofessed."[38]

Purpose makes no sense to the self that is joyfully engaged in its own activity in a world that it feels to be at its command, despite its general feelings of dread. In the technological society the notions of nature or the external world make no sense because the entire object is felt to be at the disposal of technique. There is no independent world of nature. Moral judgments or moral ends are irrelevant because the object shows no resistance. There is nothing to oppose the self in its rational activity, that is, in its activity of using reason as an instrument, a means. In a world in which all is functional, the ethical judgment makes no sense. There is only activity, and there is nothing beyond the circle of activity.

Although the technological society is a world in which there are no ethics and no true individuality, there is the continual claim of individuality. There is sustained emphasis on the individual. Each individual has his own cause, his own role, and his own matter in hand. The television talk show is the forum in which individuals are asked to voice their opinions. The individuals involved range from prominent personalities to welfare mothers, fathers who withhold child support, child abusers, thieves, bigots, street gangs, transsexuals, sufferers with bizarre mental or physical disabilities—a geek show of the human spirit. They are all blended into the moment of the medium, each to manifest his or her role and give his or her opinion. All opinions given have been heard many times before. No individual thoughts are possible, nothing can be understood. The host of the talk show emphasizes that the show is there to help others that may have the same problem. In what way this could happen is never specified, nor could it be. The talk show is a grand day out at the spiritual zoo. It is a public confessional.

Everywhere there is talk of the individual, but nowhere

is there any true value placed on the individual. Hegel says, "There thus enters a play of individualities with one another in which each and all find themselves both deceiving and deceived."[39] Individuals feign interest in each other in an effort to promote themselves. Hegel says, "A consciousness that opens up a subject-matter soon learns that others hurry along like flies to freshly poured-out milk, and want to busy themselves with it; and they learn about that individual that he, too, is concerned with the subject-matter, not as an *object*, but as his *own* affair."[40] The individuals sense that they command no substantial reality in themselves. The idea of character is irrelevant to them, to their existence in the technological world in which what counts is their role, their career, their perversion, and their ability to command some attention from others.

Individuals are just role-playing, and they will play any role so as to appear successful and real to themselves. They will appear on national television and confess their innermost secrets and deeds to no purpose and for no identifiable reason except that it is expected that they make the moment successful for television. What television and all its extensions in the personal electronic media present us with is action, which goes by the name of information. But because information is continually changing, information is in fact just activity. Anything can be information; information is an intellectual infinite. The self is attuned to this because it is in itself only matter in hand.

Ellul says, of the status of rights of individuals in technological society: "Modern society is, in fact, conducted on the basis of purely technical considerations. But when men found themselves going counter to the human factor, they reintroduced—in an absurd way—all manner of moral theories related to the rights of man, the League of Nations, liberty, justice. None of that has any more importance than the ruffled sunshade of McCormick's first reaper. When these moral flourishes overly encumber technical progress, they are discarded—more or less speedily, with more or less ceremony, but with determination nonetheless. This is the state we are in today."[41]

In the spiritual animal kingdom, any doctrine of individuality or individual rights is a deception. No empire builder, disinterested Nazi, business executive, or researcher takes ethics or individual rights seriously. What really determines the nature of things is the medium through which everything takes place—technique, the matter in hand. Hegel says: "Rather is its nature such that its *being* is the *action* of the *single* individual and of all individuals and whose action is immediately *for others,* or is a 'matter in hand' and is such only as the action of *each* and *everyone:* the essence which is the essence of all beings, viz. *spiritual essence.* Consciousness learns that no one of these moments is *subject,* but rather gets dissolved in the *universal 'matter in hand.'*"[42]

The matter in hand, like technique, dominates the activity of the individual. No genuine sense of the self is possible. All theories of the self or of rights are just projects of thought, just matters in hand. We can expect, as part of the self-deception, the humbug, of this type of consciousness, the production of all sorts of theories of justice, applied ethics, doctrines of individual creativity, plans for world peace, studies of public policy, debates on moral issues. These are all just matters in hand. They are just so much research and talk that keep the individual engaged, that give concerned individuals their own versions of the universal matter in hand, which is engagement itself.

Writers on technology believe that they must evaluate technology and its effects, offer solutions, and discuss choices. Their approach to technology is guided by the question of what is good about technology (nothing can be all bad) and how technology can best be used to maximize human choice (man is free). Such discussion is generally conducted without grounding what is said in a fully developed moral philosophy. As Ellul says: "Anybody doing that has simply no understanding of what technology is all about, and he will find lots of cheap consolations. And that is the most common error I find in practically all writings on technology. The authors wonder if we can change the use of the automobile, or if TV has a bad effect, etc. But this is meaningless."[43] Philosophy of technology that proceeds in this fashion is meaningless because it is itself technical. It approaches questions as though no metaphysics of the human or any moral vision were required. Its moral discussions often reflect no more than what is already under discussion in the newspapers.

The typical reason for rejecting a systematic account of technology is that it is a monolithic vision of technology in which technical advance is not truly subject to human choice and in which no clear solutions to the limits of technique are advocated. Here is a statement typical of this standard objection, from a recent work in the field of philosophy of technology: "Such a monolithic vision of technology is of little use in any future reform of specific technical cycles. *It* does nothing. We are responsible, and need instead an individual response to each situation, one cognizant of the dangers observed in the whole."[44]

What, we might ask, would be of more use in reforming technical cycles than a total grasp of the role of technique in modern society and consciousness? What is the evidence that we stand before technological life as free agents of choice, so that all we need to do is act "responsibly," whatever that might mean? The notion of acting responsibly in this context is like the notion of being "authentic" rather than "inauthentic." There is no way to know when one has successfully achieved either responsibility or authenticity. Technology leaves the individual completely on his own; there is no common vision of civil wisdom, as there is in traditional societies.

Writers on technology always assure us that technology is not monolithic and that the solution to all problems involved in technology is a matter of choice. These two commonplaces keep philosophers of technology in business. Most work in this field is centered on the discussion of technology and public policy, that is, on the consideration of some problematic aspect of various technologies (affecting the environment, energy, communication, and so on), and then the proposal of various possible responses.

Twenty-five years ago Alvin Toffler wrote a best-selling work, *Future Shock,* in which he speaks of "overchoice." Toffler says that many critics of the technological society regard it as a standardized society in which all will become regimented and everyone will gradually but continually be brought into a mass life. He says: "Such predictions have spawned a generation of future-haters and technophobes, as one might expect. One of the most extreme of these is a French religious mystic, Jacques Ellul."[45] Toffler says that Ellul warns of an absence of choice but that, "ironically, the people of the future may suffer not from an absence of choice, but from a paralyzing surfeit of it."[46] His example is "Design-a-Mustang," one of the most popular models of automobile ever made. We can create any kind of Mustang we want. It is the individual's choice.

For Aristotle, choice requires that we must know what we are doing, that we must do it for its own sake, and that we choose voluntarily, as the result of a permanent disposition. Let us imagine Aristotle acquiring his Mustang. He must know what he is doing. He can at least say to himself that he is doing what he is doing. He must choose which basic Mustang he wishes and what options he wishes to have on it. The options seem like virtues. Then he must choose voluntarily. This is the most difficult part. To begin with, he is not certain why he is with the salesman, designing a Mustang. There was never a choice whether or not to have cars. Cars just appeared. Henry Ford, seeing with perfect clarity into the technical process, said, "History is bunk!"

It is not Aristotle down at the car dealership. It is modern man, thrown into the conditions of his technical existence. We are there with him in the car dealer's world, about to emerge as the owner of our new Mustang with our complete set of mass options. Choices have been made; it has been a lesson in choice. This is what choice means within the technological framework of modern life: to consider one's options in any situation. For technology to be kept on the right course, Toffler suggests an ombudsman: "One step in the right direction would be to create a technological ombudsman—a public agency charged with receiving, investigating, and acting on complaints having to do with the irresponsible application of technology."[47] I like to imagine Aristotle waiting for the office to open so he can consult his state's lemon law, which would further his experience of choice.

Moral choice as conceived by the practicing applied ethicist can now be understood: it is a projection of what has happened at the car dealership. We have an idea of what we want. Then we must balance the various factors and make a decision (in medical ethics this is spoken of in terms of balancing the costs off against the needs of society, the value of the individual, and so on). In making our decision we accept what initially was held out as the likely solution. The school of applied ethics is being run by the Ford Motor Company. It is as simple as that; in this ethical world, desire replaces virtue.

Desire is a valuable passion only when it is directed by intelligence and the will. But here desire—what we want—is the guiding force, and the will is what helps us to have patience in calculating the choices in relation to what is desired. We are not quite sure where the desire came from. Could it have been from the techniques of advertising to which we have been exposed? No one is more vulnerable to the technical process than the modern liberal intellectual, who is trained in critical thinking and who believes that he or she can exercise educated choice. In modern society this means reading *Consumer Reports*.

The real reason Ellul is a pariah for the theoreticians of technology is that technology cannot be criticized. Technology does not allow criticism of itself. Technological consciousness takes itself dead seriously; it has no sense of humor. The fool can play no role in it, for there is no other realm that it can see beyond itself to which the fool can point. Consciousness in the throes of desire cannot tolerate laughter any more than criticism or laughter can be tolerated in a moment of sexual lust. Ellul's real offense is to portray technology in an unseemly way. One cannot criticize technology any more than one can criticize the media. To criticize the media is always indirectly to criticize technological life. The media, while appearing tolerant of views on both sides of any issue, is in fact completely intolerant of criticism of itself. It responds to any criticism through its power, which is absolute. The media insists that it must be taken seriously. The media is the thought-form of the technological society, and it finds nothing it does to be laughable, a sure sign that it is not human.

The philosophy of technology as a special field of thought begins in the experience of World War I and the sense of mass life that followed from it. Philosophy of technology was from its beginnings a criticism of modern life, a realization that the development of society on a technological base brought with it not simply the social ills of industrialization, which by then were well known, but also certain requirements that it made of the human spirit. Technology involved a transformation of consciousness. This is the message of Jaspers' *Man in the Modern Age* (1931), Lewis Mumford's *Technics and Civilization* (1934), Aldous Huxley's *Ends and Means* (1937), and Friedrich Jünger's *Die Perfektion der Technik* (1949 but written earlier).[48] There are also Huxley's *Brave New World* (1932) and George Orwell's *1984* (1949). The threat of "Big Brother" has now been lost in the wonder of technological surveillance. The concepts of doublethink and Newspeak, once so novel, are now simply accepted as part of modern speech: "War is peace," one says, or "Ignorance is strength" (so that a botched hostage rescue mission is announced as a "failed success" or a risky decision is considered in terms of its "deniability"). This outrageous use of language is a deformation of the human spirit; it is so much the norm that we do not hear its speech.

World War II further demonstrated the possibilities of mass organization and dedication to technical advance. Civilian populations experienced the mass order necessary to the success of modern warfare. This mass order, which was perceived in works on technology between the wars, was not simply a phenomenon of war; modern warfare is a dramatic embodiment of the general process of the managed life. Heidegger's "The Question Concerning Technology" (*Die Frage nach der Technik*) was given as a lecture in 1955.[49] Ellul's *Technological Society*, as noted above, appeared in 1954. Siegfried Giedion's *Mechanization Takes Command* appeared in 1948, Pierre Ducassé's *Histoire des techniques* in 1945.[50] Marcuse in *One-Dimensional Man* (1964) understood this transference from the mobilized population of modern warfare to life in peace time, what he calls the transformation of the Warfare State into the Welfare State.[51] Ellul points out that in technological life "never before has so much been required of the human being. . . . Never before has the human race as a whole had to exert such efforts in its daily labors as it does today."[52]

The literature on technology of the last decades of the twentieth century has forgotten what was realized by the thinkers who first noticed that technology induced transformations in consciousness and social life. The philosophers of technology have forgotten to examine the insight summed up in Jaspers' comment: "When an attempt is made to render this inevitable institution absolute, there is a danger to the selfhood that the fundamental basis of mind may be destroyed."[53] Recent analysis of technology is dedicated instead to technological apologetics.[54] Once again philosophers have failed to go to school with the poets or to listen to them. They have missed what T. S. Eliot saw in order to write *The Waste Land* and "The Hollow Men" in the 1920s. They have missed Ezra Pound's "New Cantos" of the 1930s, where he says: "Condorcet has let the cat out of the bag. He has made precious confessions. I regret that I have only an English translation of his 'Outline of the Historical View of the Progress of the Human Mind.' But in pages 247, 248 and 249 you will find it frankly acknowledged that the philosophers of the eighteenth century adopted all the arts of the Pharisees."[55] The Pharisees' arts of deception that accompany the technical arts are the Enlightenment's bluff, promising that reason can succeed in all its endeavors.

The philosophers of technology have missed Joyce's notice of this bluff in *Ulysses:* "It had better be stated here and now at the outset that the perverted transcendentalism to which Mr S. Dedalus' (Div. Sep.) contentions would appear to prove him pretty badly addicted runs directly counter to accepted scientific methods. Science, it cannot be too often repeated, deals with tangible phenomena. The man of science like the man in the street has to face hard-headed facts that cannot be blinked and explain them as best he can. There may be, it is true, some questions which science cannot answer—at present—such as the first problem submitted by Mr L. Bloom (Pubb. Canv.) regarding the future determination of sex."[56]

They have missed Henry Miller's vision, in *The World of Sex*, that "a new world is in the making, a new type of man is in the bud.... The body, of course, has long ceased to be the temple of the spirit. It is thus that man dies to the world—and to the Creator. In the course of disintegration, a process which may go on for centuries, life loses all significance. An unearthly activity, manifested with equal ferocity in the pursuits of scholars, thinkers, men of science as in the doings of militarists, politicians and plunderers, screens the ever-waning presence of the living flame. This abnormal activity is itself the sign of approaching death."[57] So, Eliot says, *"This is the way the world ends / Not with a bang but a whimper."* And Pound answers, "Yet say this to the Possum: a bang, not a whimper, / with a bang not with a whimper."[58]

In "Form und Technik" (1930), Cassirer wrote: "Man stands now by himself at that great turning point of his fate and his knowledge that Greek myth portrayed in the form of *Prometheus*. The fear of demons and gods is confronted by Titanic pride and Titanic consciousness of freedom. The divine fire is stolen from its immortal place and established in the domain of the human, in man's home and hearth."[59] Technology is a symbolic form that is understandable as one form alongside others whereby man as *animal symbolicum* creates cultural life.[60] Other forms are myth and religion, language, morals, economics, law, art, history, and science. Every organism has a "reactor system" and an "effector system," a way of responding and a way of acting. The human organism has in addition to these a "symbolic system"—the ability through images, words, and numbers to transform organic life into cultural life.

Each organism exists in terms of a particular *Umwelt*, an "environment," a surrounding world. The world of the sea urchin is full of "sea urchin things," and the world of the fly is full of "fly things."[61] The world of the human being is full of "symbolic things." The immediate flow in sense impressions can, by the human, be fixed and mediated through the power of the symbol so that what is sensed can be "found again" (*wiederfinden*) in the symbol—in the image, the word, or the formula.[62] The human never exists outside its circle of culture. All human experience, consciousness, and knowledge occur within the various powers of the symbolic process that are writ large in the basic forms of human culture. In the best of times, in a golden age, these forms are in balance and harmony, as with Heraclitus's bow and lyre (*Fr.* 51).

The unique task of philosophy is to promote an understanding of all the forms as interrelated and to promote intellectually the ideal of their harmony. But intrinsic to each symbolic form is a drive to dominate all of the cultural process. This is naturally true at the origin of human culture or the origin of any particular culture in which myth dominates, for all symbolic forms are originally mixed with myth and dialectically assert their independence from it. There is always an urge to return to myth, to the unity of the origin, just as in the individual there is always the wish to return to childhood, the state where, as Dylan Thomas says, "Time let me hail and climb / Golden in the heydays of his eyes."[63]

Instead, in the modern world we find ourselves exhausted in time, as Enrico Castelli describes in *Il tempo esaurito* (Exhausted time).[64] In the technical world of clocks and performance there is no respite, no duration in which the spirit can recover itself. Between desire and the satisfaction of desire there is only the action of the technological system; there is no duration in which examination and choice can be considered. In our age the symbolic form of technique has become successful in entering into all other forms of culture and structuring them in terms that are desirable for technical advance. How has this occurred?

Cassirer suggests the answer in *The Myth of the State* through an analysis of twentieth-century political myths.[65] The successful use of political myth by National Socialism is an example on a grand scale, but what is true of National Socialism in this regard is true of modernity in general. Ellul points out that the original theory of the concentration camp, "preventive detention" and "reeducation" (to remove the undesirable from society in order to adjust him to it), is the same as the modern theory of penology.[66] In the technological society prisons exist not for punishment but as means for managing a problematic part of society. Justice and punishment are irrelevant to crime in the technological society. The criminal, even if guilty of capital crimes, is incarcerated and released, to be with near surety incarcerated again, in a cycle.

The law becomes a form of instrumental order for embodying various moments of social ideology. The law loses its ancient connection with *ius* and becomes simply *lex*. The law has no connection with what human beings and the cosmos really are. Life in the technological society is in every sense lawless. Every individual in the society knows that should a crime be committed against him or his property, no justice will result; only the world of Franz Kafka will ensue—a series of unimaginable complications that exist in their own cycle of justification. The courts are institutions of social management and legalistics, not a theater of justice.

Technology becomes the form of modern life by joining its powers of domination and fulfillment of human desire with the powers of myth. It does this first through politics. Modern politics exists by joining the mythic image and the mythic logic of the forces of good and evil with the techniques of communication: the media. Politicians are successful only by turning themselves into media images. They hold office by being constantly "informed." Ellul says in *The Political Illusion*, "Progress is to read newspapers."[67] Propaganda in the technical society is the media. Old-fashioned propaganda, in which deliberate lies were told to influence opinions against racial groups or social classes, has no power over the masses.[68]

Attitudes are formed in advertising by telling a truth in the form of an image. In these images appear the mystic light, the magical journey, the wise figure who provides knowledge needed for life's way (this can be, for example, in the form of the druggist who recommends a hemorrhoid preparation to a grateful customer), Mother Earth, the demon (the consumer is saved from a bad situation by a new product), the divine child, the divine maiden, and Tom Thumb or Hans Brinker (something or someone very small but capable of enormous beneficial effect), the hidden king, the hermaphrodite, the magic elixir. The themes of all the archetypes of Jung's "collective unconscious" are there. What in traditional societies are formed into the narratives of myths and fairy tales are met by the modern psyche point-blank in television commercials and magazine layouts.[69]

In the print media, as it is called, journalism has ceased to exist in the classic sense of informing the reader of who, what, where, when, how, and why. Only a small portion of any daily newspaper is taken up with reports of actual occurrences; all sorts of things are written about: food, women's issues, design, education, ideas, children's news, the arts, good living, the environment, and so on. What at one time was included in the Sunday supplements is now the daily newspaper. A crime, a political event, an accident is presented as a kind of impressionistic whole; the reader is left with few specific details of the event. The reader cannot know with any precision what actually happened. Only some broad indication of how or why a crime happened is given because there is no need to think through its specifics, especially why it occurred. Its basic significance is action reported. The print media imitates television. After watching the evening news the viewer finds it impossible to remember with any precision what was reported. During the newscast the impressions are vivid, but they do not become thoughts.

In the technological world art becomes a means for advertising. The patterns of Piet Mondrian's paintings, what he called "neoplasticism" (the use of blocks of primary colors marked off with lines of white and black), become patterns for fabrics. The unique arrangement of words in e. e. cummings' poetry becomes the key to layouts for magazine advertisements. Fragrances can be sold by joining images of intimacy with a voice speaking lines from Ernest Hemingway's *The Sun Also Rises* or D. H. Lawrence's *Lady Chatterley's Lover*. The first to see these possibilities was Walter Benjamin, in his "Das Kunstwerk im Zeitalter seiner technischen Reproduzierbarkeit" (The work of art in the age of "mechanical" reproduction).[70] It is unnecessary that the viewer have any idea of the source of the images or the language used. In the technological world, art and literature become effective instruments of the media but do not offer a critical perspective on human life, society, or technology itself. Anything can be included in the medium of technical consciousness.

In the technical world, what people have most in common are the images of television commercials.[71] Every instructor in a classroom has a basis of common reference with his or her students, not by citing some work of literature, a painting, or a historical event that is part of traditional learning but by calling forth some part of a commercial. The individual eye has seen with complete precision just what the mass eye has seen and is ready to respond to its mention. History, science, morals, economics, and the law are not immune to the media.

We look into the *Wunderkammer* of television, and we find all of these forms of culture on display. There is the History Channel, on which dramatic moments of history are portrayed; undramatic moments are not. Court TV makes entertainment out of trials held all over the English-speaking world. There are programs on handling and investing money, and on the "business day." Every moral issue is handled time after time on talk shows, as mentioned above. If there is a discovery of great scientific and theoretical interest, scientists or intellectuals may be interviewed to explain, in the manner of sound bites, the nature of the discovery. There is no need to understand anything further; we have heard about it in much the same way as if we had seen a travel program on the Grand Canyon. It is not especially necessary to see the site itself. We know what it looks like. A visit to a historic site revolves around the film shown in the visitors' center. These examples will quickly become old, as would any examples that could be given; technological life and the media are in Plato's world of becoming. Technology is the cult of the new. It is impossible to talk about.

Politics is carried on by the logic of the millennium. Cassirer says: "Our modern political life has abruptly returned to forms which seemed to have been entirely forgotten. To be sure, we no longer have the primitive kind of sortilege, the divination by lot; we no longer observe the flight of birds nor do we inspect the entrails of slain animals.... Our modern politicians know very well that the great masses are much more easily moved by the force of imagination than by sheer physical force. And they have made ample use of this knowledge. The politician becomes a sort of public fortuneteller. Prophecy is an essential element in the new technique of rulership. The most improbable or even impossible promises are made; the millennium is predicted over and over again."[72]

The technological society exists by the logic of the millennium. The public, who has been deep into the quest for certainty of life and satisfaction of desires that technology provides, is periodically informed that there is irreparable damage to the ozone layer; that there is global warming and the possibility of a new ice age; that the rain forest is being depleted with unimaginable rapidity (this, for some reason, is a frequent topic of discussion in elementary schools, where it often brings children to tears and desperation); that there is a raw materials crisis; that there is an energy crisis; that the infrastructure of the utilities of large cities is deteriorating and may be too complex to repair; that there is overpopulation, pollution, multiple crises of the "environment" (whatever this term may mean); and that viruses for which there is no known cure are being released from the world's jungles, due to invasion of their ecosystems (the AIDS virus being but one example). The list only increases. It is technology's way of mobilizing an attitude of support and dependence from the individual. Each of these threats is simply a version of the apocalypse suddenly shown to the individual.

The reality of the four horsemen of the apocalypse—famine, war, pestilence, and death—was once met with religious and communal values; these were the ways that the individual could face what could not be controlled. The advent of technological society has eliminated these forces of evil, or so it announces itself. But it brings up their existence in a drama of self-fulfillment. No new choices are introduced by raising the specter of disaster. These become opportunities for swearing new allegiance to technology. The solution is to discover new technologies that will correct and modify the harm either potentially or already caused by present technologies. In a cycle, the threatening technologies continue, and new corrective ones are added.

Technology is always doubling up. This doubling up goes hand-in-hand with the "technological bluff."[73] This bluff is technology's claim, along with science, that it can offer a solution to all problems. It is the idea that "we're working on it," that nothing is beyond solution, that science marches on. It is also the claim that science and technology have done more at any moment than they actually have done, or of which they are capable. The promise of technology is to remove the division between culture and nature. Whatever part of nature that is left over as an independent force is covered by the technological bluff, which refers it to the agenda of the future and disguises the deficiencies of the present.

Ellul sees the technical phenomenon as having the property of *unicité* or *insécabilité*, that separate techniques form a whole. "It is common practice, for example, to deny the unity of the technical complex so as to be able to fasten one's hopes on one or another of its branches."[74] We need not go far to see what *unicité* means. We know that the production of goods, their marketing, their consumption, their raw materials all make up an interlocking system and that the actual production of goods requires workers who have undergone systems of education, training, and psychological conditioning and whose efforts are organized by layers of managerial order.

Technological life operates on the pleasure-pain principle. Work is pain, but not great pain; it is relieved by the coffee break, the lunch break, by company activities. The individual returns home, exhausted by time filled by performance of work. Pleasure is to eat a dinner of processed food while watching television—which at the same time will sell the viewer products and convey information. Or the evening may be spent searching for information on the Internet, which is the same as watching television. The individual is alone with the world. Television is dominated by sports, information, situation comedies, soap operas, and talk shows. Modern sports are panoramas of action; information is intellectual action; talk shows are psychic and linguistic action; situation comedies and soap operas are instructional films on the nature of citizenship in the technological society. The individual is never portrayed as the master of his or her fate, but as thrown into conditions or emotions beyond his or her control. They establish ideal forms of human interaction to be imitated, both good and bad.

The function of the music hall, originated during the Industrial Revolution to entertain workers massed in cities so that they could tolerate their hours at repetitive work, is handled by the media in contemporary electronic life. The technological life that originates in eighteenth-century Europe and America now overlays the earth. The Yanomamö, an isolated, completely primordial people discovered in the South American rain forest only thirty years ago, now wear T-shirts and have portable radios.[75] Like the perfect salesman, technology can enter any door with its products.

Ellul holds that technology involves the property of self-augmentation (*autoaccroissement*). He says: "On the whole, it is the principle of the combination of techniques which causes self-augmentation. Self-augmentation can be formulated in two laws: 1. *In a given civilization, technical progress is irreversible.* 2. *Technical progress tends to act, not according to an arithmetic, but according to a geometric progression.*"[76] Technical progress is irreversible because of the presence of rational judgment in the technical phenomenon, the choice always of the "one best means," the ideal of total efficiency. Technical progress acts in a geometric progression because of the factor of consciousness in which any technique, once established in one area of human endeavor, can leap great distances in a single bound and be applied and modified for use in a totally different area of experience. In "Travels in Hyperreality" Umberto Eco remarks on the phenomenon of "more" in American society: would you like "more coffee" (the bottomless cup); there is "more to come" (stay with the television program through its commercials, because there is more to come); "more flavor" (in a particular soft drink or coffee).[77]

Desire is governed always by "more"; nothing is ever enough. The Marquis de Sade in *Le philosophes dans le boudoir* describes the ideal state, in which desire in the form of sexual libertinage could function with perfect efficiency. He interrupts his characters in the middle of their magnificent lusts to consider the theoretical possibility that, in a utopia of libertinage, "various stations, cheerful, sanitary, spacious, properly furnished and in every respect safe, will be erected in divers points in each city; in them all sexes, all ages, all creatures possible will be offered to the caprices of the libertines who shall come to divert themselves, and the most absolute subordination will be the rule of the individuals participating."[78]

For the technological citizen, libertinage is available as a method. *The Joy of Sex* promises "more sex"; in fact, its sequel is titled *More Joy of Sex* and is followed by *New Joy of Sex*. How different from the erotic formulations of Ovid's *Art of Love,* the metaphysics of the *Kama Sutra,* or the bodily wisdom of the *Perfumed Garden.* Desire, whether for sex or power, always has the logic of "more," and so does technology.[79] As in the world of sexual seduction or corporate power, so in the world of technique—the individual lives in the world as in a menagerie of competing interests. Action has as its end more action; it does not have eros or purpose.

Technology is often understood simply as applied science. There may have been a period in the late nineteenth and early twentieth centuries when this relationship between science and technology could be said to hold. That was the age of invention, in which single individuals with a rudimentary knowledge of scientific principles and some equipment could apply such principles in order to make discoveries. In this age of invention the most important invention was the idea of invention itself. Today any philosopher of science knows, as does any philosopher of technology, that scientific research requires great technological support from the development of new types of processes and instruments, computer systems, granting agencies, personnel techniques for organizing the work of assistants, techniques of publicity, and so on. Science and technology are not distinguishable. Science requires technology to function, and technological advance continually sets up new scientific possibilities. Although seeming to be auxiliary to science, technology has in fact always been the future of science. Cassirer's analysis of concept formation makes this clear.

Cassirer shows that the shift from Aristotelian-Scholastic physics to Galilean physics is tied to a shift in symbolism.[80] The fundamental category of Aristotelian thought is substance or being. The subject of a sentence reflects the substance or substratum to which the predicate refers. Physical nature is described by Aristotle through things and their properties. The shift from Aristotelian and Scholastic physics to Galilean physics depends upon replacing the symbols of language, with its subject and predicate structure, with the symbols of mathematics, with its notational and calculative structure.

We first meet with the distinction between primary and secondary qualities in Galileo's *Il saggiatore* (The assayer). What Aristotelian science regarded as the objective properties of things—heat, cold, bitter, sweet, red, blue—become only secondary qualities of physical nature. Cassirer says nature "is an open book legible to everyone. But in order to read this book we first have to learn the letters in which it is written. These letters are not the ordinary sense-data: the perceptions of heat or cold, of red or blue, and so on. The book of nature is written in mathematical characters, in points, lines, surfaces, numbers. By this postulate Galileo removed the keystone of Aristotelian physics."[81]

The shift in the symbols by which the book of nature can be read, which is first accomplished by Galileo, develops in modern science into what Cassirer calls the functional concept.[82] The shift is from the substance-concept (*Substanzbegriff*) to the function-concept (*Funktionsbegriff*). The propositional function is the model of the significative form of thinking (*Bedeutungsfunktion*). The propositional function $\phi(x)$ is composed of two logically dissimilar factors that are yet held together in a bond. The universal element ϕ can never be a member of the series represented by x, that is, $x_1, x_2, x_3, \ldots$ In like manner the particular elements of the series $x_1, x_2, x_3, \ldots$ can never be within the particular structure transformed into the universal element ϕ, the principle of order of the series. This notion is absolutely simple, yet it holds the key for, among other things, the internal order of any form of symbolism. In the Aristotelian view of concept formation, the mind moves among particulars and articulates the property common to them. Physical events can be spoken about only in terms of generalized definitions.

The universalizing thrust of the concept has no power to connect the concept back to the particular event. In Galilean physics based on numbers and their formulas, the individual event can be followed in its motions and interactions with other events. Such notational thinking has the power at least in principle to adjust itself perfectly to the patterns of observable actions in nature. The power of the knower and the concept is greatly increased. But as a functional concept the object here is still known only through observation and calculation. Nature exists to be obeyed in order to be commanded. Nature is something independent of the knower. What I will call the technical concept emerges as a development of the functional concept. It emerges because of the technical impulse that is grounded in desire to command the object more fully and to anticipate accurately and calculate its motions.

The technical concept takes up the notion that knowledge is power in the fullest sense. The technical concept does not bridge the relation between ϕ and (x) by the adjustment of ϕ to the series of observational independent particulars that are the x series. In the technical concept reality is taken in hand from the side of the knower. The knower devises a *means* to accomplish the connection between ϕ and (x) of the functional concept. Through the power to grasp procedure, the relationship between the universal and the particular elements of this structure becomes wholly active. Through increased consciousness of technical procedure, the particular event is made to fit the law of the concept in a specific and workable fashion. This becomes the ensemble of means that is technological order.

Concept formation describes a way of thinking. Coupled to this is a way of speaking, of using language. The technological society requires a way of using language such that it follows the closed circle between the universal and the particular, between the knower and the known as dominated by the knower. This requires, in addition to what has been said above about language and images, the "humiliation of the word." It requires that the dialectical use of language be replaced with a form of procedural speech in the sphere of dealing with objects and with an imagistic speech in dealing with the human and cultural world.

Cassirer describes in *The Myth of the State* the creation of Nazi-Deutsch, of which even a dictionary could be made. Words in ordinary German were changed in meaning; for example, a sharp difference was made between *Siegfriede* and

Siegerfriede: "*Sieg* means victory, *Friede* means peace; how can the combination of the two words produce entirely different meanings? Nevertheless we are told that, in modern German usage, there is all the difference in the world between the two terms. For a Siegfriede is a peace through German victory; whereas a Siegerfriede means the very opposite; it is used to denote a peace which would be dictated by the allied conquerors. It is the same with other terms."[83] At first it seems strange that technique can merge with what would seem to be its enemy, the mythic image. The basis of this merger is the I-Thou relation that each has with the object. Both technical desire and myth, each in its own way, approach the object as an alter ego. It is this immediate merging with the object that allows them so easily to form their bond, joining technical action with imagistic thinking.

The constant redefinition of terms that refer to any human deviance from the standard is the resurgence of word-magic in technological life. The shift from *crippled* to *handicapped* to *disabled* to *physically challenged* to *differently abled* has within it the unspoken attitude that if the name for an infirmity is changed in language the actuality will somehow be improved, a medicine of words. No one is allowed to be simply blind, deaf, obese, retarded, or insane. Infirmities are accepted only as malfunctions that can be brought back to the norm, if not by procedures of modern medicine then through the politics of speech. The same is true of terms related to all social issues. Patients seeking treatment from psychiatrists or therapists are renamed *clients*, as if they were just seeking advice and not suffering from neurosis or emotional illness.

All this is done in the belief that social advance will be accomplished in formulating a nonprejudicial speech and eliminating "old ways of thinking," or "Oldspeak." In *1984*, Orwell says: "Newspeak is called *doublethink*. . . . *Doublethink* means the power of holding two contradictory beliefs in one's mind simultaneously, and accepting both of them."[84] The need for charity of spirit toward those less fortunate or those who live under injustice is made unnecessary by the act of progressive renaming. Human dignity is handed over to linguistic and social procedure. Mass life requires constant inclusion of any deviance from the normal, and this begins with the reform of language. Plain speech in which words are tied to objective conditions becomes impossible.

Words revert to word-magic when they become imagistic in the above way. In the technological world, language has been transformed to fit a world determined by technique joined to the mythical image. Ellul says: "Images are indispensable for the construction of the technological society. If we remained at the stage of verbal dialogue, inevitably we would be led to critical reflection. But images exclude criticism. The habit of living in this image-oriented world leads me to give up dialectical thought and criticism. It is so much easier to give up and let myself be carried along by the continually renewed wave of images. They provide me from moment to moment with exactly the amount of stimulus I need."[85] Dialectical speech presumes that there is something beyond, something to be reached by speech and by dialogue with other speakers. To do this language cannot be controlled in advance. How the human can reveal itself in language cannot be predetermined in dialectical speech.

Poetry, novels, philosophies upset the order of thought and transform language so that it expresses new meaning. Such works are Socratic. They have naturally within them the Socratic practice of taking a word, the meaning of which we believe we know, and taking it to the point that it must be recast many times in our mind. No great writer ever leaves language the same. One can no more steal a line of Shakespeare than steal the club of Hercules. The language of the report, the memorandum, the manual, and the media is procedural, actional. In such speech meaning is superseded by function. It is what Anton Zijderveld calls "clichégenic."[86] In participating in E-mail "discussions," a new duty of the academic, everyone is a journalist, typing thoughts and responses just as they come, producing the daily column, full of the matter in hand. Any thought can enter into E-mail. In cyberspace anyone can have a home page. Everyone is an entry in technique's filing cabinet. Everyone is handling information, the commodity of the technological universe. Everyone is inspecting the merchandise.

Technological society is Leviathan. Hobbes is the first to use this term in a secular sense. The frontispiece of the 1651 *Leviathan* has at its top edge a line from the Book of Job in the Latin Bible: "Non est potestas Super Terram quae Comparetur ei." The top half of the frontispiece is a depiction of the "artificial man," a sovereign whose body is composed of tiny drawings of the human populace and who holds in his right hand a sword symbolizing the power of the state and in his left a crosier symbolizing the power of the church.

In the bottom half of the frontispiece are depicted ten analogical scenes of civil and ecclesiastical power, five on the right and five on the left. For example, a scene with banners, muskets, swords, and pikes, the paraphernalia of war, is depicted, and opposite it is a scene with wooden pikes on which are written various logical and theological terms. A trident has "syllogis-me" inscribed by syllables on each of its tines. On the two prongs of another are written "real" and "intentional." On a larger two-pronged staff is the distinction between "spiritual" and "temporal"; another has "direct" and "indirect" (referring to forms of proof). These are the instruments of ecclesiastical battle or dispute — the tools of Scholastic logic and metaphysics. The bottom frame opposes a scene of battle among knights, with an army in the background, against a scene of theological disputation or perhaps a court of canon law. War versus words: we are reminded of Hobbes's view that only power, not words, maintains social order.

The line Hobbes quotes from Job is the description the Lord gives of the Leviathan, the subject of chapter 41: "Upon the earth there is not his like." The second line completing the verse is "a creature without fear" (Job 41:33). The forty-first chapter begins with the Lord asking, "Can you draw out Leviathan with a fishhook, or press down his tongue with a cord?" (41:1). It ends, "He beholds everything that is high; he is king over all the sons of pride" (41:34). Leviathan is king over all proud creatures. There are basically two reasons for the Lord to call attention to Leviathan and to the other great beast, Behemoth (the crocodile and the hippopotamus), but more fully they are mythical beasts involved in a long tradition. *Behemoth* is the title of another of Hobbes's works. The first reason is that man is only one of God's creatures and is not the measure of all things. Leviathan cannot be made to do or be whatever man desires. This is the point of the Lord's series of questions in the first verses of chapter 41. The second reason is that man's suffering is not unique; it must be understood with the total perspective of the cosmos.

Hobbes's *Leviathan* is the Book of Job for modern man. It is a book of wisdom for the citizen of the modern state. In his work on the citizen, *De cive*, Hobbes says in his preface to the reader: "In this Book thou shalt finde briefly described the duties of men, First as Men, then as Subjects, Lastly, as Christians."[87] The Book of Job is advice on how to live in terms of the absolute power of nature. *Leviathan* is advice on how to live in terms of the absolute power of the state. The Leviathan of nature and the Leviathan of the state are both powers that are blind to the individual. The individual must, by studying the Book of Job, learn the art of ancient life and, by studying the book of Hobbes, learn the art of modern life. Hobbes's advice holds true for the technological order that succeeded the order of the modern state as he knew it. Technological order is absolute.

The covenant that man has with God causes man to give up his right to be the measure of all things. The Lord reminds man of this with Leviathan. Hobbes says that every man makes a covenant and gives up his right concerning his self to the commonwealth: "This done, the Multitude so united in one Person, is called a COMMON-WEALTH, in latine CIVITAS. This is the Generation of that great LEVIATHAN, or rather (to speake more reverently) of that *Mortall God,* to which wee owe under the *Immortall God,* our peace and defence."[88] In his discussion of books of the Bible in part 3 of *Leviathan,* Hobbes says that he regards the Book of Job as a moral treatise: "concerning a question in ancient time much disputed, *why wicked men have often prospered in this world, and good men have been afflicted.*"[89]

Technological society is Leviathan. The covenant was made without our knowledge in the twilight of the Renaissance and the dawn of the modern world. Descartes was there. It was a covenant of method: that truth would always be a matter of right reasoning, that nature was a machine. Vaucanson's mechanical figures and duck were there.[90] Condorcet was there, with his confession to using the deceptive art of the Pharisees. John Wyatt was there, with his machine made "in order to spin without fingers." Machines were transformed from a matter of curiosity into a means of production. Once begun, none of this was reversible. Social order followed the machine, and all, including man's identity, had to be rethought: man a machine, the brain a computer.

The computer has become the meaning of technology in the way that the machine originally was what technology meant. As with the machine before, there is now the constant assertion that the computer is just an instrument and that it is at the direction of its users. Ellul says: "The computer is nothing but, and nothing more than technology. Yet it performs what was virtually the action of the technological whole, it brings it to its bare perfection; it makes it obvious."[91] Neil Postman in *Technopoly* says: "I am constantly amazed how obediently people accept explanations that begin with the words 'The computer shows . . .' or 'The computer has determined . . .' It is Technopoly's equivalent of the sentence 'It is God's will.' "[92] All is united in one Person, the technical man.

Ellul says: "Man's central, his—I might say—metaphysical problem is no longer the existence of God and his own existence in terms of that sacred mystery. The problem is now the conflict between that absolute rationality and what has hitherto constituted his person."[93] The medium of the technological commonwealth is the ensemble of means, the certainty that is achieved in all parts of life without need of wisdom or virtue. Now what do you say? "Can you draw out Leviathan with a fishhook, or press down his tongue with a cord? . . . Upon the earth there is not his like, a creature without fear. He beholds everything that is high; he is the king over all the sons of pride."

In his modern version of the story of Job, *J. B.: A Play in Verse*, Archibald MacLeish reminds us that Job is also modern man. As J. B. listens, Nickles says: "None of them knew the truth as Job does. / None of them had his cause to know."[94] J. B.'s wife, Sarah, says: "Cry for justice and the stars / Will stare until your eyes sting." She continues: "I couldn't help you any more. / You wanted justice and there was none—Only love."[95] Technique holds dominion. But it cannot be so. If it did, none of what can be said of its presence could be said. No one would know enough to find anything wrong with it. No one would know enough to listen.

We are thrown back on the old Socratic spirit of the examined life that can be discussed among friends. In his preface to the reader of *De cive,* Hobbes says: "But in after times, *Socrates* is said to have been the first, who truly loved this civill Science, although hitherto not thoroughly understood, yet glimmering forth as through a cloud in the government of the Common weale, and that he set so great a value on this, that utterly abandoning, and despising all other parts of Philosophy, he wholly embraced this, as judging it onely worth the labour of his minde."[96]

The problem philosophy faces is how to keep itself alive in the age of technology—how, that is, to keep the questions of self-knowledge and civil wisdom alive in an age that has no apparent need for them. Contemporary philosophy illustrates Hegel's dictum that philosophy is its own time apprehended in thought, for in our age philosophy yields to the objectifying technical impulse and loses its ancient task of pursuing the Socratic ideal of the wisdom of the examined life. The problem becomes how to reconceive philosophy as rooted in memory as opposed to method. To accomplish this, philosophy must reestablish its connections to poetry.

4

Philosophical Memory

> Socrates was the first to call philosophy down from
> the heavens.
> —Cicero

Giulio Camillo, near the end of his life, dictated on seven mornings at Milan a little work entitled *L'idea del theatro*, published at Venice and Florence in 1550. Camillo was one of the most famous men of the sixteenth century, known to his contemporaries as "the Divine Camillo." This great figure of memory was forgotten by posterity, except for some brief recollection of him in the eighteenth century. Camillo's work contains details of his theater of memory, which was constructed in both France and Italy. The theater contained a memory system based on rhetorical commonplaces and mythological images, through which the properly attuned spectator could remember the entire universe, beginning from first causes, as if he were the deity.

Camillo's work begins with the claim: "The most ancient and wisest writers have always had the habit of entrusting to their writings the secrets of God under obscure veils, so that they are not understood except by those who (as Christ says) have ears to hear, namely who by God are chosen to grasp his most sacred mysteries."[1] In issuing this warning Camillo is echoing Plato's admonition to Dionysus of Syracuse, in his *Letters* (2.314A), that he should be cautious and not let his teaching be disclosed among untrained people. Camillo is also echoing the warning of Hermes Trismegistus in the prologue to the *Asclepius* in the *Hermetica*, that a discourse of such lofty themes should not be profaned by a throng of listeners. The *Zohar* of the Cabala contains a warning to those who would disclose secrets. The Bible is metaphorically described as a woman hidden under many veils who is revealed by lifting them one by one. Marsilio Ficino (in the *Banquet of Plato*) and Giovanni Pico della Mirandola (in the *Dignity of Man*) anticipate Camillo's beginning sentence.[2] Those "who have ears to hear" are mentioned in many places in the Books of Matthew, Mark, and Luke.[3]

Who is the divine and forgotten Camillo? Lina Bolzoni gives us a description: "Fat and stammering, speaking like someone possessed and thus reducing to silence skeptical men of letters and refined courtiers; of an obscure family, with little disposable money, fabled of wealthy Croatian origins, of a splendid erudition that waits only to be recouped, and on this basis asks for a loan from an unfortunate admirer who, in the hope of rejuvenation, drank one of his miraculous discoveries, a 'potable gold' that reduced him to the end of his life." Unlike Vico, who remained throughout his career in Naples, "he moves with a great natural ease, from distant Friuli to the intellectual circles of Venice and Padua, to Bologna with the daring *'notomisti'* and heretical groups, to Rome with the 'Ciceronians' (and then within the conclave that elects Pope Farnese), to the villas of the patricians of Genoa, to the splendid French court of Francis I, the Geneva of Calvin, to the Milan of D'Avalos, where he dies as a result of excessive amorous exercise with two women, he who transported himself from Venice to France and back again to Italy."

Camillo, Bolzoni continues, is the universal figure: "Man of letters and philosopher, orator and poet, magician, alchemist and cabalist, friend (and enemy) of *letterati* and artists (Titian himself says he had done a portrait of him); much admired among French reformists, gambler and libertine at

Venice; discoverer, by divine grace, of the miraculous invention that secured universal dominion over words and things, that reveals, he writes, access to all the most beautiful secrets of the tradition of letters, Latin and vulgar." Bolzoni concludes, "Giulio Camillo appears on first impression as one of those many charlatans, more or less ingenious, who between the Quattro and Cinquecento (he was born about 1480 and died in 1544) frequented the courts of Italy and Europe to earn themselves a livelihood."[4]

In 1532 Viglius Zuichemus wrote to Erasmus of the existence of Camillo's theater.[5] Viglius went to Venice and visited the theater, which was built of wood and large enough at least for himself and Camillo to be together in it. The spectator entered onto the stage, occupying the place of the actor, and looked upon an audience of *pitture* (images) arranged on seven grades divided into seven sections by aisles. The whole system rested on a representation of the seven pillars of Solomon's House of Wisdom (Proverbs 9:1), a pillar standing before each of the seven sections. Within each of the sections were images rising up before the spectator on the seven grades. Marking the beginning of each of these sections were the seven Sephiroth of the supercelestial world.

The first grade depicted first causes, with the sun as a central image; the second was the first day of creation (the banquet); the third was the mixing of elements (the cave); the fourth was the creation of man's *mens* and soul (the Gorgon sisters); the fifth was the joining of man's soul and body (Pasiphae and the bull); the sixth represented the things man can do by his natural abilities (the sandals of Mercury); and the seventh was the Promethean grade, containing all the arts and sciences "both noble and vile."[6] The grades were associated with the seven planets, the signs of the zodiac, and the archangels as well as with the elements of the Cabala and figures of classical mythology.

Camillo says that ancient orators were accustomed to associating the subjects upon which they wished to speak with "frail" places, so that thinking of these places would allow them to recall the points of their speech. This was known as the art of "artificial memory," the invention of which is attributed to the poet Simonides of Ceos, who is said to have identified the dead crushed in the collapse of a banquet hall by recalling, for their grieving relatives, the place at which each was seated, as Cicero relates (*De orat.* II. 86.351–54). The theater is a system of commonplaces or *topoi*, but these are not frail or arbitrary places. They are eternal places captured through master metaphors that are the keys to the nature of things. They are the first language of the mind, the words closest to the origin. Camillo says: "Our high labor, therefore, has been to find an order in these seven measures, capacious and distinct from one another, and which will keep the mind awake and move the memory."[7] The proper grasp of the significances captured in the arrangement of the *pitture* of the theater will allow the spectator to achieve the complete speech of wisdom.

In addition to the depictions were drawers or coffers that held texts by Cicero. Viglius writes, "He gives a place to each individual figure and ornament, and he showed me such a mass of papers that, though I always heard that Cicero was the fountain of richest eloquence, scarcely would I have thought that one author could contain so much or that so many volumes could be pieced together out of his writings."[8] The theater was a system of word and thing, a complete metaphysics of memory. Camillo had produced the *clavis universalis*, the key to the alphabet of the world, whereby the grand book of nature and man could be read through the signs impressed by the divine mind. What Leibniz later sought through logic as *characteristica generalis*, Camillo had already discovered through poetic and rhetoric.[9]

Camillo said he would reveal the secret of the theater only to the king of France in exchange for a pension, but this pension was not forthcoming, and he returned to Italy where the Marchese del Vasto, the Spanish governor of Milan, offered him support in return for the secret. Camillo spent the remainder of his life discoursing before del Vasto and various academies. Did he reveal the secret of the theater to the Marchese? There is no report of it. If his secret survives it is to be found within his little book, which contains only a description of the specific contents of the theater itself, with practically no theoretical comment.

Camillo's theater is a divine machine; it is a place within the place of the world, a commonplace that unites all the commonplaces of the mind. It is a microcosm. In it the divine *mens* of man can be aligned with the divine *mens* itself. The key to the image and to the speech, I believe, is proportion. The spectator stands in the theater looking directly at the seven grades, times the seven aisles, times the seven pillars, the seven planets, and so on. Number is proportion. The key to any visual work of art is proportion; to any oration the key is proportion. The balanced speech is what affects the soul, its inner eye as well as its outer eye. Proportion is the key to architecture.

Camillo's theater is the inner architecture of the mind produced as an outer one wherein the human can encounter itself. The key faculty is memory. To remember is to keep things in proportion. To forget is to allow things to become out of proportion, to become one-sided and not to see the whole. Memory balances the world. It is the agent of harmony and thus the agent of human prudence, the guide to harmonious action in the world. We must thank Camillo for such architecture.

To live in a technological world is to live in a world without memory. Desire cuts off wonder and hence leads away from memory. The things of perception, words of languages, and other persons are approached as objects without histories. Thoughts are understood as instruments and persons as agents in a field of action and problem-solving. Desire for control of the object puts thought into action, for the object cannot be dominated simply in thought. Action is needed to complete the desire for mastery. Camillo reminds us that the world can be approached differently, that each thing in the world has memory within it. With Camillo's truth in hand, we move within the world as in a great theater. This architecture of the theater of the world as present has within it an architecture of the past, reachable by memory. This inner architecture of memory takes us back to the origin of things.

In the technological world there is no sense of origin, nor need there be. In such a world all beginnings are provisional; they are points at which a new course of action is initiated, nothing more. A sense of beginning that is satisfying to memory requires a grasp of the place at which the divine, the natural, and the civil meet. Once this place is reached by the mind, the world can unfold before us in a new way. The present ceases to be simply a world of action and becomes a world of meanings. Memory encounters the object as an other that is not to be manipulated but revived within the mind. The present is enriched with the past. The past is not a special question for investigation but a constant way of knowing to which the mind naturally resorts when confronted with anything to be known. Memory is a form of meditation in which thought, in contrast to desire, attempts to enter into the inner life of the object.

With these words on the importance of memory in *exordium*, I bring my case, in this last chapter, before the court of the reader, for the reader must decide whether the events of my whole discourse in this work convey truths that are useful to life. In this last chapter I wish to employ the forensics of Quintilian (IV. 1-3) to which the reader was alerted in Chapter 1. I have begun with Camillo to remind us that memory is divine and that it penetrates throughout the human world. Memory takes us to the eternal places and thus to "first philosophy."[10] The facts upon which this case rests concern the nature of the Muses, the nature of time, and the relation of philosophy to the arts that the Muses govern. From my statement of these facts I will proceed to the proofs that define and support the centrality of memory for philosophy. Should the reader find my proofs laborious, my peroration shall be brief.

I wish the reader to consider three questions: How can we have a doctrine of philosophical memory? How can philosophy go to school with the poets? How does philosophical memory provide a basis for a doctrine of prudence? I intend these questions to revive interest in the ancient doctrine of self-knowledge and in the humanist doctrine of wisdom, eloquence, and prudence. I wish to reconceive philosophy, the love of wisdom, as based in the mimetic impulse (*mimēsis*), which is natural to human beings. In so doing, philosophy may remember who it is and begin again to have an identity for itself as opposed to being simply the present reflected in thought.

Let us consider the facts about the Muses and time, upon which philosophy and all humanistic thinking rests. Quintilian says: "I shall, I think, be right in following the principle laid down by Aratus in the line 'With Jove let us begin,' and in beginning with Homer" (X. 1.46). With this Quintilian begins his elucidation of the canon of those authors a speaker must know in order to achieve eloquence. Eloquence is not simply to speak finely but to speak wholly, to put the whole of a subject into words. Prior to Quintilian, Cicero writes: "Begin then, for we grant you the entire day. 'With Jove the Muses commence their song,' to quote from my version of Aratus' poem" (*De Leg.* II. 3.7). With this Cicero begins his elucidation of the laws and the meaning of law.

Aratus's *Phaenomena* was translated by Cicero in his early youth. Aratus begins his poem: "From Zeus let us begin; him

The Nine Muses depicted in relief on a Roman sarcophagus

do we mortals never leave unnamed; full of Zeus are all the streets and all the market-places of men; full is the sea and the heavens thereof; always we all have need of Zeus" (1–4). Aratus's poem describes the whole cycle of the heavens, the stars, the constellations, the circles of the celestial sphere. He concludes his poem with an account of weather signs. He explains the importance of these divine signs as a guide for human prudence in reading the symptoms of the seasons and the motions of the weather. Thus Aratus begins his account of the heavens with Zeus. It is a fact that Zeus is a true beginning.

Zeus copulates on nine nights with Mnemosyne, Memory. From these nine copulations are born the nine Muses, who govern the arts of humanity. From them is born the place of the arts, the museum. The Muses are Jove's legacy, but they are the very parts of Mnemosyne that number themselves the same as the letters of her name. Plutarch says, "Nine Muses were born because their mother's name is spelled with that number of letters" (*Mor.* IX. 744). The mother, the alma mater of the humanist, is Memory. Plato's academy, the first school of the humanist, contained a museum.

Philosophical Memory / 199

Vico says that the "first Muse must have been Urania, who contemplated the heavens to take the auguries" (*NS* 391).[11] Homer defines the Muses as giving the poet knowledge of "both good and evil" (*Ody.* 8.63). This is the knowledge of foretelling, of reading the signs Jove has put in the sky. This divination is the first metaphysics and may be characterized as "scienza in divinità" (*NS* 365). Urania is the first Muse because she is closest to Jove, who hurls his thunderbolts from the sky. Foretelling gives us knowledge of good and evil. Hesiod, who first tells us of the Muses, says: "Now let us begin with the Olympian Muses who sing for their father Zeus and delight his great soul, telling with harmonious voices of things past and present and to come" (*Theog.* 36-39).

The Muses are the first to order time; they do this by making time a song. The Muses order time but not neutrally, for they can sing "both true and false songs." The Muses are thus a guide to eloquence. They do not sing in a monotone but pass between the true and the false and speak out the whole, which contains both what is positive and negative. They are guides to what is probable in speech. Their speech is melodic because it is mixed, in the way good and evil are mixed in the whole of things. Hesiod says further that the Muses can sing true songs when they will. In their songs the true can govern, but how are we to determine this or imitate it? If we can learn this power of the true song we can master many things, including prudence, for prudence is the ability to govern ourselves in terms of a whole action, an action grasped in terms of what was, is, and is to come.

How do the Muses stand to each other? As said above, Urania is the first Muse because she is the Muse of astronomy, the subject closest to the domain of Jove. Vico says that Clio must be the second Muse, for she is the "narrator of heroic history" (*NS* 533). Clio is second because she is closest to the power distinctive to the Muses themselves—the power of foretelling, of time. To narrate, whether truly or falsely, is to sing of what was, is, and is to come. To narrate not merely historically but to make such narration metaphysical is to add the idea of necessity to what was, is, and is to come. Metaphysical narration tells of what had, has, and will have to be. This is a true song and it is the basis of wisdom and prudence.

The third Muse must be Polyhymnia, whose name means "many songs." Polyhymnia is mime. Through *mimēsis* all the arts achieve their power of making. Aristotle recognizes this, saying, "Imitation is natural to man from childhood, one of his advantages over the lower animals being this, that he is the most imitative creature in the world, and learns first by imitation" (*Poet.* 1448b6-9). *Mousikē*, "art of the Muses," requires the power of the mime both to begin and to govern the *poiēsis* of the poet. The other Muses bless poetic making in its various forms: Euterpe (flutes), Thalia (comedy), Melpomene (tragedy), Terpsichore (lyric, dance), Erato (lyric, hymns), and Calliope (epic) (*Anth. Pal.* 9.504, 505). Hesiod says that Calliope is chief among the Muses, for "she of the noble voice" attends worshipful princes and gives them the guide of gracious words to declare all decisions (*Theog.* 79f). The Muses are present wherever there is melodious, harmonious speech. We depend on them once a beginning has been made. We become the agent of the making they inspire and of their *mousikē*.

In their primal art of song the Muses set the conditions of human life after the beginning, that is, life as measured by past, present, and future. Augustine says, "We do not measure poems by pages, for that would be to measure space not time; we measure by the way the voice moves in uttering the poem" (*Conf.* XI. 26). We know one thing of time, Augustine says: that it passes. We know this because the mind has three kinds of acts: "The mind expects, attends and remembers: what it expects passes, by way of what it attends to, into what it remembers" (XI. 28). The first form of language is the song. Vico says the founders of the gentile nations "formed their first languages by singing" (*NS* 230).

Augustine demonstrates the order of time through his example of the psalm: the song, *psalmos*, the Greek rendering of the Hebrew *mizmōr*. Augustine says: "Suppose that I am about to recite a psalm that I know. Before I begin, my expectation is directed to the whole of it; but when I have begun, so much of it as I pluck off and drop away into the past becomes matter for my memory; and the whole energy of the action is divided between my memory, in regard to what I have said, and my expectation, in regard to what I am still to say" (*Conf.* XI.28). Augustine's recitation divides between what his mind *expects* and what it *remembers;* one passes into the other and makes his song possible. He continues: "But there is a present act of attention, by which what was future passes on its way to becoming past. The further I go in my recitation, the more my expectation is diminished and my memory lengthened, until the whole of my expectation is used up when the action is completed and has passed wholly into my memory" (XI. 28).

The psalm requires attention as the "place" at which expectation passes into memory. When the mind holds something in its attention, it makes it possible for what is to come to pass into what now was. A song is never sung only once; songs achieve their truth by repetition. Repetition trains the mind in attention. To give attention is to fix the moment when expectation passes into memory. This is the activity of attention. It is not a passive state.

Calliope, as the queen of epic, gives a noble voice to this; she governs the speech of this passing. Augustine concludes: "And what is true of the whole psalm, is true for each part of the whole, and for each syllable: and likewise for any longer action, of which the canticle may be only a part: indeed it is the same for the whole life of man, of which all a man's actions are parts: and likewise for the whole history of the human race, of which all the lives of all men are parts" (XI. 28). The psalm, the song in each of its parts and in its whole, is the structure of the whole life of a man and of the whole history of the human race. What the Muses teach in the Greco-Roman world is taught in the psalm of the Judeo-Christian tradition.

Vico says, "Therefore, if one does not begin from—'a god who to all men is Jove,'—one cannot have any idea either of science or of virtue" (*NS* 1212). "From Jove the Muse began" (Vergil, *Eclogue* 3.60) (*NS* 391). Urania, Clio, Polyhymnia, all assisted by Calliope, are Jove brought within the conscience of the human race. Urania governs divine knowledge, the understanding of the heavens and of the signs of good and evil. Clio governs human knowledge of what occurs in history, the signs of good and evil in the affairs of men. Polyhymnia governs the many songs that imitate the human condition, including man the *archimimus*, who plays all roles. Calliope governs the noble voice that must exist in each and in the arts of accompaniment, comedy, tragedy, lyric, and her own distinctive art of epic.

The sense of epic is the sense of tale, of the narrative order of past, present, and future upon which all acts play, some focusing on one rather than another (as lyric on the present) and others on the connection of all three (such as tragedy). The poets, like the good prince of whom Hesiod speaks, have always taken inspiration from the Muses to discern good and evil and to speak in a harmonious way. The power of the song has never been eschewed by the poet or the true prince. Wisdom, eloquence, and prudence, buried deep within the Muses, invested in Memory by Zeus, have been implicit in the beginning of philosophy. Philosophy begins in the reformulation of the pictures of Being we find in myth. Myth portrays for us a dynamics of opposites that philosophy transforms into an intellectual unity that governs the opposites, the famous ones-in-the-many of the pre-Socratics.

It is a fact that philosophy as a whole speech of the human self begins with Socrates. This is a second beginning of philosophy, the pre-Socratic cosmologies being the first. The Socratic standpoint rests on an act of memory. Socrates conceives the love of wisdom as the pursuit of self-knowledge. Socrates locates the intersection of things human and divine in the task of self-knowledge.[12] His dedication to self-knowledge as the subject of philosophy is achieved through an act of memory. In declaring that life is to be examined, Socrates remembers what is already stated on the Temple of Apollo at Delphi, attributed to the Seven Sages: *gnothi seauton*, "know thyself." The second famous inscription—*mēden agan*, "nothing too much"—indicates that self-knowledge requires proportion or harmony, more specifically *sophrosynē*. Socrates' act of memory to recover self-knowledge brings with it the offspring of Memory, namely, the art of the Muses or the arts of humanity.

The Muses dwell with Apollo, the god of light and truth, on Mount Parnassus, which towers over Delphi. Vico says: "Apollo is the founding god of humanity and of its arts, the Muses. These arts the Latins call *liberales* in the sense of noble" (*NS* 537). Pico calls attention to a third Delphic precept, saying that to know the nature of man requires that we investigate nature, of which man is a part: "When we are finally lighted in this knowledge by natural philosophy, and nearest to God are uttering the theological greeting, *ei*, that is, 'Thou art,' we shall likewise in bliss be addressing the true Apollo on intimate terms."[13]

Socrates is the first humanist, the true follower of the Muses who admits that he is wise in human things (*Apol.* 20D) but preserves Pythagoras's denial of divine wisdom. Philosophers from Thales to Socrates struggled in their own ways with the work of the poet, with the myth. They attempted to formulate mythic oppositions of being and mythic vivifications of multiple causes into consistent orders. They attempted to think of things as connected through ultimate unities. Philosophy's second beginning in Socrates leads to the statement in *Republic* X: "Let us say that there is an old quarrel between philosophy and poetry" (607B).

It is a well-known fact that this quarrel is with Homer and Hesiod, principally Homer, whose works among the Greeks were quoted as a matter of daily wisdom and were recited by rhapsodes, in a way analogous to the use of the Bible as the source of wisdom in traditional societies of the Judeo-Christian world. The Renaissance humanists would add Zoroaster and the bearer of Egyptian wisdom, Hermes Trismegistus, as, for example, Pico does in the *Dignity of Man* and as does Ficino, the translator of the *Pimander* of the *Corpus hermeticum*.[14] Hermes was thrice-great because he was the greatest philosopher, the greatest priest, and the greatest king. He entered into the Christian doctrine so much that his image is the first on a ladder of depictions of human and divine wisdom inscribed in the floor of the cathedral of Siena.

Are the philosophers a new school of poets, or do they bring a new form of knowledge? The friends of wisdom must set their inspiration off against the inspiration of the poets, the tellers of myths, the rhetoricians, the *logopoioi*, and all others who are makers of knowledge and wisdom in words. Philosophy is a linguistic art. The arts of the Muses are in large part linguistic arts, meanings conveyed by the spoken voice and written word. The agenda of all later philosophy is set in *Republic* X. Philosophy attempts to separate itself from poetic and rhetoric. This separation is advocated by the founders of modern philosophy, Descartes and Locke, and by the adherents to the barbarism of reflection in philosophy today. Such a separation is an impossible goal, for philosophical reason can never do without the metaphor or rhetorical structure. Plato is not truly an enemy of poetry but an enemy of the false claims about poetry. His *Dialogues* are based throughout on both mythos and logos.[15]

The only problem that philosophy ever has to solve is its relation to poetry, to the myth. From its stand on this problem follow the solutions to all its other concerns. The "quarrel with poetry" is present in every philosophy in every age, whether acknowledged or not. Philosophy can be understood at any point in its development in terms of how it stands with regard to the conditions of its birth. Philosophy must come to terms with its birth in poetry, in the way any person must come to terms with his or her own autobiography and with the autobiography of humanity that is the history of the human race.

This is my statement of facts concerning the divine birth of the Muses, the divinity of Memory herself, how time is held within her daughters' songs, and how philosophy is born from myth and the Muses' music. I turn now to my proofs. They concern memory, poetic, and prudence.

Memory

Joyce thought the most important sentence in Vico's *New Science* to be "Memory is the same as imagination" (*La memoria è la stessa che la fantasia; NS* 819).[16] Vico held that the "first science to be learned should be mythology or the interpretation of fables" (*NS* 51). He said, "The theological poets call Memory the mother of the Muses" (*NS* 699).

Hegel in the *Phenomenology of Spirit* made "absolute knowing," philosophical consciousness, the same as memory, "recollection" (*Erinnerung*).[17] He knew Mnemosyne as the "Absolute Muse."[18] In one of his earliest fragments he called for a "mythology of reason" (*Mythologie der Vernunft*), thus joining philosophy that is reason with the primordial form of imagination that is mythology.[19] In the thought of these two great heroes of education in memory is preserved the syllogism:

> Imagination is memory.
> Philosophy is imagination.
> ___
> Philosophy is memory.

Self-knowledge is based on memory. Memory is memory when it remembers things, imagination (what Vico calls *fantasia*) when it alters or imitates them, and ingenuity (*ingenium*) when it gives them a new turn or puts them into proper order (*NS* 819). These three aspects of memory, taken together, I call recollection or philosophical memory. They constitute the life of the self to the extent that the self is responsive to the Delphic inscription "know thyself." At the end of *Finnegans Wake* Joyce states for the modern world the principle of self-knowledge: "Mememormee!"[20]

To remember is to live in time. In his short treatise *On Memory* Aristotle says: "The object of memory is the past. All memory, therefore, implies a time elapsed; consequently only those animals which perceive time remember, and the organ whereby they perceive time is also that whereby they remember" (449b27-30). The human animal is both in time and has a power over time. Aristotle says in the *History of Animals:* "Many animals have memory, and are capable of instruction; but no other creature except man can recall the past at will" (488b25-26). To remember in a human sense is to be able to recall the past at will, to know that one was born and has lived through time. To remember is to have memories and, further, to employ them as a basis of education and practical life.

Aristotle says: "If asked, of which among the parts of the soul memory is a function, we reply: manifestly of that part to which imagination [*phantasia*] also appertains; and all objects of which there is imagination are in themselves objects of memory" (450a21-23). Both memory and imagination originate in sense perception: "As to the question of which of the faculties within us memory is a function, it has been shown that it is a function of the primary faculty of sense-perception, i.e., of that faculty whereby we perceive time" (451a17-19).

Memory depends upon the power of the imagination to form sense perceptions of things into images in which it alters or imitates them. Both memory and imagination are active forces. In the *Topics* Aristotle says: "Perception is a state, whereas movement is an activity, . . . for memory is never a state, but rather an activity" (125b17-19). In the *Posterior Analytics* he says: "So from perception there comes memory, as we call it, and from memory (when it occurs often in connection with the same thing), experience; for memories that are many in number form a single experience" (100a3-6).

Imagination is the middle term within the three aspects of memory. It is the way memory in its activity fixes and retains the sense perception. The imagination is an active force. This is evidenced by the fact that imagination can be employed by the poet in the act of making. Through the power of the imagination the poet makes metaphors. In the *Theatetus*, Plato understands *phantasia* as a blend of judgment and perception (195D). In the *De anima*, Aristotle understands it as intermediary between perceiving (*aisthēsis*) and thinking (*noēsis;* 427b-29a). Cicero says that it is an "impulse from the outside" that can be grasped by the soul (*Acad. post.* I. 11.40-42). Aristotle says: "Imagination must be a movement resulting from an actual exercise of a power of sense. As sight is the most highly developed sense, the name *phantasia* (imagination) has been formed from *phaos* (light) because it is not possible to see without light" (*De an.* 429a1-4).

Gianfrancesco Pico in *De imaginatione* accepts Aristotle's views and adds to them that "*phantasia* shall be applied to virtue."[21] He says: "The spiritual eye, joined to the body, makes use of images to contemplate the truth, as the eye of dull vision uses glass lenses to gaze at a sensible object."[22] From the ancients we see that imagination is intermediate in the process of knowledge. From the humanist tradition we see that imagination can be also the basis of virtue.[23]

As the middle term between remembering and ingenuity, imagination is tied to the power of the Muses. Bacon states this aspect of imagination in *Sylva sylvarum:* "Imagination, is of three kinds: the first joined with belief of that which is to come: the second joined with memory of that which is past: and the third is of things present, or as if they were present."[24] The song of the Muses, with its three moments of time, suggests from the beginning that memory in its full capacity is not simply recalling past impressions or remembering things. Memory in its fullest sense is recollection. This means that the things remembered and formed by the imagination must be put into a proper order.

A song has an order; like a narrative, it has a beginning, middle, and end. Aristotle says, in *On Memory:* "When one wishes to recollect, that is what he will do: he will try to obtain a beginning of movement whose sequel shall be the movement which he desires to reawaken. This explains why attempts at recollection succeed soonest and best when they start from a beginning" (451b29-32). To recollect requires the location of the beginning of a thing and the formation of it in the mind as it develops from its past to the present and anticipates a future.

Aristotle says: "But one must get hold of a starting-point. This explains why it is that persons are supposed to recollect sometimes by starting from 'places.' . . . It seems in general that the middle point among all things is a good starting-point" (452a14-19). In the *Rhetoric* Aristotle speaks of *topoi* or commonplaces from which the speaker can draw forth what is needed for his speech. Characteristic of Aristotle's thought at this point is the preposition ἐκ, meaning "from" or "out of."[25] The *topos* is the middle term from which the speaker can draw his beginning; it is a commonplace, or something held as common opinion. In a speech of philosophical importance this commonplace will be part of the *sensus communis,* the "communal sense" of mankind. The communal sense of humanity contains those places from which all language and things arise for the human mind, as Camillo portrays in his theater.

The author of the *Ad herennium* says: "Now let me turn to the treasure-house of the ideas supplied by Invention, to the guardian of all the parts of rhetoric, the Memory" (III. 16.28). He says further that those who know the letters of the alphabet can write out what is dictated to them and read aloud what is written. Those who know mnemonics, whether the "frail" or artificial *loci* of ordinary rhetoric or, we could add, the eternal places of Camillo, can speak from memory. "For the *loci* are very much like wax tablets or papyrus, the images like the letters, the arrangement and disposition of the images like the script, and the delivery like the reading" (III. 17.30). Socrates asks us in the *Theatetus* to consider that our minds contain a block of wax: "Let us call it the gift of the Muses' mother, Memory, and say that whenever we wish to remember something we see or hear or conceive in our own minds, we hold this wax under the perceptions or ideas and imprint them on it as we might stamp the impression of a seal ring" (191D). In *Hamlet* we find: "the table of my memory" (I.V.98).

Ingenuity (*ingenium*) is the power to perceive connections between things that issue on the one hand in metaphor and on the other in scientific hypotheses. As an aspect of memory, ingenuity is that power needed to arrange the things remembered into a proper order of recollection. Aristotle says: "The act of recollecting differs from that of remembering, not only in respect of time, but also in this, that many also of the other animals have memory, but, of all that we are acquainted with, none, we venture to say, except man, shares in the faculty of recollection. The cause of this is that recollection is, as it were, a mode of inference" (453a6-10). The element of inference that is in recollection depends upon the art of the middle term, to which the other two terms of the syllogism can be connected, and this depends upon that power of wit or ingenuity that allows us to perceive connections between things held in memory.

Without *ingenium* recollection could not take place. In largest terms, *ingenium* lets us make the connections needed to recollect an order among things past, present, and to come. The Muses offer us the power of memory as *narratio*. Within *narratio*, philosophically understood as within the word itself, is *ratio*. The song of the Muses has an order, but it does not have a necessary order of causes. The sense of ratio, of an "account," a "reckoning," an "order," is the specific philosophical element. Philosophy seeks a knowledge of events *per causas*. Vico, in quoting the Muses, transforms their song into a proof by adding to their three moments the principle of necessity. The philosopher aims at knowing what "had, has, and will have to be" (*dovette, deve, dovrà; NS* 349).

Every event that occurs at any moment for the human has entered into the great theater of memory; it is impressed like a ring seal on its great tablet. Nothing occurs without precedent. All has in some sense been in the past and will be again in the future. Novelty exists only in the present. All words, even those just coined, have histories because they are part of language. All images of the plastic arts have precedents; all laws and customs have been in some form before. All intellectually organized religions have been before in the primordial religious experiences. The present is a middle term connected to past and future; it never stands alone.

True philosophy begins in the insight that all things act in accordance with what Vico speaks of in relation to the common nature of nations—that all things known to us have within them an "ideal eternal history" (*storia ideale eterna*). This first principle depends upon our power of *ingenium* to see that all things in the civil world are like our own being, that within them there is a kind of self-writing, an autobiography. The inner writing of any event means that it has a birth, a maturity, and a death. To know requires a metaphysics of memory. We must perceive all things in terms of the Muse's song; each is an arrangement of causes emanating from its origin. Further, all things in the civil world can be the subject of *oratio*. Any subject can be put into a speech that places beginning against present and these against an end. Vico says, "Doctrines must take their beginning from that of the matters of which they treat" (*NS* 314). This sense of *oratio* is achieved by the union of *narratio*, the story that each thing has within it, and *ratio*, the arrangement or order of causes distinctive to it.

The art of philosophical memory is *mimēsis*, "imitation." The philosopher aims at an imitation in words (*verba*) of the reality of the thing (*res*). The philosopher must speak about the thing in such a way that the mind's eye can "spy out" its inner nature. In this way true philosophy is *speculatio*, speculating, not reflecting. Reflection presupposes recollection because recollection is required to have the thing before the mind. Recollection is required for the knower even to be present, for the knower's reality is tied to memory. Reflection would act as if the mind functions just in the present and that thought is novelty. But the present is tied to the past and future in a bond of memory. The thing is born through the act in perception of "finding-again." The stream of sensation is fixed, and through the fixed sensation the other moments of what is sensed can be found again. This is what Cassirer calls "symbolic pregnance" (*symbolische Prägnanz*).[26] It is a structure of memory: what was is held together in a present, and that present is part of a totality of sensation that is ongoing.

Below language in consciousness is the gesture. We meet with two forms of the gesture or bodily sign.[27] One is the imitative sign, from which comes sign language. In it the body is used to imitate the thing meant. The body takes the shape of the thing, such as hands moving in imitation of the flow of water or a face changing to express the emotion felt. The other sign is indicative, the act of "pointing out." With it, meaning is achieved by the repetitive act of pointing to what is there. The same indicative gesture is used over and over to direct attention to different things. Meaning is accomplished operationally. From the imitative sign comes the language of the humanist, who wishes to portray the world in words. From the indicative sign comes the language of the scientist, whose concern is to have the world at a permanent distance, to delimit and refer to the world.

In philosophy the humanist wishes to grasp the thing in terms of its own history. The literal-minded philosopher, if asked what something is, engages only in an act of pointing, using logic to define and point out the nature of what is there. What is known is known, not on its own terms, but on the terms of the knower. The falseness of this literal-minded philosophy becomes plain when we consider that it can offer no self-knowledge. It is dedicated to method and has no method by which to know the reality of the knower. For the knower to put himself into words, an autobiography is required. He must imitate in words his own reality. The author is like his book. This sense of things is ignored in the literal act of pointing.

The difference between these two responses to the world

underlies the difference between critical and topical philosophy. Critical philosophy is dedicated to the principle that a method or criterion can be formulated to separate out true from false knowledge. Once in possession of this, philosophy would have accomplished its task. It would possess the master key to human knowledge and to what is real. Philosophy becomes identical to the art of criticism, a "science of science" necessary to all other sciences. As the art of criticism, philosophy understands its task to be to distinguish the true from the false in every part of human knowledge.

Critical philosophy has a high aim, but it is bought at the price of turning its back on the original wisdom of the Seven Sages inscribed at Delphi. Critical philosophy can offer no account of self-knowledge. It can never be Socratic in a true sense, as the bringer of civil wisdom. Critical philosophy prefers to see Socrates as the great critic of established beliefs and to regard him only as the gadfly of Athens, a thinker without positive doctrine, the seeker of the final criterion of which he professes ignorance. It ignores Socrates' claims, in the *Charmides* and the *Phaedrus*, that he is not a maker of theories or a seeker of science but a seeker of the wisdom that resides in the self and that concerns the knowledge of things divine and human.[28]

POETIC

In the *Tusculan Disputations* Cicero says, "Wisdom [*sapientia*] is the knowledge of things divine and human and acquaintance with the cause of each of them" (IV. 26.57). He repeats this claim in *De officiis*, saying that *sapientia* has been defined this way "by the philosophers of old" (II. 2.5). Vico, referring to Varro's lost work on *The Antiquities of Divine and Human Institutions,* says: "True wisdom, then, should teach the knowledge of divine institutions [*cose*] in order to conduct human institutions [*cose*] to the highest good" (*NS* 364). Vico adds, "Wisdom among the gentiles began with the Muse defined by Homer in a golden passage in the *Odyssey* [8.63] as 'knowledge of good and evil,' and later called divination" (*NS* 365).

As mentioned above, Vico says that the Tuscans called this knowledge of good and evil "science in divinity" (*scienza in divinità;* ibid.). Quoting Vergil (*Eclogue* 3.60), Vico says, "From Jove the Muse began (*A Iove principium musae*)," and he warns that "at this point it was all too easy for the philosophers later to intrude the dictum that the beginning of wisdom is piety" (*NS* 391). Also quoting Vergil (*Aeneid* 10.112), Vico says, "If one does not begin from—'a god who to all men is Jove,'—one cannot have any idea either of science or of virtue" (*NS* 1212). He says that the Muses "'sing' in the sense in which the Latin verbs *canere* and *cantare* mean 'foretell'" (*NS* 508).

For Vico there is a wisdom that is poetic: *sapienza poetica*. This wisdom, as well as a *sapienza filosofica*, is based on a knowledge of things divine and human. Thus:

> Knowledge of things divine and human is wisdom.
> Poetic is knowledge of things divine and human.
> ―――――――――――――――――――――――――――――
> Poetic is wisdom.

The idea of "poetic wisdom" recasts the ancient Platonic quarrel between philosophy and poetry of *Republic* X and allows philosophy to recover its relation to poetry and to understand that poetry is the "teacher of mankind." Vico says: "For the metaphysics of the philosophers must agree with the metaphysic of the poets, on this most important point, that from the idea of divinity have come all the sciences that have enriched the world with all the arts of humanity: just as this vulgar [poetic] metaphysic taught men lost in the bestial state to form the first human thought from that of Jove, so the learned must not admit any truth in metaphysic that does not begin from true *Being*, which is God" (*NS* 1212).[29]

Collingwood says: "The philosopher must go to school with the poets in order to learn the use of language, and must use it in their way: as a means of exploring one's own mind, and bringing to light what is obscure and doubtful in it. . . . The principles on which the philosopher uses language are those of poetry."[30] The greatest principle that the philosopher shares with the poets is metaphor. Aristotle says: "The greatest thing by far is to be a master of metaphor. It is the one thing that cannot be learnt from others; and it is also a sign of genius" (1459a5-7). In his conception of "poetic logic" Vico regards metaphor as the first trope: "The most luminous and therefore the most necessary and frequent is metaphor" (*NS* 404). He says that the first poets, the makers of the myths of mankind, used metaphor to give sense and passion to insensate things, thus attributing to such things their own capacities. Vico says, "Every metaphor so formed is a fable in brief" (ibid.).

As mentioned above, "the first science to be learned should be mythology or the interpretation of fables." The poets with whom Platonic philosophy quarrels are Homer and Hesiod, who are the conveyors of these fables of the Greeks, the origins of which are lost in antiquity. In his discovery of the true Homer, Vico finds that Homer is the Greek people themselves and that "the fables, which at their birth had come forth direct and proper, reached Homer distorted and perverted" (*NS* 808). Vico says that "the fables in their origin were true and severe narrations, whence *mythos*, fable, was defined as *vera narratio*" (*NS* 814). The fable is *vero e severo*. It states an unmediated truth.

Myths are first thoughts. They are born from fear. Their trope is metaphor. *Metaphysics* is second thoughts. It is born from wonder. Its device is the question. *Method* is third thoughts. It is born from doubt and is sustained by suspicion. Its form of expression is theory and the criticism of theories.

Myths or first thoughts: fear and metaphor. Myths are the first thoughts of humanity, and they are the thought-form of childhood. In Vico's "poetic metaphysics," the *giganti* or *bestioni* who wander the earth for two centuries after the biblical flood form the first metaphor from the thundering sky. The world dries out to a point at which there can be thunder and lightning. This new perception causes the protohumans to feel fear for the first time. They are all body, senses, and passion, and they take the sky to be an alter body. They shake in fear and flee into their caves in order to be out of sight of the god.

Their twofold reaction embodies the imitative and the indicative sign. Their bodies shake in sympathetic imitation of the great body of the sky, and their primal cries of fear, onomatopoeic of the rumbling and noise of the thunder, begin to form the first name of Jove. They flee into caves in order not to fornicate in the sight of Jove, and they form marriages. Their act of flight is an indicative sign of the presence of Jove. Thunder, Jupiter Tonans, is pointed out in their act of fleeing. In these bodily actions and in the cries that become the name of Jove, a first truth is made.

Jove is an "imaginative universal" (*universale fantastico*), a first metaphor. This metaphor is not that of the classical tradition, in which "metaphor consists in giving the thing a name that belongs to something else" (*Poet.* 1457b7–8). The sky does not exist as an empirical thing designated by the common name *sky* that is then given the sacred name *Jove*. The process is not accomplished by the likening in thought of two givens of different orders. In Jove the "given" itself appears for the first time. The sky as something natural is not likened to something divine, the god. The metaphor present in the imaginative universal is based on "is" or identity, not on "likeness" or analogy.

For the first time, something "is." The first humans are poets and masters of metaphor, which in this case is to say they are masters of being. Jove *is*, where before there was only immediacy.[31]

The Muses are present even to these first poets, because memory is present. The *giganti* are the offspring of the sons of Noah, the sons of the earth, and in them the dim memory of their earlier human state is awakened. But memory is present also as remembering, in that the flow of the immediate sensations of thunder are found again in the poetic character of Jove. This poetic character is made not by cognition but by the middle term of memory, imagination, or *fantasia*. Jove is formed as an image, a metaphor, which is a fable in brief. The myth always holds together opposites, and within the Jove experience are the opposites of the imitative and the indicative. Fear is allayed only by the transformation of the fear into an image, an object made in *fantasia*. Petronius says that religion originates in fear: "Primus in orbe deos fecit timor" ("It was fear first created gods in the world, when the lightning fell from high heaven"; *Poet. Lat. Min.* 76; Fr. 27 Müller). Vico says, "It was fear which created gods in the world; not fear awakened in men by other men, but fear awakened in men by themselves" (*NS* 382).

Ingenuity, the third aspect of memory, is active in the metaphor of Jove, for Jove, who is the sky, divides the sky from the earth. Things divine and things human are separated in this primordial act. Once the power of the name is attained, all things can be seen as full of Jove and can be named. The world is given a new turn and its contents put into proper arrangement. In the Jove experience memory is born, and the protohumans become humans and begin to make sense together. Jove is a *topos* formed through the senses; what Vico calls *topica sensibile* (*NS* 495). Vico says that the human mind first "began to hew out topics, which is an art of regulating well the primary operation of our mind by noting the commonplaces that must all be run over in order to know all there is in a thing that one desires to know well; that is, completely" (*NS* 497). This thought of topics is the common sense of mankind: "Common sense is judgment without reflection, shared by an entire class, an entire people, an entire nation, or the entire human race" (*NS* 142). Mythology is the first common sense of any form of humanity. It is its first thoughts.[32]

Myth is the first complete speech. In the myth the true is the whole, but the whole is not accomplished by the application of a single principle that unifies opposites. Opposites are totalized in the myth simply through its power to form images or metaphors that are elaborated in fables. Myth is the counter to ratiocination in that, the more opposites present in the myth, the richer its statement. Further, myth loves the multiplicity of causes. The categorical drive toward the reduction of a multiplicity of phenomena to a single cause is for myth a poverty of thought. The mythic event is the more rich for its having a multiplicity of causes.[33] Myth is memory.

To forget is to allow the mind to adhere to a single understanding of the world. This single understanding requires the elimination of opposites in thought. Through critical philosophy the true is separated from the false, and the real in its fullness disappears from our horizon. The myth renews the mind by its example of opposites expressed in a single speech. A myth, like a song, can be spoken, sung, in many ways. It is not the single speech of the Understanding. Vico says understanding (*intendimento*) "is neither memory nor imagination" (*NS* 662). The myth acts against forgetting as it acts against the original world of the *giganti* in which there is no memory.

The barbarian is always there, with no interest in the past or future, always there ready to mold the mind as an instrument of desire that can be satisfied in the present. Memory takes us back to beginning, the place where time originates for a given topic, and from this beginning we can speak wholly on it, relieving ourselves from the erosion of the time that goes on from one moment to the next, in what Hegel calls a "bad infinity" (*schlechte Unendlichkeit*). At the beginning is always the myth again, and it is the beginning of wisdom for the self. For in myth the self can recontact its original bond with the world, although we can never attain the myth itself, any more than we can attain the world of the child. Myth and the child are before time and before self.

Metaphysics or second thoughts: wonder and question. F. H. Bradley says, "Metaphysics is the finding of bad reasons for what we believe upon instinct, but to find these reasons is no less an instinct."[34] Metaphysics is second thoughts. Myth is at the origin of things, but once the origin is past, myth is inaccessible in its own terms. Metaphysics is the attempt to recover in thought what the myth possesses immediately in the metaphor and fable. Metaphysics begins in the difference between *seems* and *is*. Myth is *vera narratio* because myth is the attempt of the mind to have something before the mind, to capture opposites in language. The mythical image gives form to fear, but once the fear of the beginning is gone, the mind gives way to wonder. Wonder begins in the apprehension of the difference between *seems* and *is*. Wonder requires a sense of the real that can appear, that can be found by the mind in appearance.

In the *Rhetoric* Aristotle says, "Learning things and wondering at things are also pleasant for the most part; wondering implies the desire of learning, so that the object of wonder is an object of desire; while in learning one is brought into one's natural condition" (1371a31–34). Wonder is tied to the love of learning. This is desire, not in the sense of domination of the object but in the sense of discovering the source or cause of the wonder. In *Metaphysics* I, Aristotle says: "For it is owing to their wonder that men both now begin and at first began to philosophize.... And a man who is puzzled and wonders thinks himself ignorant (whence even the lover of myth is in a sense a lover of wisdom, for myth is composed of wonders); therefore since they philosophized in order to escape from ignorance, evidently they were pursuing science in order to know, and not for any utilitarian end" (982b12–23). The lover of myth is a lover of wisdom and finds myth to be composed of wonders. Because the lover of myth is looking back at myth from the love of wisdom, myth is a source of wonder. In the *Theatetus*, Socrates says that the "sense of wonder is the mark of the philosopher" and that "philosophy indeed has no other origin" (155D).

Vico associates the trope of irony with the arrival of reflective thought in the course of a nation's life: "Irony certainly could not have begun until the period of reflection, because it is fashioned of falsehood by dint of a reflection which wears the mask of truth" (*NS* 408). He says that the "first fables could not feign anything false; they must therefore have been, as they have been defined above, true narrations" (ibid.). We learn from Quintilian that irony involves an element of *illusio* (VIII. 6.54). He says, "A man's whole life may be colored with *irony*, as was the case with Socrates, who was called an *ironist* because he assumed the role of an ignorant man lost in wonder at the wisdom of others" (IX. 2.46). Socrates assumed the metaphysical distinction between appearance and reality within his own being. Socrates is never what he appears to be. The real is always something beyond appearance, to which Socrates' questions are alluding. Quintilian says, "By far the most artistic device is to indicate one thing by allusion to another" (IX. 2.97).

When philosophy arrives in human affairs, the stories of the poets come into question. Philosophy depends upon metaphor for its own starting points. The *topos* from which we can speak about any subject recapitulates the original *topos* of Jove. The metaphor is the transferring (*metaphérein*) of meaning from one thing to another. This is first enacted completely within the tension of the elements of the Jove experience. Later, when the things of the world are named, metaphor can occur in the classical sense of using the name of one thing for another. Irony follows the same logic as metaphor but requires a reflective moment so that the two things in the irony are kept apart, not merged into one. Irony used philosophically allows us to indicate truths that cannot be said literally. What keeps philosophy from being poetry is not its use of prose or argument but its use of irony and the question.

As a trope, irony is closely tied to the question. The pre-Socratics craft philosophy from myth by insisting on the discovery of the one-in-the-many, of a single cause or principle through which the oppositions of the world can be mediated rather than just held together in the mythic narration.[35] To this concern for the discovery of Being Socrates adds the device of the question. When Being can be questioned, it can become a problem. Philosophy is kept separate from poetry by the use of the question. Because reflection and irony, as Vico says, always bring with them deception by dint of the mask, the ethos of the speaker is crucial. Quintilian says, "More closely dependent on *ethos* are the skillful exercise of feigned emotion or the employment of irony in making apologies or asking questions, irony being the term which is applied to words which mean something other than they seem to express" (VI. 2.15-16). Socrates' irony is successful because he will make no one the worse for knowing him and because he believes that "no harm can come to a good man."

Speculation offsets the reflection and the mask that resides in irony. Speculation promotes the dialectic that is indigenous to irony. Irony always points to an opposite meaning, and speculation, with its power of dialectic present in the question, moves thought through opposites and toward the True as the whole. The philosopher is like the fool in that the beginning of metaphysics is the power of inversion. The fool can begin the process of metaphysical speculation, but that is all the fool can do. The fool, like the philosopher, acts against forgetting by calling attention to the reality of the opposite of any settled meaning. The philosopher accomplishes this through the application of the question. Wonder is the passion naturally tied to the question. Wonder motivates the question and the dialectic of questions and answers. The question calls for the cause of what is before the mind. In myth, thunder is given being, brought before the mind, and named as a god, which forms the fear of the thunder as a thought. As an object of wonder, thunder is the subject of the question. Lear says: "First let me talk with this philosopher. / What is the cause of thunder?" (*King Lear* III.iv.161–62).

Philosophy is the product of the mimetic impulse, and true philosophy remains an expression of this impulse. In "Fable About Man" Juan Luis Vives shows that man realizes his humanity through his distinctive power to imitate things around him in the natural and civil worlds, even to imitate the gods, including Jove.[36] Man is the imitative animal. He is the archmime, demonstrating his social nature by creating society as imitative of the cosmos. Man demonstrates his rational nature by imitating thought in language. Philosophy is the culmination of the mimetic impulse that is at the center of human nature, for philosophy, when practiced rightly, transforms the theater of the world into the theater of ideas, which imitates for the human self "all that there is."

Method or third thoughts: doubt and suspicion, theory and criticism. Third thoughts produce method. Whitehead says: "Every method is a happy simplification. But only truths of a congenial type can be investigated by any one method, or stated in terms dictated by the method. For every simplification is an over-simplification. Thus the criticism of a theory does not start from the question, True or false? It consists in noting its scope of useful application and its failure beyond that scope. It is an unguarded statement of a partial truth."[37] Method arises as an answer to doubt. Socrates' quest for self-knowledge is not a quest for certainty. The Socratic question arises, not from doubt, but from the attempt to establish the meaning of the wisdom of the poets, of the myth. The so-called Socratic method is no method at all, for like the poets' art of metaphor it cannot be learned from others. Irony cannot be learned any more than metaphor can be learned. We can learn from Socrates only by attempting to imitate Socrates. Unlike Descartes, he has no method that can be exposited in steps and learned from others. Socrates poses his questions, creates his metaphors, and relates his "likely stories" by memory, imagination, and ingenuity.

When the project of speculative conversation and noetic truth wanes, method comes to fill their place, motivated by doubt. Truth becomes a concern with what is partial because critical philosophy, with its concern to distinguish knowledge from ignorance, must lose the speech that wishes through opposites to show the whole in words. What answers doubt is certainty, but certainty is not truth because it is not a knowledge of causes. All that can be said of self-knowledge from the standpoint of certainty is *Si fallor, sum; dubito, ergo sum; cogito, ergo sum.* This becomes the "I think" that can be appended to all acts of reflective knowledge. The self becomes inaccessible. Reflection, which is originally born in the trope of irony, separates from irony and from all such rhetorical forms of speech. Reflection becomes a thing unto itself, tied to logic and to the category. Chained to the Caucasus of the category, the self is bound to a one-sided grasp of the world and suffers the loss of the whole. Wisdom is unobtainable, and thought is surrounded by forgetting.

Method, as Whitehead indicates, goes hand-in-hand with theory. In philosophy, once it is dedicated to method, theory replaces the metaphysics of wonder as well as the love of wisdom that is developed from the poets through the question and the trope of irony. Theory is an "unguarded statement of a partial truth." Theory is the product of reflective understanding. It knows nothing of world inversion except that doubt has raised the question of dread through the possibility of an anti-God or deceiver, who gives cause to doubt even the truths of pure thought.

Reflection produces the theory that can be grounded only in application. Theory does not begin from Jove. It has no claim to the origin. Its basis is reflection alone and its application of the concept to the content of perception. Theory is without memory and without the Muses. Theory cannot speak outside its own confines, the confines of the method that supports it. Wittgenstein gives sage advice in the famous seventh proposition of the *Tractatus logico-philosophicus:* "What we cannot speak about we must pass over in silence."[38] Outside the theory all is silence or is humbug and deception.

Once the truth of "know thyself" is given up, all appears to be theory or potential theory. The result is suspicion. Doubt, which can be satisfied by certainty, gives way to suspicion. What answers suspicion? Nothing answers suspicion but power: the "hermeneutics of suspicion," the "school of resentment."[39] The great narratives of metaphysical wonder are unmasked by considering their opposites to be true. Deconstruction arises from disenchantment with the results of reflection, and then it itself fails to escape a reflective understanding. It remains just another form of critical philosophy. All is reflection, and when reflection finds an opposite to its certainties, it declares itself to be in possession of an untruth. It has unmasked the object of wonder. Its heroes are Kant (for critique), Nietzsche (for power), and Heidegger (for concealment and interrogation).

Speculation is never deceived, for it works through the phenomena of illusion, deception, and inversion toward the true as the whole speech. Inversion is a principle deep within human consciousness that consciousness itself works through in the production of human culture. Lévi-Strauss, in what he calls the "Opossum's Cantata," speaks of the "opossum's proof" found in the mythology of the Tacana, Caraja, and other native peoples of central Brazil, where the opossum is the symbol of an inversion through which civilization arises. In this myth, "the opossum personifies a kind of anti-agriculture which is at one and the same time pre- and pro-agriculture. For, in the 'upside down' world that was the state of nature before the birth of civilization, all future things had to have their counterpart, even if only in a negative form, which was a kind of guarantee of their future existence."[40] The opossum is the instrument of inversion whereby men attain agriculture and hence make culture from nature. The opossum is a trickster, a Promethean figure.

Speculative philosophy is the mimetic impulse of the poets, transformed from imitating the objects of the senses to imitating the whole. Like the poet, the philosopher is a maker in words, and this making is always sublime because the object philosophy wishes to imitate is noetically known. The philosopher strives to bring the absolute into words. The philosopher, through contact with the origin and depths of consciousness, becomes a remaker of culture at a point when culture is threatened by its own disintegration. Words are to imitate the thing, not to represent it but to represent its reality in the word, the complete speech.

The true philosopher has an impossible task. The temperament of the true philosopher is one of melancholy, as Aristotle explained in *Problems* XXX (953a10-11). Cicero says: "Aristotle indeed affirms, all ingenious men to be melancholic" (*Aristotles quidem ait omnes ingeniosos melancholicos esse; Tusc.* I. 33.80). The Cartesian world of methodological thinking is comic in form. Method and theory by definition have a happy ending in store for any subject matter to which they are applied, for method and theory accept from the start only what can be managed by them to a successful result. The isms captured in the family portrait of the positions of contemporary philosophy have given up the comic for the banal. Outside contemporary philosophy stands the humanist grounding of philosophy in the ironic and the melancholic.

Suspicion trades in power and regards all thought as disguised ideology that must be unmasked. Philosophy becomes a world of competing ideologies and the unmasking of ideologies, in a cycle without exit. Once philosophy becomes theory, there is no truth of the whole or of the self to be had. Thought becomes analytic and deconstructive, which are the same activity. In this way, third thoughts are last thoughts. There is nothing to think after them. At the point of these last thoughts, in which all is method and theory, concern with virtue and the real is gone. Eloquence, the concern with the complete speech, in which piety and wisdom are joined, is of no special interest. Analytic and deconstructive thought by nature are the thought of the part, not the whole, and so eloquence is of no importance to such philosophy.

Joyce has given the answer to the banality of method. He says: "Chance furnishes me with what I need. I'm like a man who stumbles: my foot strikes something, I look down, and it's exactly what I'm in need of."[41] The true method, for the things that matter, is epiphany and the ingenuity that answers to it.

PRUDENCE

In *De partitione oratoria*, Cicero says: "Eloquence [*eloquentia*] is nothing else but wisdom delivering copious utterance" (XXIII. 79). Eloquence is to speech what virtue is to human life and thought: "Virtue has a twofold meaning, for it is exhibited either in knowledge or in conduct. The virtue that is designated prudence [*prudentia*] and intelligence and the most impressive name of all, wisdom [*sapientia*], exercises its influence by knowledge alone.... The virtue of prudence when displayed in a man's private affairs is usually termed personal sagacity and when in public affairs political wisdom" (XXII. 76–77).

Vico says that "the whole is really the flower of wisdom."[42] He asks, "What is eloquence, in effect, but wisdom, ornately and copiously delivered in words appropriate to the common opinion of mankind?"[43] Eloquence is putting the whole into words; it is not simply the formation of elegant and ornate phrases. Eloquence does require *copia*, in that it joins together many aspects of its subject. Cicero was renowned for the felicity of his copiousness, and Demosthenes could speak of quite distant things, going outside his case only to bring his audience back with the lightning flash of his mighty enthymeme. Quintilian says: "The verb *eloqui* means the production and communication to the audience of all that the speaker has conceived in his mind, and without this power all the preliminary accomplishments of oratory are as useless as a sword that is kept permanently concealed within its sheath" (VIII. pr. 15–16).

Vico says that, in accordance with the humanist ideal, when teaching the young he "never discussed matters pertaining to eloquence apart from wisdom" and always would say that "eloquence is nothing but 'wisdom speaking'" (*la sapienza che parla*).[44] In his sixth oration, Vico says: "Having been imbued with the knowledge of divine things, may you learn prudence in human affairs, first, the moral, which forms man, then the civil, which forms the citizen."[45] In the *Study Methods* Vico says: "There is only one 'art of prudence' and this art is philosophy" (*Quamquam quid hoc verbi est "ars prudentiae," cuius una ars est philosophia*).[46] Vico is alluding to the first line of the *Digest* of Roman law, which claims that jurisprudence is true philosophy.[47] Eloquence is the middle term in the ideals that guide humane education and civil life: *sapientia, eloquentia, prudentia.* Thus:

> Eloquence is wisdom.
> Prudence is eloquence.
> ―――――――――――
> Prudence is wisdom.

In *Ars poetica* Horace says that the role of poetry is to teach, delight, and move (333). These functions attributed to poetry are taken over from rhetoric. In *Brutus* Cicero says: "Now there are three things in my opinion which the orator should effect: Instruct his listener, give him pleasure, stir his emotions" (185; see also *De orat.* II. 27.115). Rhetoric and poetic become part of a common process that parallels the ideals of wisdom, eloquence, and prudence.

In his address to the Academy of Oziosi, Vico quotes from Horace (*Ars. poet.* 309–11) on the art of properly using language in verse as well as prose: "'Right thinking is the first principle and source of writing,' because there is no eloquence without truth and dignity; of these two parts wisdom is composed." Thinking of the writings of Plato, Xenophon, Aeschines, and perhaps Antisthenes, Horace says, as Vico quotes: "'Socratic writings will direct you in the choice of subjects,' that is, the study of morals, which principally informs the wisdom of man, to which more than in the other parts of philosophy Socrates divinely applied himself, whence of him it was said: 'Socrates recalled moral philosophy from the heavens.'" Vico concludes with Horace's third principle: "And 'when the subject is well conceived, words will follow on spontaneously,' because of the natural bond by which we claim language and heart to be held fast together, for to every idea its proper voice stands naturally attached. Thus, eloquence is none other than wisdom speaking."[48]

When Socrates recalls moral philosophy from the heavens, he also recalls the knowledge of good and evil from the poets and makes it a subject of eloquence. Cicero says: "Socrates was the first to call philosophy down from the heavens and set her in the cities of men and bring her also into their homes and compel her to ask questions about life and morality and things good and evil" (*Tusc.* V. 410–11). Cicero in *De oratore* says that Socrates "in his discussions separated the science of wise thinking from that of elegant speaking, though in reality they are closely linked together" (III. 16.60). Cicero says that it is absurd to sever the tongue from the brain; he says that Socrates is in fact the most eloquent of speakers. He asks: "What of Critias? and Alcibiades? these though not benefactors of their fellow-citizens were undoubtedly learned and eloquent; and did they not owe their training to the discussions of Socrates?" (III. 34.139; see also III. 32.129).

Socrates' own obvious eloquence, coupled with his reputation for putting philosophy against rhetoric, is one of the many paradoxes of his identity. We cannot classify Socrates as belonging to either the theoretical or the practical world. All attempts at such classification immediately turn to the opposite. Cassirer says: "As soon as we believe that we have grasped the 'true' face of Socrates and of Socratic thought, then this 'truth' dissolves. Our 'knowledge' is transformed into 'ignorance.' Socrates seems to defy every attempt to 'pin him down'; his every aspect immediately turns into its opposite. This is a fundamental part of Socratic irony. This 'irony' has been borne out again and again in the historical interpretations of the figure of Socrates."[49]

Cassirer says that Socrates can be seen as Aristotle describes him in the *Metaphysics,* as the discoverer of the concept (978b3). In Plato's early dialogues Socrates appears as the discoverer of the logos, *ratio,* the concept. He appears, as Cassirer says, as the first great "artist of reason." Sharply opposed to this is Xenophon's picture of Socrates as the moralist and the teacher of "practical wisdom." Cassirer sees this as evidence "that the unique problem Socrates poses has not yet been fully understood. This problem consists in the fact that the opposition between theory and practice—the opposition between knowledge and action—has been denied and overcome by Socrates, raising it in a synthesis to a new level. Socrates seems to reject the opposition; for him all knowing is doing. Virtue ($\mathit{\dot{α}ρετή}$) is knowledge" (*Meno* 98D).[50]

Socrates raises the problem of the opposition of knowledge and action to a new level. Cassirer regards the key to this to be the Delphic oracle's instruction to "know thyself." He says Socrates "does not call for 'self-knowledge' in the sense of some pure (monadic) looking inward (intro-spection, intuition of the I in the pure act of the *cogito*); instead, it means something completely new and unique for him. This call now means: know your *work* and know 'yourself' *in* your work; know what you do, so you can do what you know."[51] Cassirer conceives *Werk* as a "basis phenomenon," a fundamental way in which the self realizes itself. Cassirer's *Werk* corresponds to civil wisdom as made by the self acting out of tradition, custom, and culture. In the *Phaedrus* Socrates describes himself as a "lover of learning" (230D).

Aristotle says that "in the moral character there are two qualities, natural virtue and virtue in the full sense; and of these the latter implies prudence. This is the reason why some people maintain that all the virtues are forms of prudence; and why Socrates, though partly right, was also partly wrong in his inquiries, because he was mistaken in thinking that all the virtues are forms of prudence, but he was quite right in asserting that they *imply* prudence" (*Nic. Eth.* 1144b15-20, trans. Thomson). Aristotle says that Socrates was wrong to hold that virtues are principles, but they do imply principles. Socrates was wrong, in Aristotle's view, because he held that virtues are forms of knowledge. Aristotle concludes: "Thus we see from these arguments that it is not possible to be good in the true sense of the word without prudence, or to be prudent without moral goodness" (1144b30-32, trans. Thomson). There is a prudential sense of wisdom (*phronēsis*) that is crucial to moral goodness and that connects knowledge to action.

Prudence is deliberation, and we do not deliberate about the past, as Aristotle says (*Nic. Eth.* 1139b6), or about what is necessary and cannot be changed. To deliberate we require a knowledge of what is both noble and base (*Topics* 137a12), and, as with wisdom in general, we require both memory and experience. Deliberation requires the art of the Muses, because, in relation to any course of action, we must understand it in terms of what was, is, and is to come. To deliberate is to foretell through contemplation. It is to be able to narrate what is at issue in terms of time, and this requires a grasp of the subject as a whole. Tradition, custom, law, and habit are themselves embodiments of prudence. They are embodiments of practical wisdom that the individual and the society have proven in action over time.

The *Institutes* of Justinian state, "The commandments of the law are these: live honorably; harm nobody; give everyone his due" (*Iuris praecepta sunt haec: honeste vivere, alterum non laedere, suum cuique tribuere*).[52] The jurisprudence of positive law and the habits that form our character from our education and social customs are our guides to human action. When we can act in accordance with these guides, there is no need for deliberation. They provide an eloquence of life that is present at least in traditional societies. Prudence is simply to follow their prudence.

All the art of life is not directed by a knowledge of the jurisprudence of one's nation or even, as Vico would call it, of the "jurisprudence of the human race," which is a knowledge of the actions of providence throughout the world of nations, a knowledge of the principles of their ideal eternal history. The individual, guided by "know thyself" as a principle of his action in the world and by "nothing too much" as a principle of moderation in that action, must take a specific course of life toward goodness and must act in individual occasions that require deliberation. Prudence is not mere cleverness or self-interest, as it has come to be understood from the standpoint of modern ethics that exists "after virtue."[53] How is prudence in this sense to be learned?

The key to virtuous human action is eloquence. Moral goodness is what we tell ourselves after we have acted. The learning of prudence requires us to make a moral act for ourselves in a manner similar to making an intellectual truth for ourselves. The act comes first, but the word is not separate from the act. We act, and the act must then be held in memory. The act must be made into a narration whereby the act can be held in mind as a moral truth. Eloquence is wisdom speaking or putting the whole into words. Every action so held in the memory as a narration is a guide to future action. Memory is the basis of deliberation.

At the basis of the moral-act-remembered is poetic, for the course of the action must be formed as a true story, a *vera narratio*. It must enter the imagination. But the narration must be joined with *ratio;* that is, it must be put into proper arrangement. It must be tested by ingenuity, and the similarities in its dissimilars must be perceived such that the course of action has a necessity of its internal elements. They must be seen as a harmony, grasped in proportion. When we are prompted to deliberate, we find ourselves in the middle of a course of events that has already begun and that is moving on its own toward an end. At the origin there is never need for deliberation.

A set of conditions is born and develops within history toward a point of maturity or crisis, unless it is interrupted from without. The conditions are tied to all the other events affecting them in history. But they have their own history. The point of maturity is potentially the heroic moment of such a course, and it may be naturally dissipated into its future and end. If the course of events in which we find ourselves becomes problematic, it becomes so just past the midpoint, when the course would naturally begin to dissipate and finally find its death among the larger scene of human events.

When events call out for deliberation, we face the problem of the identification of the moral. The moral is an act of seeing. Either we see the presence of the moral or we do not. If we do not see the moral dimension, we may simply become a person. To become a person is to practice the art of overlooking. Every society practices the art of overlooking in that it orders the civil world in a specific way. The vision of the individual is directed by this order, and the problem of good and evil is solved by this order. Society does not engage in dialectics to show itself what has been left out. The individual who identifies the moral and perceives it as counter to the social order has a dialectical vision. The individual sees more than has been seen by society.

The fact that there are other cultures calls every culture into question. But what calls culture into question in ultimate terms is not the fact that there are other cultures, other societies and customs whereby life is actually lived. That there is a way things ultimately are calls any moral state of events into question. Prudence in an ultimate sense is to act in accordance with the way things are, and this is to act absolutely and beyond opposites.

In the *Tao Te Ching* are the lines: "*T'ien ti pu jen:* Heaven and Earth are not kind: The ten thousand things are straw dogs to them. The Sage is not kind: People are straw dogs to him."[54] The art of the Sage is *wu wei*, "actionless action," which acknowledges that there is a course that anything takes that is natural to it. The problem of prudence in this sense is to remain in accord with it. As with the art of the Muses, one must know the nature of things well enough to act in accordance with them, to foretell. This depends upon memory and eloquence in speech. Argument will not help us, because for every argument there is a counter argument. From this process we can never reach the whole of anything that the deliberation is about.

The passage from the *Tao Te Ching* quoted above ends with the lines: "Longwinded speech is exhausting. Better to stay centered." Argument is endless. Eloquent speech brings things together, as does wisdom. Prudence is eloquence in action. The prudent action, like the perfect word or perfect brush stroke, is completely natural. In this sense we can say that the fool practices true prudence, because the fool simply acts in accordance with what is actually there. The fool is not a moral agent, but the moral agent can benefit from studying the fool's grasp of events, as we can benefit from paying attention to the ruthlessness of the action of the Sage.

Like the action of the Sage, the moral act has an absoluteness about it. Prudence comes into conflict with justice when prudence is understood as simply taking a temperate course of action in order to reduce conflict and opposition. The moral act, if it is truly such, cannot be understood simply as one possible course of action in relation to a given state of affairs. If so, it is a prudent act in the trivial sense of prudence. The intent of the truly moral act is to act in accordance with the good; the good is understood as something beyond opposites. The moral course taken claims to be absolute in relation to what is to be done in this specific case. Justice is the proper harmony or proportion of things, and when the proper harmony has been violated, injustice is perceived. The just man acts in accordance with the good, and no harm can come to a good man.

The distinction made in modern ethics—between *is* and *ought* as the fundamental opposition within which any moral deliberation takes place—ignores the need for a middle term between what is the case and what ought to be the case. In order to pass from one side of this opposition to the other, we must consider what *might* be the case. To do this requires imagination connected to memory. To deliberate and to act in moral terms require the moral imagination. When the injustice of a given order of things is seen, it must be seen in terms of what can be imagined otherwise. What might be or might have been provides the concrete sense of the possibilities in which the deliberations of practical wisdom can occur.

The moral philosophy I am suggesting is topical, not critical, in form. The self, by acting and narrating to itself the truth of its actions, by placing them under the good, and by formulating these actions in terms of the virtues, develops itself as a theater of communal sense from which it can draw forth the moral places from which to act. This process is like the law, in which the meaning of any case and the presence of any specific law in it, as well as the law itself, are grasped by finding precedents from which to understand the present case. To seek the prudent life when deliberation is not called upon to confront extremes, such as the presence of injustice, is to seek a life in accordance with what Cicero calls decorum. He says that with decorum we seek considerateness and self-control that give a sort of polish to life.

Such life embraces the cardinal virtues, especially temperance (*temperantia*). Cicero says: "Under this head is further included what in Latin may be called *decorum* (propriety); for in Greek it is called πρέπον. Such is its essential nature, that it is inseparable from moral goodness; for what is proper is morally right, and what is morally right is proper" (*De off.* I. 27.93–94). Decorum or propriety is something that cannot be taught by any critical method of reasoning. It comes from human beings acting in any situation in terms of their own human dignity. It is a sense of the civil applied in life and brought forth from it. Cicero says, "This propriety, therefore, of which I am speaking belongs to each division of moral rectitude; and its relation to the cardinal virtues is so close, that it is perfectly self-evident and does not require any abstruse process of reasoning to see it" (I. 27.95).

For decorum we must go to school with the poets. The propriety we seek is that which "we may infer from that propriety which poets aim to secure. . . . Now, we say that the poets observe propriety, when every action is in accord with each individual character" (I. 28.97). The poet can only say what is fitting of any character. In terms of propriety we might say of moral activity what Horace in the *Ars poetica* says to the poet about presenting lives on stage: "Either follow tradition or invent what is self-consistent" (119).

This completes my proofs to the reader of the true nature of philosophy. I turn to my peroration. Concerning the soundness of the proofs and of others that they may imply, the reader must convince himself of them by making and remaking them for himself. I can offer no more than does Vico for his account of civil wisdom: that the reader must meditate and narrate to himself their truth by the proof that such "had, has, and will have to be." This necessary order is the philosopher's version of the original truth of the three moments of the song of the Muses. To motivate such making I can only hold out the Vichian promise of provision: "These proofs are of a kind divine and should give thee a divine pleasure" (*NS* 349). Philosophy rests on piety toward human excellence and acceptance of the boundaries of the whole of things.

The reader must consider that the civil world rests either on fire or on logos. If it rests on fire it rests on desire, on the inner fire of the self. When desire as the passion of fire is coupled with technique as the instrument of intelligence, the civil world is put to work. Technique is ingenuity (*ingenium*) divorced from its natural bond with memory and imagination. The modern technological world is a theater of ingenuity separated from tradition or human image. It is ingenious ingenuity, that is to say, ingenuity for the sake of ingenuity. Like desire that is never satisfied, ingenuity knows no limits in itself. Only memory as the order of the past and imagination as the formation of the present can direct ingenuity back to necessity, the mother of invention. Only memory and imagination can supply the sense of to what ingenuity need be applied. The gift of the Promethean fire is the gift of pure mastery, without civil wisdom. It is the gift of action. This is not action in accordance with virtue but action in accordance with desire.

There is a second Promethean commonplace that is not as well known as that of *Prometheus Pyrphoros* and its variations. This is the commonplace that civil wisdom and society itself rest on logos become eloquence.[55] This second Promethean commonplace is found in Cicero, before Cicero in Isocrates, and before Isocrates in Protagoras, who says: "Toil and work and instruction and education and wisdom are the garland of fame which is woven from the flowers of an eloquent tongue and set on the head of those who love it. Eloquence however is difficult, yet its flowers are rich and ever new" (Fr. 12).

In the *Nicocles* Isocrates says that it is this power of logos that sets man apart from the beasts: "For in the other powers which we possess we are in no respect superior to other living creatures; nay, we are inferior to many in swiftness and in strength and in other resources" (*Nic.* 5-9). We should not be hostile to eloquence: "Because there has been implanted in us the power to persuade each other and to make clear to each other whatever we desire, not only have we escaped the life of wild beasts, but we have come together and founded cities and made laws and invented arts; and generally speaking, there is no institution devised by man which the power of speech has not helped us to establish" (ibid.).

Isocrates says eloquence not only is needed to speak before others but also is required when we deliberate in private with ourselves on the problems before us. He concludes, "We shall find that none of the things which are done with intelligence take place without the help of speech, but that in all our actions as well as in all our thoughts speech is our guide, and is most employed by those who have the most wisdom" (ibid.). Isocrates repeats this passage in the *Antidosis* (253-57).

Cicero in *De inventione* expresses this view of logos as eloquence in terms of the Promethean commonplace: "If we wish to consider the origin of this thing we call eloquence—whether it be an art, a study, a skill, or a gift of nature—we shall find that it arose from most honorable causes and continued on its way for the best reasons" (I.2-3). Cicero says that there was a time when men wandered at large in the fields like animals and did nothing by reason. There was no legitimate marriage and no equitable code of law. He says: "At this juncture a man—great and wise I am sure—became aware of the power latent in man and the wide field offered by his mind for great achievements if one could develop this power and improve it by instruction" (ibid.). At first these bestial humans cried out against this man's teaching: "Then when through reason and eloquence they listened with greater attention, he transformed them from wild savages into a kind and gentle folk" (ibid.).

This original "Promethean" orator conveys the gift of eloquence, which is both the origin and the medium of civilization. Cicero says: "To me, at least, it does not seem possible that a mute and voiceless wisdom could have turned men suddenly from their habits and introduced them to different patterns of life" (ibid.). He concludes: "This was the way in which at first eloquence came into being and advanced to greater development, and likewise afterward in the greatest undertakings of peace and war it served the highest interests of mankind" (ibid.).

Cicero goes on to say that as some men lost their attachment to virtue they corrupted the use of eloquence because they did not combine it with the study of philosophy. This brought eloquence into disrepute. This accords with Aristotle's claim in the *Rhetoric* (1356a1-14) that the truth of what is said depends upon the ethos of the speaker and reflects the first sentence of this work—"Rhetoric is the counterpart of dialectic"—that is, rhetoric and dialectic stand to each other as do strophe and antistrophe (1354a1). In the *De officiis*, Cicero says that some men persist on a level of beasts in the field and thus cannot be reached: "For some people are men only in name, not in fact" (I. 30.105). In *De oratore* Cicero relates a eulogy of the rhetoric of Crassus, in which he speaks of the marvel of the single being who can arise and, with a few others, through wisdom joined with eloquence move things in a prudent manner (I. 30-34).

Vico's primal scene is of Jove the thunderer, whose presence creates fear for the first time in the *bestioni*, who roam the earth for two centuries after the universal flood and who have no marriage, burial, or religion. With his noise of thunder, shaking of the sky, and discharge of lightning bolts, Jove is a transformation and a joining of the two versions of the Promethean commonplace: Prometheus as fire-bringer and Prometheus as the man who brings logos. The fire comes directly from Jove from whom "the Muse began," not from a theft by Prometheus from Jove's domain.

Vico says: "The first theological poets created the first divine fable, the greatest they ever created: that of Jove, king and father of men and gods, in the act of hurling the lightning bolt" (*NS* 379). Jove was for the gentile peoples the first word, the logos of the world. Vico says: "This is the civil history of the expression 'All things are full of Jove' (*Iovis omnia plena*) [Vergil, *Eclogue* 3.60] by which Plato later understood the ether which penetrates and fills everything [*Cratylus* 412D]" (ibid.). Possessing the divine fable of Jove, the founders of the first families of the gentile nations institute civil wisdom, religion, marriage, and burial, through their ability to make altars and take the auspices of the actions of Jove in the heavens: "They believed that Jove commanded by signs, that such signs were real words, and that nature was the language of Jove" (ibid.).

In Vico's doubling of the Promethean commonplace, the founders of the first families practice a "science in divinity" by finding the logos in the real words of nature, guided by the wisdom of the first theological poets. These founders are the first orators, able to civilize and foretell. The thunderbolts of Jove do not produce a mastery over material conditions purely and simply through the power of fire. The mastery is produced through the real words. The fire of the thunderbolt of Jove is not separate from his logos.

The first word is *Jove*, formed directly from his nature: "Awakened in men by the first thunderbolts, these interjections of Jove should give birth to one produced by the human voice: *pa!;* and that this should then be doubled: *pape!*" (*NS* 448). From the power of logos first families were formed, and then cities. Eloquence takes its first form from poetic wisdom. Even ethos comes from Jove: "Jove was equal [just] to all. This is the civil history of the expression *Iupiter omnibus aequus*" (*NS* 415). All the arts of material comfort presuppose Jove the bringer of logos through his fire, and they presuppose Jove the bringer of the arts of humanity, the Muses, through his coupling with Mnemosyne.[56] This is the Vichian reading of the "Promethean grade" of Camillo's theater of memory.

In Vico's frontispiece, the *dipintura* that heads the text of the *New Science,* we see the divine providential eye sending light down to Dame Metaphysic, who stands upon the globe of nature; the convex jewel on her breast reflects this light onto the statue of Homer, whose blind gaze transfers it to the world of civil things, the symbols of which are arranged along the bottom of the scene. Vico confronts us, in this emblem, with the three worlds in juxtaposition: the divine, the natural, and the human. In the first sentence of this work Vico says, "As Cebes the Theban made of moral, we present for view here a Tablet of civil things, as will serve the reader to conceive the idea of this work before reading it, and to bring it back most easily to memory, with such aid as the imagination may afford, after he has read it." In the final paragraph of his commentary on this scene, Vico says, "The entire engraving represents the three worlds in the order in which the human minds of the gentiles have been raised from earth to heaven."

All true philosophies are theaters of memory. Memory is the master key to the wisdom that Socrates loves. For he says that he is a "lover of learning," and learning is the memory of the thinker.

Epilogue:
The Tablet of Philosophy

In October I entered a London bookshop specializing in antiquarian texts and noticed a small work, bound in mottled calfskin, by an anonymous eighteenth-century author. The work was a commentary on Tommaso Campanella's *La città del sole*, composed in a fine Italian style. The author maintained that the work not only described a utopia but contained a system of memory based on the concentric circles of the city walls. He drew certain connections to the use of occult memory in the doctrine of heliocentricity in Giordano Bruno's *La cena de le ceneri*, which were highly original and learned. In the back of the work were bound a number of pages that composed a second text, written in an uneven style. The volume seemed to have come from a private library. It bore no mark of a printer or editor.

The second text was untitled, and by its first sentences it appeared to be an Italian translation of the Tablet of Cebes, but this text broke off, and it continued as a description of the travels of a group of scholarly thinkers. These were citizens of the Republic of Letters who had entered Italy through Milan and were making their way southward in order to view the site of Pompeii and, farther on, the remains of the Greek temples at Paestum. They broke their journey halfway at Cortona, climbing, from Terontola on the plain below, up the hill on which Cortona sits. These were citizens of the North: a Jew from Breslau, a Celt of Catholic birth, and a Protestant from Swabia who understood only some Italian and communicated with the others mostly in his native German and in Latin. In Florence they met a handsome woman, a Mediterranean of admirable temperament who was traveling with several of her daughters. The two groups decided to travel on together, and she enlivened the evenings with her excellent memory, recalling stories and facts regarding the places through which they passed. The daughters had become worldly like their mother, and they willingly ministered to the wants of the gentlemen of letters, relieving their every care, much to the satisfaction of their learned mother, who was not above joining her daughters in their liaisons.

Cortona, their Mediterranean companion recalled to them, originally bore the name of its founder, Corythus, reputedly the father of Dardanus, the mythical ancestor of the Trojans. In speaking with the citizens of Cortona they learned of a particular phenomenon, the *Tanella di Pitagora,* located below the town, on the hillside. They asked the mother of the delightful daughters if she knew of this cave of Pythagoras. She explained that it is believed by most to be an Etruscan hypogeum of the fourth century B.C., a place mistakenly associated with Pythagoras because of a confusion between Cortona and Cortone, where Pythagoras lived in southern Italy and which was classically known as Croton. It is held that Pythagoras died in the neighboring city of Metapontium, having withdrawn there to escape the Crotoniates, who had risen up against his authority. But, she said, there are some who believe that when Pythagoras left Croton he fled beyond Metapontium, north to Corythus, and died there.

Hearing this, the gentlemen of letters were more than eager to make the short descent to view the *tanella.* They expected to see nothing more than a simple cave in the side of the hill. Each had to stoop to enter the low opening, and as they looked up they were surprised to see a picture inscribed on one wall. They and their female companion were greeted by an old man, thin and adust in appearance. He addressed them in broken Tuscan, a language he knew but did not speak easily. They communicated with him in Tuscan and in Latin, which he knew as if it were his native tongue. They had noticed that those who stood around the entrance addressed him as Mastro Vicus, or some name that sounded like this. He was from one of the cities of the South, the region called the *Mezzogiorno*. Like all from his *patria* he was by birth a master of the *narratio fabulosa* that Macrobius describes.

The senex explained that among the ancients the full wisdom of the tablet was known, to the extent that it ever could be known. But as these citizens of letters, to which Republic the old man must also have belonged, knew well from the tenth book of the *Rules of Pedagogy* of Aristoxenus, not all the doctrines of Pythagoras were for all men to hear; that is, if this picture did indeed contain such doctrines. A doctrine of this magnitude was to be expected from one of the Seven Sages, who some say left no writings, although this is called absurd by Diogenes, on the authority of Heraclitus. Whether Pythagoras left writings or not, it is reported by Iamblichus that Pythagoras considered most necessary the use of symbols in instruction. Was this perhaps the one formulation that Pythagoras left, in the last days of his life, while in asylum and hiding from those in revolt against his authority?

The senex said that there are those who hold that Pythagoras was a disciple of Isaiah, but this is firmly denied by Lactantius in the *Divine Institutions*, and some claim that his view can be supported by a passage of Josephus in the Jewish *Antiquities*. The senex said also that there are those who hold that Pythagoras was the teacher of divination to Numa, but this is denied by Livy, who places Pythagoras at the time of Servius Tullius and claims further that, because of the barbarous character of Italy at that time, it was impossible for Pythagoras or even his name to reach Rome from Croton, passing through so many peoples of varying languages and customs.

Against such restricted views, the senex then reminded them, are the long journeys that Pythagoras had the power to undertake through many nations, visiting the disciples of Orpheus in Thrace, the mages in Persia, the Chaldeans in Babylonia, and the gymnosophists in India; and then, on his return, the priests of Egypt and, after crossing Africa at its widest point, the disciples of Atlas in Mauretania and, crossing the sea, the Druids in Gaul. Pythagoras is said to have returned to his fatherland having become rich in wisdom from those barbarous nations, where, long before, Hercules the Theban had gone on a civilizing mission, slaying monsters and tyrants. These were the same nations to whom the Greeks had taught culture, as they later bragged, but not with such profit that these nations did not remain barbarous. Porphyry reports that Pythagoras learned the mathematical sciences from the Egyptians, the Phoenicians, and the Chaldeans, for the first excelled in geometry, the second in numbers and proportions, and the third in astronomical theorems and divine rites. Other secrets of life, Porphyry says, he learned from the Magi.

The senex faced them and said, "I must convey to you a danger." Before he would relate the essence of the tablet to them, he said, they must decide whether they wished to hear it. He did not begrudge them their curiosity and wonder, from which all knowledge originates, but he said they must know that should any one of them listen and fail to understand, he would become unhappy, vicious, and ignorant and would pass his days wretchedly. If they did give attention and understand all the speculation told in the picture, they would derive great benefit and become wise and possessors of virtue. This was a choice, he said, over which he had no control; each must make his own decision.

In other words, each must be his own Hercules in this matter, for, as they recalled from Dio Chrysostom and from Xenophon before him, Hercules had faced a similar choice in his training.

The old man's warning reminded them of the sphinx, who put riddles to travelers and slew them if they failed to find solutions. Here they did not fear that physical death might be the result of failure to comprehend the picture. Instead, the result could be the agony, relieved only by death, of being bound to inquiry that goes on and on in an unceasing attempt to find the literal truth of a doctrine that has none. They could be bound to the rock of cognition. At this moment, the learned spectatrix of memory who accompanied them encouraged them, recalling a line by Gianfranceso Pico concerning the fact that the spiritual eye, joined to the body, uses images to contemplate the truth.

The citizens of letters had little trouble in urging the senex to proceed. Each had taken a similar risk when entering the pursuit of truth itself. The misery of which he warned was not worse than the melancholy each had already experienced as a thinker dedicated to the whole of truth. This prior dedication did not eliminate the danger of the Pythagorean threshold, but his auditors were prepared for it. Each swore his willingness for the ingenious old man to proceed. Because of the weight of this oath, he asked each to voice his acceptance four times, in accord with Pythagorean custom. This done, he took up a wand and began to relate a tale of the philosophical life.

He first called their attention to the picture as a whole. It showed a hill of perfect dimensions, a triangle of equal sides with four levels running across it, the fourth being almost at the top. On these levels or grades were figures of men and women grouped in various ways, their number decreasing as their procession moved along the grades and toward the top. The figures were distributed throughout each grade; the movement from one grade to another was through a center aisle that ran to the top grade. Gates and figures appeared to control the two entrances to the first grade and subsequently to this aisle. The figures at these gates had the appearance of gods or heroes. Between the grades on the hill were areas of forest.

The human figures on the first level fell into four groups, with two groups on the left of the great vertical aisle and two on the right. On the second level the number of groups reduced to three, with the middle group arranged inside a circle that obstructed the aisle itself. On the third grade, the figures were divided into two groups, one on each side of the aisle, and on the final grade the aisle culminated in a one small group. Each group was arranged around a single point on the grade that was its center. Many figures seemed content to remain where they were. Only a few appeared to be attempting to view the fourth grade and to undertake the ascent. Most could see this final possibility if they raised their eyes, even in the chiaroscuro of the first grade. But most looked horizontally along their own grade or focused on their own group. Some were in attitudes of conversation, some were meditating, and some were listening. Others seemed active merely with their own work.

When the senex had finished pointing out the four grades and their representations, he called his auditors' attention to a large group at the foot of the hill and off to the right. This seemed to depict a school, with two instructors speaking to the assembled group. They recognized one as Cicero; the other, the old man explained, was Heraclides of Pontus. This scene was a kind of annex to the scene of the main picture, and he explained that it was of later origin, added at some point during the Roman colonization of this region. To his auditors the text of this scene was now evident, but the old man turned to them and, with perfect clarity, recalled the following.

"While we see that philosophy is something very ancient, we admit that its name is of recent origin. For who can deny that wisdom is ancient, not only the thing, but the name as well? It gained this glorious name among the ancients for its apprehension of things divine and human and of the origin and causes of all that exists. Hence arose the tradition that the famous Seven and, many generations earlier, Lycurgus and, even earlier, in the heroic age, Ulysses and Nestor were, and were thought to be, wise. Nor would the stories of Atlas holding up the sky and Prometheus chained to the Caucasus and Cepheus transformed into a star together with his wife, his daughter, and her husband have arisen if their superhuman knowledge of heavenly things had not caused their names to become legends. After these men, all who showed zeal for contemplation and study were thought to be and were called wise, and this designation continued in use until the time of Pythagoras. As Heraclides of Pontus, a pupil of Plato and one of the most learned of men, writes, Pythagoras is said to have visited Phlius and to have spoken learnedly and eloquently with Leon, the ruler of the Phliasians. Leon, admiring his genius and eloquence, asked him what skill he professed, and he replied that he knew no skill but was a philosopher. Leon wondered at the novel word and asked what philosophers were and how they differed from other men, but Pythagoras replied that life seemed to him like the gathering when the great games were held, which were attended by the whole of Greece. For there some men sought to win fame and the glory of the crown by exerting their bodies, and others were attracted by the gain and profit of buying and selling. But there was one kind of man, the noblest of all, who sought neither applause nor profit but who came in order to watch, wanting to see what was happening and how. So too among us, who have migrated into this life from a different life and mode of being as if from some city to a crowded festival, some are slaves to fame, others to money; but there are some rare spirits who, holding all else as nothing, eagerly contemplate the universe. These he called 'lovers of wisdom,' for that is what *philosopher* means; and as at the festival it most becomes a visitor to be a spectator without thought of personal gain, so in life the contemplation and understanding of the universe is far superior to all other pursuits."

They recognized these words, which the senex quoted to them in Latin. The senex called their attention to a path leading from the school of philosophy to a vestibule located at the beginning of the aisle at the base of the hill. In the vestibule was a throng of figures, and before them, his back to the hill, was a figure who appeared to be an auctioneer. The old man informed them that this was indeed an auctioneer who was rapidly presenting ideas of the universe, man, and the gods. He was a spieler of ideas, turning each over and over and showing its attractions and advantages. The audience was pushing forward to hear better his descriptions. To the old man's auditors, the scene recalled Lucian's *Sale of Philosophers:* "All shapes and sizes!" "Assorted doctrines!" The vestibule was in the form of a square. There was no direct entrance from the square into the aisle. Any entrance was blocked by a low wall and by the auctioneer, but the audience could see how the aisle led upward toward the light and could see the procession of figures ascending. There were two side doors or gates issuing from this auction square; one gave entrance onto the left side of the first grade, the other onto the right.

The senex explained that when members of the audience tired of the confusion and *pseudopaideia* of the auction, and he said that some never did, they would naturally turn their attention to the two side doors. At the one on the left stood Hermes, the lackey of Zeus, speaking in a rote and conventional way, extolling the wonders of a second figure beside him. This figure they recognized as Narcissus, who was posing before various mirrors and a pool in a way that fascinated the onlookers. The process apparently had the approval of Zeus, which pleased those attracted to Narcissus even more. The old man explained that the ability both to lose and to enjoy the ego in a single act was a power these onlookers much desired. That such a pleasure could be spoken of by Hermes as also respectable and pleasing to Zeus was decisive for them. He explained that Hermes in his contrived speech does not tell them that the soul can be lost in the reflection, and he does not mention that Narcissus languished and died through seeing his reflection in the water. His soul was carried off in it.

The senex explained that these figures listening to Hermes had found many of the ideas to which they were exposed in the auction upsetting, and they now turned a deaf ear to these ideas, feeling that such thoughts might also be upsetting to the gods and to the state. They were attracted to the clarity of Hermes' words and to the clarity of Narcissus's mirrors and reflection. Through the threshold of the left gate they could perceive figures that looked just like themselves, the old man said, and one could see many figures entering happily.

Before the gateway on the right side stood a woman of great beauty and composure, brightly dressed, with an aura of possessing elemental powers. The senex pointed to the figure with his wand and said it was Eros, masked as Aphrodite. The old man said that those few who approached and asked admission to the right side of the grade were embraced by the Eros figure, with such affect as to arouse both their minds and their bodies. It inflamed their passions and quickened the circulation of their blood. The *philia* they had understood as the friendship to be had with wisdom and with others who shared it was now grounded in the elemental force of Eros's embrace. All this the senex related.

Although the auditors thought they knew, they asked the old man what choice was being made between the two doors.

Without hesitation he replied: "It is the choice between true and false philosophy. Those who pass into the left door are philosophers of the part, and they can never become wise. They can only think of this-and-that and mine-and-thine, and in so doing they can discover truths, but they can never make these truths into the True. Philosophy must for them remain forever only an expertise. Those who pass through the door on the right are philosophers of the whole. Although their thinking moves through arguments and definitions and the facts and the connections these entail, the truths generated are never the final end of philosophy for them. They know that to love wisdom is to love the whole of things."

He then called their attention to the activities of the two groups of figures depicted on the left side of the first grade, those who had passed through the door of Hermes and Narcissus and taken up permanent residence in this place. To the far left were advocates of facts, he said, and of theories. They had no special sense of history or letters and spent their time developing arguments and solutions to problems they noticed around them. They were thinkers of the real object, material men of method, elaborators of the certainties of sense coupled with ratiocination. Some held that language itself is a theory. Some held that there are facts in the world independent of thought. Some held that the mind is the behavior of the limbs and organs of the body and not more. "Problems of their own identity or of human conduct," he said, "are discussed among them with logic and with little else. Most questions which appear to be the result of their dedication to argument are in fact decided by authority and convention." As the auditors now realized, they were gazing on a great workshop in which all were busy, each with his own project, that never required justification beyond a kind of common approval. Their goal was the matter-at-hand.

This same general goal was also that of the second group,

that closest to the left doorway, the senex explained. Here, too, was a workshop, but one of more superficial refinement. Wine was being served and consumed, but no figure could be seen pouring a libation. Here the exchanges concerned not facts and theories, but phenomena, structures, and texts. The object was the center of attention, but it was a subjectivized object. It was, the old man explained, nonetheless kept at full distance from the human. Although everywhere the "human sciences" were discussed among these figures, nowhere was the human itself truly to be found. It was of no real concern. "Those in this place," the senex explained, "can be described as transcendental reflectors."

In the first group there was a belief that if enough facts were analyzed and brought together under theories, there would be a world, and if enough words were analyzed, there would be language. In the second group there was the belief that if enough phenomena were examined, or enough structures described, or enough texts dismantled, there would be meaning. But some among them had given up the notion of meaning as being of any importance; they spoke only of "interpretations" and "readings." Some saw all thought as the shadow of politics. The old man explained that no concern existed for the discovery of sources or origins, for the noetic, or for narration. "Such never enters their minds or their words," he said. The auditors noted that both parts of this great workshop had a kind of monotone that concentrated on the representation of *res*, or whatever stood in its place as the object of thought. Even if the thinkers thought about themselves, they were there only as another *res*. The senex pointed out that this was the legacy of Narcissus: philosophy done in a hall of mirrors.

Above the left side of the first grade, in the forest on the hillside between it and the second grade, were two pockets of figures whose significance the auditors could not immediately make out. In an illuminated clearing were seated figures with folded hands, in deep thought, but in another area, toward the center of the hill, the figures seemed suspended in an enclosure. The senex explained that those seated in the patches of light were seekers of being, who had become disenchanted with the representations of truth that many on the first grade sought. They were, he explained, troglodytes of a sort, who lived in caves in the hill and were thus constantly attracted to the patches of light. They seek a presence of being in their own being, and they wait for it, going into the caves when it is dark and returning to their positions each morning.

The other area, he explained, is intended to depict an aviary, in which those who were unable to subscribe to the literal-mindedness of the workshop of the first grade sought refuge. These are aviators, floating, so to speak, in an air of suspicion. They have the jargons. They are sure that there are no final meanings to be found. Any meaning can be changed to its opposite through the jargons. "But," the old man said, "they are not skeptics." The skeptic seeks a certainty to answer his doubts, but these suspicionists, he explained, hold to an infinity of readings and speakings for which there is no terminus in principle. In this way, he said, they practice their own kind of waiting.

The senex then turned his wand to the two groups arrayed along the right side of the grade, to those who had entered through the door of Eros. Here was depicted not a workshop but a journey. There was a procession of figures that wound through this grade and back into the great aisle above the low wall of the auction square. They passed on to the second and third grades and upward to the fourth grade, at the head of the hill. "This pattern of movement," the old man said, "shows the stages of true philosophy." It was a course that he could relate to them in no more than its barest outlines, for although the full meanings of each of its stages were second nature to many of the ancients, those meanings could be recaptured now only by meditation and memory of the most devoted sort.

"Here," he said, "is the first group closest to Eros. They are gaining experience in the art of comprehending images. They are finding their way through the great forest of depiction and emblem." Within this group the auditors noticed another group, and they asked who they were. He replied that these were poets and tellers of tales, whom the lovers of wisdom were consulting. By their gestures some of the poets appeared to be mad; others appeared calm but unresponsive to the apparent questioning of the philosophers. The philosophers were regarding them very carefully.

The senex moved his wand horizontally along the grade to the second group. "These are philosophers listening to lawgivers and jurisconsults," he said. "They are intent on learning the arts of rhetoric and jurisprudence that are the basis of all moral thought. The images are keys to the cosmos, but the laws are the keys to the soul and to successful action in the world of civil things." Within this group the auditors observed another group of figures. Some of these seemed keen-eyed, and others seemed dull in their manner. The senex said, "These are politicians and administrators. Those who are keen-eyed rule by instinct, and have some respect for justice. Those who are dull are administrators and hold positions by convention. Neither has knowledge. The administrators regard justice as unimportant for their actions." He said that although there is nothing to be learned from them, the lover of wisdom must learn to recognize them, for they often form a bond with false philosophy, or false philosophy seeks out their position. The true philosopher recognizes that the true teacher of politics is the law itself. This is what must be learned on this part of the journey, the old man said.

Then he moved his wand quickly along the line of figures that were ascending the center aisle toward the second grade. There, directly in the middle of the great aisle, was a circle, and within its space was a group of figures in animated conversation. To the left and right of this circle along the grade were two other groups, one flanking the circle on each side. As the auditors carefully viewed the whole grade, they saw that it depicted figures moving freely back and forth, around and among these three groups. The senex explained that this grade is where method is learned by the lovers of wisdom. "The group to the left of the circle is engaged in the formulation of arguments and their testing. Here training is offered in *ars critica*. Judgments are tested, and the imagination is disciplined. The group to the right of the circle is engaged in the art of formulating questions, the key to dialogue and inquiry." He said that here the *ars topica* is taught, which trains in the use of the image to establish beginning points for thought and in the use of the question to draw forth from the image the idea that is the medium of reason. It is a scandal to logic that it cannot guarantee the truth of the premises of its own arguments. To learn the art of wise speech, the figures must pass back and forth between the two groups.

The senex then turned to the group in the circle, saying that this group is concerned with dialectic, the apprehension of opposites as found in thought and in experience. This was the art of the *coincidentia oppositorum*. The lovers of wisdom applied themselves here to learning in common the art of the complete speech: the speech that moves from opposition to opposition throughout experience, recalling the whole of things and imitating its truth in words. Within this process, the senex explained, thought moves from the finding of *topoi* to the judgments of reason that follow from them and issue in *argumenta*. These *argumenta* are at the same time enclosed in a course of higher speech that is the true narration of what is. This is the thought of the circle, the perfect motion that runs from beginning to middle to end, and in the end is its beginning. The art of the philosopher is the art of circular thinking, or what is called speculation.

Speculation is insight into inner form. It sees, the senex said, the nature of a thing through its opposite and forms a circle of thought. The danger here, he warned, is that the lover of wisdom may become fascinated with system and locked into this second grade forever. The system builders can become infatuated with a narcissism of internal relationships and thus lose the wonder of the *Jenseits*. The cure for this, he said, is for the practitioner of dialectic to notice how language speaks of all opposites but never unifies them. Language is a field of transference and metamorphoses, but it is never a unity. The speakers of system, he said, are closer to the truth than are the watery souls carried off in the mirrors and pools of reflection. But system is not the final embodiment of philosophy.

The old man now confessed that he was not sure if what he had said up to this point was what the picture intended. He insisted that his account might be only approximate. Whatever was the case, the traveling friends agreed that it was a speech of great interest and urged him to go on. The ingenious old man then pointed to the figures leaving the circle and proceeding up the aisle to the third grade, on which there were two groups, one on each side of the aisle. "This," he explained, "is the grade of the tropes. Here style appropriate to wisdom is imparted." On the left side, he said, was a concentration on the mastery of metaphor, the trope of the poet. On the right the figures were learning to become masters of irony, the trope of the philosopher proper.

Both of these tropes, he explained, depend upon *ingenium*, a faculty largely lost to the pursuers of false philosophy, who do require and employ *ingenium,* as does all human thought, but they never know it or acknowledge it. Metaphor and irony are the slayers of literal-mindedness; they locate meaning beyond the appearance. The true philosopher's speech moves between the origination of a truth in a metaphor and a reformulation of it through irony. In metaphor and irony, things are brought together that can never be spanned by logic alone. They allow the philosopher to stand common sense on its head. "Style is the end of the philosopher's education," the senex explained.

The scene depicted on the fourth and final grade is not a part of the philosopher's education, but the result of it. "It is," he said, "the depiction of the philosopher's persona." This final part of the tablet had become quite faded with the effects of time. Barely anything of the attitudes of the figures could be discerned. Here, the senex said, he could tell his hearers very little, for he, too, had come upon the picture in this faded condition. As they had noticed when first regarding the picture as a whole, the fourth grade was illuminated by a light from above and behind the hill. The figures were arranged in a semicircle and appeared to be engaged in friendly conversation, to speak easily with one another.

The senex said it was a scene of talk among friends, who shared a noetic power to grasp essentials. Their ideal was to be wisdom that speaks. Wisdom was here both an inner and an outer light. In this light could be seen, he said, the interdependence of virtue and the real. Metaphysics becomes a guide to life through their common speculations. They practice a poetic learning. They join the poetic eye of the immediate with a learned memory. He said that each of these philosophers was like a spirit whom it pleases to visit the world and stay for a while. "But," he said, "they are not kindly spirits. They teach a jurisprudence of the soul, and their words are often a severe narration. They transport a civil wisdom, a justice, that is not always pleasing to those who hear it."

The auditors asked the old man if these friends could be the Platonic friends of the forms. He answered that it was possible that this was what was depicted, but it was also possible that they were the followers of numbers, from the teachings of Pythagoras. "Or they may be followers of other doctrines," he said, "for there are many ways to traverse the grades and places of the hill, but there is only one love of wisdom." The figures in the final group had nearly reached the apex of this mount of joy, and they shared the whole as the flower of this *colonna* of wisdom. "The name *philosophos*," he said, "is the name of all philosophers." The auditors, having arrived at the end of their journey with the senex, looked upon the ten places of the tablet and took pleasure in its music.

They were much impressed with the possibilities of the final group, who were a republic to themselves. Yet the senex pointed out that the figures were grouped just below the peak of the hill. They could go no further, as the aisle ended with them. The group's circle did not enclose the top itself. In the calm voice in which he had spoken throughout, the senex claimed that he could not say what the meaning of this final moment of separation was but that to attain its meaning would surely hold the key to the entire tablet. Beyond this he could offer them no instruction. "To know the significance of this separation," he said, "is the same as to grasp the instruction on the Temple of Apollo at Delphi: *gnothi seauton*, 'know thyself.' Only in it, and in its corresponding instruction in virtue—*mēden agan*, 'nothing too much'—can true philosophy expect to live."

Notes

Citations to Greek and Latin authors are to editions of the Loeb Classical Library (Cambridge: Harvard University Press); *The Collected Dialogues of Plato,* Bollingen Series LXXI, ed. Edith Hamilton and Huntington Cairns (New York: Pantheon, 1961); *The Complete Works of Aristotle: The Revised Oxford Translation,* Bollingen Series LXXI.2, ed. Jonathan Barnes, 2 vols. (Princeton: Princeton University Press, 1984).

Introduction
Prometheus and Descartes

1. Jean-Jacques Rousseau, *The First and Second Discourses,* trans. Roger D. Masters and Judith Masters (New York: St. Martin's, 1964), 30; Rousseau, *Discours sur les sciences et les arts,* ed. George R. Havens (New York: Modern Language Association of America, 1946), following p. 88.
2. Rousseau, *Discourse,* 47; Rousseau, *Discours,* 127.
3. Rousseau, *Discourse,* 45 n; Rousseau, *Discours,* 127 n.
4. For the order of Aeschylus's four plays, see Carl Kerényi, *Prometheus: Archetypal Image of Human Existence,* trans. Ralph Manheim (New York: Pantheon Books, 1963), 69–76.
5. Rousseau, *Discours,* 227.
6. Baldesar Castiglione, *The Book of the Courtier,* trans. George Bull (New York: Penguin, 1976), 290.
7. *L'idea del theatro dell'eccellen. M. Giulio Camillo* (Florence: Lorenzo Torrentino, 1550), 71–86.
8. Giovanni Boccaccio, *Genealogia Deorum gentilium,* IV, cap. 44, as cited by Olga Raggio, "The Myth of Prometheus," *Journal of the Warburg and Courtauld Institutes* 22 (1958): 53–54.
9. Marsilio Ficino, "Five Questions Concerning the Mind," trans. Josephine L. Burroughs, in *The Renaissance Philosophy of Man,* ed. Ernst Cassirer, Paul Oskar Kristeller, and John Herman Randall, Jr. (Chicago: University of Chicago Press, 1948), 208.
10. *The Letters of Marsilio Ficino,* trans. members of the language department

of the School of Economic Science, London, vol. 1 (London: Shepheard-Walwyn, 1975), 41.
11. Francis Bacon, *De sapientia veterum*, in *The Works of Francis Bacon*, ed. James Spedding, Robert Leslie Ellis, and Douglas Denon Heath, vol. 6 (New York: Garrett Press, 1968), 747.
12. Francis Bacon, *De augmentis scientiarum*, in *The Works of Francis Bacon*, ed. James Spedding, Robert Leslie Ellis, and Douglas Denon Heath, vol. 1 (New York: Garrett Press, 1968), 649.
13. Sigmund Freud, "The Acquisition and Control of Fire," in *The Standard Edition of the Complete Psychological Works of Sigmund Freud*, ed. and trans. James Strachey, vol. 22 (London: Hogarth Press, 1964), 183–93.
14. G. W. F. Hegel, *Lectures in the Philosophy of Religion*, ed. Peter C. Hodgson, vol. 2 (Berkeley: University of California Press, 1987), 467.
15. Mary W. Shelley, *Frankenstein, or The Modern Prometheus*, ed. M. K. Joseph (London: Oxford University Press, 1969), 228–29. Shelley's subtitle was prefigured but probably not influenced by Shaftesbury's *Moralists* (1709).
16. Edith Braemer, *Goethes Prometheus und die Grundpositionen des Sturm und Drang* (Weimar: Arion, 1963); Raymond Trousson, *Le thème de Prométhée dans la littérature européenne* (Geneva: Droz, 1964).
17. Friedrich Nietzsche, *The Birth of Tragedy Out of the Spirit of Music*, ed. Michael Tanner, trans. Shaun Whiteside (New York: Penguin, 1993), 48.
18. Immanuel Kant, *Kant's Werke*, Prussian Academy Edition, vol. 1 (Berlin: Reimer, 1910), 472.
19. Karl Marx, *Capital*, vol. 1 (Moscow: Foreign Language Publishing House, 1954), 645.
20. Karl Marx, *The Communist Manifesto* (Chicago: Regnery, 1954), 54.
21. Giacomo Leopardi, "The Wager of Prometheus," in *The Moral Essays: Operette morali*, trans. Patrick Creagh (New York: Columbia University Press, 1983), 77–84.
22. Jacques Ellul, *The Technological Society*, trans. John Wilkinson (New York: Random House, 1964), 111–12.
23. Siegfried Giedion, *Mechanization Takes Command* (New York: Oxford University Press, 1948), 15–17, 34–36.
24. Julien Offray de La Mettrie, *Man a Machine* (French-English), ed. and trans. Gertrude Carnab Bussey et al. (La Salle, Ill.: Open Court, 1961), 70.
25. Louis Dupré, *Passage to Modernity: An Essay in the Hermeneutics of Nature and Culture* (New Haven: Yale University Press, 1993).
26. See, for example, Gregor Sebba, *Bibliographia Cartesiana: A Critical Guide*

to the *Descartes Literature, 1800–1960* (The Hague: Nijhoff, 1964), and *Bulletin cartésien* (supplement to *Archives de philosophie*).
27. René Descartes, *Oeuvres de Descartes*, ed. C. Adam and P. Tannery, 12 vols. with suppl. (Paris: Cerf, 1897–1910), 3:247–48. My translation. Descartes' reference is to Augustine's *City of God* XL.26; see also *De trinitate* X.10 and *De libero arbitrio* II.3.7.
28. Giambattista Vico, *On the Most Ancient Wisdom of the Italians Unearthed from the Origins of the Latin Language, Including the Disputation with the Giornale de' Letterati d'Italia*, trans. L. M. Palmer (Ithaca: Cornell University Press, 1988), 54–55.
29. Johann Caspar Lavater, *Essays on Physiognomy*, trans. Henry Hunter, vol. 3 (London: John Murray, 1792), 251.
30. Ibid., 246.
31. G. W. F. Hegel, *Phenomenology of Spirit*, trans. A. V. Miller (Oxford: Oxford University Press, 1977), 190.
32. Elizabeth S. Haldane, *Descartes: His Life and Times* (London: John Murray, 1905), 358.
33. René Descartes, *Cogitationes privatae*, in *Oeuvres* 10:213. My translation. See also John R. Cole, *The Olympian Dreams and Youthful Rebellion of René Descartes* (Urbana: University of Illinois Press, 1992).
34. René Descartes, *The Philosophical Writings of Descartes*, trans. John Cottingham, Robert Stoothoff, and Dugald Murdoch, 3 vols. (Cambridge: Cambridge University Press, 1984–91), 1:125.
35. Ibid., 1:112.
36. Ibid., 1:185.
37. Antonio Mattei, *L'homme de Descartes* (Paris: Aubier, 1940), 179–230.
38. Leo Spitzer, "Le *poêle* de Descartes," *Modern Language Notes* 56 (1941): 110–13.
39. Fernand Braudel, *Capitalism and Material Life, 1400–1800*, trans. Miriam Kochan (New York: Harper and Row, 1973), 218.
40. For Rembrandt's etching, see the French edition: Fernand Braudel, *Civilisation materiélle et capitalisme*, vol. 1 (Paris: Armand Colin, 1967), facing p. 288.
41. "Descartes à Mersenne," Endegeest, October 20, 1642, in *Oeuvres* 3:587–90.
42. Michel de Montaigne, *The Complete Works of Montaigne*, trans. Donald M. Frame (Stanford: Stanford University Press, 1957), 828; Montaigne, *Essais*, ed. Albert Thibaudet, Pleiade edition (Paris: Gallimard, 1950), 1213–14.
43. Montaigne, *Works of Montaigne*, 885; *Journal de voyage de Michel de Mon-

taigne, ed. François Rigolot (Paris: Presses Universitaires de France, 1992), 24.
44. Mircea Eliade, *The Forge and the Crucible: The Origins and Structures of Alchemy,* trans. Stephen Corrin (New York: Harper, 1971), chap. 8.
45. William J. Hynes and William G. Doty, eds., *Mythical Trickster Figures: Contours, Contexts, and Criticisms* (Tuscaloosa: University of Alabama Press, 1993).
46. Paul Radin, *The Trickster: A Study in American Indian Mythology,* with commentaries by Carl Kerényi and C. G. Jung (1956; reprint, New York: Greenwood Press, 1969), ix.
47. Descartes, *Philosophical Writings* 2:3.
48. Ibid.
49. Miguel de Unamuno, *The Tragic Sense of Life in Men and Peoples,* trans. J. E. Crawford Flitch (London: Macmillan, 1931), 35.
50. Descartes, *Philosophical Writings* 1:15.
51. Ibid., 1:186.
52. Ibid., 1:122.
53. Albert William Levi, *Philosophy as Social Expression* (Chicago: University of Chicago Press, 1974), chap. 4.
54. Jacques Ellul, *The Technological Bluff,* trans. Geoffrey W. Bromiley (Grand Rapids, Mich.: Eerdmans, 1990).
55. Descartes to Huygens, December 4, 1637, quoted in Jack Rochford Vrooman, *René Descartes: A Biography* (New York: Putnam, 1970), 142.
56. Descartes to Mersenne, January 9, 1639, quoted in ibid., 142–43.
57. Quoted in G. A. Lindeboom, *Descartes and Medicine* (Amsterdam: Rodopi, 1978), 95; Descartes, *Oeuvres* 11:671.
58. Ernst Cassirer, *The Philosophy of Symbolic Forms,* vol. 4, *The Metaphysics of Symbolic Forms,* ed. John Michael Krois and Donald Phillip Verene, trans. John Michael Krois (New Haven: Yale University Press, 1996), 110–11. See also Johann Wolfgang von Goethe, "Prometheus: Dramatic Fragment," trans. Frank Ryder, in *Goethe's Collected Works,* vol. 7, *Early Verse Drama and Prose Plays,* ed. Cyrus Hamlin and Frank Ryder (New York: Suhrkamp, 1988), 239–50.
59. Bacon, *De sapientia veterum,* in *Works* 6:751.
60. Ibid., 6:751–52.
61. Thomas Hobbes, *Leviathan,* ed. C. B. Macpherson (New York: Pergamon, 1979), 169.
62. Descartes, *Philosophical Writings* 1:39.
63. Bacon, *De sapientia veterum,* in *Works* 6:751.

64. Carl Kerényi, "The Trickster in Relation to Greek Mythology," in Radin, *The Trickster*, 181.
65. André Gide, *Le prométhée mal enchaîné* (Paris: Gallimard, 1925), 80.
66. Ernesto Grassi, "The Originary Quality of the Poetic and Rhetorical Word: Heidegger, Ungaretti, and Neruda," *Philosophy and Rhetoric* 20 (1987): 258.
67. C. G. Jung, *Symbols of Transformation*, trans. R. F. C. Hull, 2d ed. (Princeton: Princeton University Press, 1956), 169-70.
68. See the discussion of the Muses in Chap. 4.
69. Giuseppe Ungaretti, in a lecture on Vico in São Paulo, Brazil, in 1937. See *Vite d'un uomo: Saggi e interventi* (Milan: Mondadori, 1974), 345.
70. Carl Kerényi, *The Gods of the Greeks*, trans. Norman Cameron (London: Thames and Hudson, 1951), 104.
71. Claude Lévi-Strauss, *The Raw and the Cooked: Introduction to the Science of Mythology*, trans. John Weightman and Doreen Weightman (New York: Harper, 1969), 16.

Chapter 1
Barbarism of Reflection

1. *The New Science of Giambattista Vico*, trans. Thomas Goddard Bergin and Max Harold Fisch (Ithaca: Cornell University Press, 1984), par. 1106.
2. Robert Pogue Harrison, *Forests: The Shadow of Civilization* (Chicago: University of Chicago Press, 1992).
3. On the "barbarism of reflection," see Donald Phillip Verene, *Vico's Science of Imagination* (Ithaca: Cornell University Press, 1981), chap. 7; and Alain Pons, "Vico et la 'barbarie de la réflexion,'" in *La pensée politique (revue annuelle)*, ed. Marcel Gauchet, Pierre Manent, and Pierre Ronsanvalln (Paris: Gallimard, 1994), 178-97.
4. Juan Luis Vives, *De disciplinis*, in *Opera omnia*, vol. 6 (London: Gregg Press, 1964), 8. My translation.
5. Niccolò Machiavelli, *Discourses on the First Decade of Titus Livius*, in *The Chief Works and Others*, trans. Allan Gilbert, vol. 1 (Durham, N.C.: Duke University Press, 1989), bk. 1, chap. 2.
6. Vico, *New Science*, par. 241.
7. Francesco Guicciardini, *Ricordi* (Milan: Rizzoli, 1977), 131. My translation.
8. James Joyce, *Ulysses* (London: Bodley Head, 1960), 42.

9. See Donald Phillip Verene, "Imaginative Universals and Narrative Truth," *New Vico Studies* 6 (1988): 1–19.
10. Vico, *New Science*, par. 7.
11. Giambattista Vico, "All'Abate Esperti in Roma," in *Autobiografia, seguita da una scelta di lettere, orazioni e rime,* ed. Mario Fubini (Turin: Einaudi, 1965), 109–12.
12. Vico, *New Science*, par. 979.
13. *Cinque libri di Giambattista Vico de' principj d'una scienza nuova d'intorno alla comune natura delle nazioni* (Naples: Felice Mosca, 1730), 457. My translation.
14. *Le Grand Robert de la langue française*, 12th ed., vol. 8 (Paris: Robert, 1985), 148, s.v. *réflexion*.
15. René Descartes, *The Philosophical Writings of Descartes*, trans. John Cottingham, Robert Stoothoff, and Dugald Murdoch, 3 vols. (Cambridge: Cambridge University Press, 1984–91), 1:131; Descartes, *Oeuvres de Descartes*, ed. C. Adam and P. Tannery, 12 vols. and suppl. (Paris: Cerf, 1897–1913), 6:41.
16. Ibid., 1:127, 6:33. Descartes uses *réflexion* in the *Discours* to refer to mental activity in three places other than those discussed above (see ibid., 1:115, 125, 143; 6:9, 28, 63).
17. Ibid., 3:357, 5:220–21.
18. For corresponding expressions in going from English to Greek, see S. C. Woodhouse, *English-Greek Dictionary: A Vocabulary of the Attic Language* (London: Routledge and Kegan Paul, 1964), s.vv. *reflect; reflection*.
19. See, e.g., Plato, *Republic* 510A, *Sophist* 266B, and *Timaeus* 71B; Aristotle, *Meteorology* bk. 1 (chaps. 5–8), bk. 2 (chap. 9), and bk. 3 (chap. 4); Aristotle, *De anima* bk. 2 (chap. 8) and bk. 3 (chap. 12); Aristotle, *Sense and Sensibilia*, chap. 2.
20. *Oxford Latin Dictionary*, ed. P. G. W. Glare (Oxford: Clarendon, 1982), s.v. *reflecto*.
21. *The Revised Medieval Latin Word-List from British and Irish Sources*, comp. R. E. Latham (London: Oxford University Press for the British Academy, 1965), s.v. *reflexio*.
22. "The power of reflecting on the contents of consciousness is more fully described in the passage: 'In anima . . . reflexio potest fieri vel conversio intellectus supra speciem absolute, non considerando cuius rei sit illa species vel ymago, et sic fit pura apprehensio speciei et non memoria, vel potest fieri reflexio supra illam considerando cuius rei sit, et conferendo ad rem cuius est, et sic fit cum apprehensione memoria.' *Quaest. Met.*, xi,

p. 88:25" (E. D. Sharp, *Franciscan Philosophy at Oxford in the Thirteenth Century* [Oxford: Oxford University Press, 1964], 165).
23. *The Opus majus of Roger Bacon*, trans. Robert Belle Burke, vol. 2 (Philadelphia: University of Pennsylvania Press, 1928), 499.
24. Ibid., 580.
25. *Basic Writings of Saint Thomas Aquinas*, ed. Anton C. Pegis, vol. 1 (New York: Random House, 1945), 817 (Q.85, art. 2); see also 830 (Q.86, art. 2).
26. Ibid., vol. 1, 841 (Q.87, art. 4).
27. John Locke, *An Essay Concerning Human Understanding*, ed. Alexander Campbell Fraser, 2 vols. (Oxford: Clarendon, 1894).
28. *The Oxford English Dictionary*, 2d ed., vol. 13 (Oxford: Clarendon, 1989), s.v. *reflection* (8.c).
29. Locke, *Essay* 1:122.
30. Ibid., 1:123.
31. Ibid., 1:123-24.
32. *Oeuvres philosophiques de Condillac*, ed. Georges Le Roy, vol. 1 (Paris: Presses Universitaires de France, 1947-51), 21-23.
33. G. W. Leibniz, *New Essays on Human Understanding*, ed. and trans. Peter Remnant and Jonathan Bennett (Cambridge: Cambridge University Press, 1981), 51.
34. Salvatore Battaglia, *Grande dizionario della lingua italiana*, vol. 16 (Turin: UTET, 1992), s.v. *riflessione*.
35. José Ferrater Mora, ed., *Diccionario de filosofía*, vol. 4 (Madrid: Alianza, 1979), 2807-11. *Diccionario de la lengua castellana*, vol. 5 (Madrid: La Real Academia Española, 1737), contains the following passage that connects light, reflection, and reason: "No sus luces, sus refléxos / solo es razón que te copie, / que no es tratable la llama, / por no es los resplandóres"; s.v. *reflexo*.
36. Locke, *De intellectu humano*, trans. Ezekiel Burridge (London, 1701), was reviewed in the *Acta eruditorum* in 1702 and reprinted in Leipzig (1709) and Amsterdam (1729). Vico used the Latin edition of Locke's *Essay;* see Gustavo Costa, "Vico e Locke," *Giornale critico della filosofia italiana* 3 (1970): 344-61, and *Vico e l'europa: Contro la "boria delle nazioni"* (Milan: Guerini, 1996), chap. 2.
37. Paolo Sarpi, *Scritti filosofici e teologici*, ed. R. Amerio (Bari: Laterza, 1951), 130.
38. Alexander Robertson, *Fra Paolo Sarpi*, 2d ed. (London: Sampson Low Marston, 1894), 53.
39. Immanuel Kant, *Critique of Pure Reason*, trans. Norman Kemp Smith

(London: Macmillan, 1958), A262, B317; Kant, *Kritik der reinen Vernunft* (Hamburg: Meiner, 1956), A262, B317. Kant's term for reflection here is *Überlegung*, which he is using as the equivalent for the Latin *reflexio*. He makes this clear in the first sentence of the "Amphiboly of Concepts of Reflection": "Die Überlegung (*reflexio*) hat es nicht mit den Gegenständen selbst zu tun" (A260, B316).

40. Ibid., A51, B75.
41. Ibid., A235-36, B294-95.
42. Descartes, *Philosophical Writings* 1:114; Descartes, *Oeuvres* 6:7.
43. Immanuel Kant, *Critique of Practical Reason and Other Writings in Moral Philosophy*, ed. and trans. Lewis White Beck (Chicago: University of Chicago Press, 1949), 188-89; Kant, *Kritik der praktischen Vernunft*, in *Immanuel Kants Werke*, ed. Ernst Cassirer, vol. 5 (Berlin: Bruno Cassirer, 1922), 90.
44. Descartes, *Philosophical Writings* 1:384; Descartes, *Oeuvres* 11:445.
45. David Hume, *A Treatise of Human Nature*, ed. L. A. Selby-Bigge (Oxford: Clarendon, 1960), 484.
46. Kant, *Critique of Practical Reason*, 172-73; Kant, *Kritik der praktischen Vernunft*, 71.
47. Immanuel Kant, *Critique of Judgment*, trans. J. H. Bernard (New York: Hafner, 1951), 172 n. 50; Kant, *Kritik der Urteilskraft*, in *Kants Werke* 5:404 n.
48. Kant, *Critique of Judgment*, 4; Kant, *Kritik der Urteilskraft*, 236.
49. Kant, *Critique of Judgment*, 15; Kant, *Kritik der Urteilskraft*, 248.
50. Ernst Cassirer, *Kant's Life and Work*, trans. James Haden (New Haven: Yale University Press, 1981), chap. 6.
51. Susanne Langer, *Philosophy in a New Key* (New York: Penguin, 148), 75-79.
52. Kant, *Critique of Judgment*, 128-29, 135-38; Kant, *Kritik der Urteilskraft*, 360-61, 367-70.
53. Kant, *Critique of Judgment*, 129; Kant, *Kritik der Urteilskraft*, 361.
54. Kant, *Critique of Judgment*, 129; Kant, *Kritik der Urteilskraft*, 361.
55. Kant, *Critique of Pure Reason*, A84, B117.
56. See Donald Phillip Verene, *Vico's Science of Imagination* (Ithaca: Cornell University Press, 1981), chap. 3.
57. Anthony Ashley Cooper, third earl of Shaftesbury, "*Sensus Communis:* An Essay on the Freedom of Wit and Humor," treatise 2 of *Characteristics of Men, Manners, Opinions, Times*, ed. John M. Robertson (Indianapolis: Bobbs-Merrill, 1964).
58. Vico, *New Science*, par. 142.

59. Immanuel Kant, *Prolegomena to Any Future Metaphysics* (Indianapolis: Bobbs-Merrill, Liberal Arts Press, 1950), 4.
60. See Donald Phillip Verene, "The Bodily Logic of Vico's *universali fantastici*," in *Vico und die Zeichen, Vico e i segni*, ed. Jürgen Trabant (Tübingen: Gunter Narr, 1995), 93–100.
61. Vico, *New Science*, par. 382. See also the discussion of the Jove experience in Chap. 4.
62. Pierre Adler, "G. W. F. Hegel: Philosophical Dissertation on the Orbits of the Planets (1801), Preceded by the Twelve Theses Defended on August 27, 1801," *Graduate Faculty Philosophy Journal* 12 (1987): 269–309.
63. G. W. F. Hegel, *Phenomenology of Spirit*, trans. A. V. Miller (Oxford: Oxford University Press, 1977), 38; G. W. F. Hegel, *Phänomenologie des Geistes*, ed. Johannes Hoffmeister, 6th ed. (Hamburg: Meiner, 1952), 51.
64. Kant, *Critique of Pure Reason*, A50–64, B74–88.
65. Hegel, *Phenomenology*, 38; Hegel, *Phänomenologie*, 51.
66. Hegel, *Phenomenology*, 39; Hegel, *Phänomenologie*, 52.
67. Dante Alighieri, *The Divine Comedy: Paradiso*, trans. Charles S. Singleton (Italian-English) (Princeton: Princeton University Press, 1975).
68. Giambattista Vico, *On the Most Ancient Wisdom of the Italians Unearthed from the Origins of the Latin Language, Including the Disputation with the Giornale de' Letterati d'Italia*, trans. L. M. Palmer (Ithaca: Cornell University Press, 1988), 77.
69. G. W. F. Hegel, *Science of Logic*, trans. A. V. Miller (London: Allen and Unwin, 1969), 45; G. W. F. Hegel, *Wissenschaft der Logik*, ed. Georg Lasson, vol. 1 (Hamburg: Meiner, 1971), 26.
70. Edmund Husserl, *Ideas: General Introduction to a Pure Phenomenology*, trans. Fred Kersten, in *Collected Works*, vol. 2 (The Hague: Nijhoff, 1982), sec. 77.
71. Hans-Georg Gadamer, *Truth and Method*, 2d rev. ed., trans. Joel Weinsheimer and Donald G. Marshall (New York: Crossroad, 1992), 569.
72. Maurice Merleau-Ponty, *Phenomenology of Perception*, trans. Colin Smith (London: Routledge and Kegan Paul, 1962), 62.
73. Marvin Farber, "Modes of Reflection," *Philosophy and Phenomenological Research* 8 (1947–48): 588.
74. Descartes, *Philosophical Writings* 1:152; Descartes, *Oeuvres* 6:81.
75. Thomas Hobbes, "Tractatus opticus," in *Thomae Hobbes Malmesburiensis opera philosophica quae Latine scripsit omnia*, ed. William Molesworth, vol. 5 (London: John Bohn, 1845), 215–48. Hobbes's "Tractatus" was published in Mersenne's *Cogitata physico-mathematica*.

76. James P. C. Southall, *Mirrors, Prisms, and Lenses: A Textbook of Geometrical Optics*, 3d ed. (1918; reprint, New York: Dover, 1964), 86.
77. Locke, *Essay* 1:123.
78. Ibid., 1:124 n. 1.
79. *The Works of George Berkeley*, ed. A. A. Luce and T. E. Jessop, vol. 1 (London: Nelson, 1948). Note Berkeley's use of Descartes in the appendix, 237-38.
80. See Johannes Hoffmeister's "Einleitung" to Hegel, *Phänomenologie des Geistes*, vii.
81. Ibid., viii.
82. Ibid., xiii. My translation.
83. Ibid., xiv.
84. See Donald Phillip Verene, *Hegel's Recollection: A Study of Images in the Phenomenology of Spirit* (Albany: State University of New York Press, 1985).
85. R. G. Collingwood, *The New Leviathan, or Man, Society, Civilization, and Barbarism*, ed. David Boucher, rev. ed. (Oxford: Clarendon, 1992), 6-7.
86. On *sophrosynē*, see Stanley Rosen, *The Ancients and the Moderns: Rethinking Modernity* (New Haven: Yale University Press, 1989), 83-106.
87. Kant, *Critique of Pure Reason*, A108.
88. Ibid., B135.
89. Gilbert Ryle, *The Concept of Mind* (London: Hutchinson, 1949), 197-98.
90. Ibid., 198.
91. William James, *The Principles of Psychology*, auth. ed., vol. 1 (New York: Dover, 1950), 370.
92. Leon Battista Alberti, *Momo o del principe* (Latin and Italian texts), ed. Rino Consolo (Genoa: Costa and Nolan, 1986). As the second part of the title indicates, Alberti's fable of Momus is a treatise on government. My remarks are not intended to comment on the larger purpose of this complex work, but only to focus on the figure of the vagabond. For another treatment of Momus, see Thomas Carew, "Coelum Britannicum: A Masque at Whitehall in the Banqueting House on Shrove Tuesday Night the 18th of February, 1634," in *Court Masques: Jacobean and Caroline Entertainments, 1605-1640*, ed. David Lindley (Oxford: Oxford University Press, 1995), 168-86. In this play Momus engages in a series of satirical exchanges with Mercury.
93. *The Fragments of Sophocles*, ed. A. C. Pearson, vol. 1 (Amsterdam: Hakkert, 1963), 77-78 (no. 418).

94. *Aesopica*, vol. 1 (Greek-Latin), ed. Ben Edwin Perry (Urbana: University of Illinois Press, 1952), 360.
95. Alberti, *Momo*, 34–35.
96. Ibid., 38–39.
97. On the expulsion of Momus, see Ernesto Grassi, *Renaissance Humanism: Studies in Philosophy and Poetics*, trans. Walter F. Veit (Binghamton, N.Y.: Center for Medieval and Early Renaissance Studies, 1988), 97–100.
98. Leon Battista Alberti, *On Painting and on Sculpture: The Latin Texts of De pictura and De statua*, ed. and trans. Cecil Grayson (London: Phaidon, 1972), 61.
99. Alberti, *Momo*, 122–23. My translation.
100. Ibid., 100–101. Translation of these lines is from Mark Jarzombek, *On Leon Baptista Alberti: His Literary and Aesthetic Theories* (Cambridge: MIT Press, 1989), 165.
101. *The Autobiography of Giambattista Vico*, trans. Max Harold Fisch and Thomas Goddard Bergin (Ithaca: Cornell University Press, 1963), 113. See Donald Phillip Verene, *The New Art of Autobiography: An Essay on the Life of Giambattista Vico Written by Himself* (Oxford: Clarendon, 1991), chap. 6.
102. Descartes, *Oeuvres* 10:213. See also my remarks on Descartes' mask in the Introduction.
103. Jarzombek, *Alberti*, 165.
104. Vico, *Autobiography*, 199.
105. Hegel, *Phenomenology*, 317; Hegel, *Phänomenologie*, 371.
106. Hegel, *Phenomenology*, 317; Hegel, *Phänomenologie*, 372.
107. Hegel, *Phenomenology*, 317–18; Hegel, *Phänomenologie*, 372–73.
108. Carl Sandburg, "Momus," in *The Complete Poems of Carl Sandburg*, rev. ed. (New York: Harcourt Brace Jovanovich, 1970), 45.

Chapter 2
Metaphysics of Folly

1. William Willeford, *The Fool and His Scepter: A Study of Clowns and Jesters and Their Audience* (Evanston, Ill.: Northwestern University Press, 1969), 226. Willeford states that *Babinian* is from *Baba*, an old woman, and was intended to characterize the run-down manor house in which the society met. Willeford gives his source for the Babinian Republic as Carl Friedrich Flögel, *Geschichte des Groteskekomischen* (Liegnitz: Siegert,

1788), 350-52; Flögel's source is Stanislaus Sarnicius, "Annales Polonici," appended to Joannes Dlugossius, *Historia Polonica*, vol. 2.

2. Desiderius Erasmus, *The Praise of Folly*, trans. Clarence H. Miller (New Haven: Yale University Press, 1979), 58-59. In Horace, *Epistles* II. 2.128-40.

3. *The Complete Works of François Rabelais*, trans. Donald M. Frame (Berkeley: University of California Press), 198-201; Rabelais, *Oeuvres de Rabelais en français moderne*, ed. Jean Garros (Paris: Henri Bézait, 1936), 175-79.

4. Paul V. A. Williams, ed., *The Fool and the Trickster: Studies in Honour of Enid Welsford* (Cambridge, U.K., and Totowa, N.J.: D. S. Brewer and Rowman and Littlefield, 1979).

5. Sandra Billington, *A Social History of the Fool* (Sussex, U.K., and New York: Harvester Press and St. Martin's, 1984), 2.

6. One of the most interesting and excellent analyses of humanism and folly is a little-known collection of essays edited by Enrico Castelli, *L'Umanesimo e la Follia* (Rome: Abete, 1971), with essays by Castelli, Maurizio Bonicatti, Pierre Mesnard, Rubina Giorgi, Irving L. Zupnick, Ernesto Grassi, André Chastel, François Secret, and Robert Klein.

7. Enid Welsford, *The Fool: His Social and Literary History* (Gloucester, Mass.: Peter Smith, 1966), 4-5.

8. Sebastian Brant, *The Ship of Fools*, trans. Edwin H. Zeydel (New York: Dover, 1962); *Sebastian Brants Narrenschiff*, ed. Friedrich Zarncke (Hildesheim: Olms, 1961); Sebastian Brant, *Das Narrenschiff* (based on the original edition [Basel, 1494], with the additions of the editions of 1495 and 1499, and including the woodcuts of the original German edition), ed. Manfred Lemmer, 2d ed. (Tübingen: Niemeyer, 1968).

9. Erasmus, *Praise of Folly*, 1.

10. Walter Kaiser, *Praisers of Folly* (Cambridge: Harvard University Press, 1963).

11. Voltaire, *Candide, or Optimism*, 2d ed., trans. Robert M. Adams (New York: Norton, 1991), 70.

12. Jonathan Swift, *Gulliver's Travels*, ed. Herbert Davis (Oxford: Blackwell, 1959), 179-86.

13. Nicholas Breton, *The Good and Bad in Archaica*, ed. E. Brydges, vol. 1 (London, 1815), 23-24. Quoted in Barbara Swain, *Fools and Folly During the Middle Ages and the Renaissance* (New York: Columbia University Press, 1932), 185.

14. Anton C. Zijderveld, *Reality in a Looking-Glass: Rationality Through an Analysis of Traditional Folly* (London: Routledge and Kegan Paul, 1982), 162.

15. Ibid., 35.
16. Wolfgang Promies, *Die Bürger und der Narr oder das Risiko der Phantasie: Sechs Kapitel über das Irrationale in der Literatur des Rationalismus* (Munich: Hanser, 1966).
17. Desiderius Erasmus, *Praise of Folly*, 42; Erasmus, *Encomium moriae* in *Colloquia familiaria et Encomium moriae*, vol. 2 (Leipzig, 1829), 324.
18. Hans-Georg Gadamer, "Die verkehrte Welt," *Hegel-Studien*, Beiheft 3 (1966): 137. My translation.
19. Bertolt Brecht, *Flüchtlingsgespräche* (Frankfurt: Suhrkamp, 1961), 111. My translation.
20. John H. Smith, *The Spirit and Its Letter: Traces of Rhetoric in Hegel's Philosophy of Bildung* (Ithaca: Cornell University Press), 1988.
21. See Donald Phillip Verene, *Hegel's Recollection: A Study of Images in the Phenomenology of Spirit* (Albany: State University of New York Press, 1985), chap. 4.
22. A production of Tieck's *Die verkehrte Welt*, with a large cast and full program notes, premiered at the Schiller-Theater in Berlin on December 22, 1975. Prior to this an abridged version was performed in a student production in Berlin in 1963.
23. Ludwig Tieck, *The Land of Upside Down*, trans. Oscar Mandel (London: Associated University Presses, 1978), 19. For the original of Tieck's play see *Ludwig Tieck's Schriften*, vol. 5 (Berlin: Georg Reimer, 1828), 283–433.
24. Tieck, *Land of Upside Down*, 20.
25. Ibid., 121.
26. John N. Findlay, *The Discipline of the Cave* (London: Allen and Unwin; New York: Humanities Press, 1966); Findlay, *The Transcendence of the Cave* (London: Allen and Unwin; New York: Humanities Press, 1967); Findlay, *Ascent to the Absolute* (London: Allen and Unwin; New York: Humanities Press, 1970).
27. Findlay, foreword to G. W. F. Hegel, *Phenomenology of Spirit*, trans. A. V. Miller (Oxford: Oxford University Press, 1977), xiii.
28. Hegel, *Phenomenology*, 97–98; G. W. F. Hegel, *Phänomenologie des Geistes*, ed. Johannes Hoffmeister, 6th ed. (Hamburg: Meiner, 1952), 122–23.
29. Hegel, *Phenomenology*, 103; Hegel, *Phänomenologie*, 128.
30. *Hegel: The Letters*, trans. Clark Butler and Christiane Seiler (Bloomington: Indiana University Press, 1984), 591.
31. Billington, *Social History*, 5.
32. Zijderveld, *Reality*, 60–64; Welsford, *The Fool*, 202–6.
33. Karl Rosenkranz, *Geschichte der deutschen Poesie im Mittelalter* (Halle, 1830), 586–94.

34. Jacob Grimm and Wilhelm Grimm, *Deutsches Wörterbuch*, vol. 12, pt. 1 (Leipzig, 1951), s.v. *verkehren*.
35. Michel Foucault, *Madness and Civilization: A History of Insanity in the Age of Reason*, trans. Richard Howard (New York: Random House, 1973), 11. Zijderveld finds no evidence for so strong a claim as Foucault makes regarding the actual existence of such boatloads of fools (*Reality*, 36), although the idea of such boats was widespread, a point discussed below in relation to Brant's work.
36. Hegel, *Phenomenology*, 15.
37. Johannes von Saaz, *The Plowman from Bohemia* (German-English), trans. Alexander Henderson and Elizabeth Henderson (New York: Ungar, 1966), 103-4.
38. Ibid., 49.
39. Willeford, *The Fool*, 92.
40. Rosenkranz, *Geschichte*, 592. My translation.
41. Hegel, *Phenomenology*, 19.
42. Rosenkranz, *Geschichte*, 592. My translation.
43. See the discussion of Hegel's speculative sentence in Chap. 1.
44. Willeford, *The Fool*, 57.
45. René Descartes, *The Passions of the Soul*, in *The Philosophical Writings of Descartes*, trans. John Cottingham, Robert Stoothoff, and Dugald Murdoch, 3 vols. (Cambridge: Cambridge University Press, 1984-91), 1:371.
46. See, e.g., Frederic R. Stearns, *Laughing: Physiology, Pathophysiology, Psychology, Pathopsychology, and Development* (Springfield, Ill.: Thomas, 1972), chap. 1.
47. *The Chief Works of Benedict de Spinoza*, trans. R. H. M. Elwes, vol. 2 (New York: Dover, 1951), 173.
48. Descartes, *Philosophical Writings* 1:372.
49. Francis Bacon, *Sylva sylvarum, or A Natural History in Ten Centuries*, in *The Works of Francis Bacon*, ed. James Spedding, Robert Leslie Ellis, and Douglas Denon Heath, vol. 2 (New York: Garrett, 1968), 570-71.
50. Thomas Hobbes, *The Elements of Law Natural and Politic*, ed. J. C. A. Gaskin (Oxford: Oxford University Press, 1994), 54-55.
51. Thomas Fuller, *The Holy State and the Profane State*, ed. Maximilian Graff Walten, vol. 2 (New York: Columbia University Press, 1938), 156.
52. Giambattista Vico, "A Factual Digression on Human Genius, Sharp, Witty Remarks, and Laughter," trans. Antonio Illiano, James D. Tedder, and Piero Treves, *Forum Italicum* 2 (1968): 312. This is a translation of the

digression in Vico's *Vici vindiciae* (1729), in *Opere di G. B. Vico*, ed. Fausto Nicolini, vol. 3 (Bari: Laterza, 1931), 302-7.
53. Laurent Joubert, *Treatise on Laughter*, trans. Gregory David de Rocher (Tuscaloosa: University of Alabama Press, 1980), 17.
54. Louis Poinsinet de Sivry, *Traite des causes physiques et morales du rire relativement a l'art de l'exciter*, ed. William Brooks (Exeter, U.K.: Exeter University Publications, 1986), 26.
55. Hegel, *Phenomenology*, 205.
56. Ibid., 210; Hegel, *Phänomenologie*, 254. My translation.
57. Paul Reps, *Zen Flesh, Zen Bones: A Collection of Zen and Pre-Zen Writings* (Rutland, Vt.: Charles E. Tuttle, 1957), 25.
58. Pico della Mirandola, "Oration on the Dignity of Man," trans. Elizabeth Livermore Forbes, in *The Renaissance Philosophy of Man*, ed. Ernst Cassirer, Paul Oskar Kristeller, and John Herman Randall, Jr. (Chicago: University of Chicago Press, 1948), 235-36.
59. Henri Bergson, *Laughter: An Essay on the Meaning of the Comic*, trans. Cloudesley Brereton and Fred Rothwell (London: Macmillan, 1911), 186.
60. *Jokes and Their Relation to the Unconscious*, vol. 8 of *The Standard Edition of the Complete Psychological Works of Sigmund Freud*, trans. James Strachey and Anna Freud (London: Hogarth Press and the Institute of Psycho-Analysis, 1960), 45.
61. James Joyce, *Finnegans Wake* (London: Faber and Faber, 1939), 593.
62. With appreciation to "The Firesign Theatre."
63. Johann Caspar Lavater, *Essays on Physiognomy*, trans. Henry Hunter, vol. 1 (London: John Murray, 1792), 59.
64. Helmuth Plessner, *Laughing and Crying: A Study of the Limits of Human Behavior*, trans. James Spencer Churchill and Marjorie Grene (Evanston, Ill.: Northwestern University Press, 1970), 29-32.
65. Umberto Eco, *The Name of the Rose*, trans. William Weaver (New York: Harcourt Brace Jovanovich, 1983), 491; Eco, *Il nome della rosa* (Milan: Bompiani, 1980), 494. See Donald Phillip Verene, "Philosophical Laughter: Vichian Remarks on Umberto Eco's *The Name of the Rose*," *New Vico Studies* 2 (1984): 75-81.
66. Eco, *Name of the Rose*, 477; Eco, *Il nome della rosa*, 481.
67. Eco, *Name of the Rose*, 477; Eco, *Il nome della rosa*, 481.
68. Eco, *Name of the Rose*, 474-75; Eco, *Il nome della rosa*, 477-78.
69. G. W. F. Hegel, "Who Thinks Abstractly?" trans. Walter Kaufmann, in *Hegel: Reinterpretation, Texts, and Commentary* (New York: Doubleday,

1965), 461–65; G. W. F. Hegel, "Wer denkt abstrakt?" in *Werke,* vol. 2 (Frankfurt: Suhrkamp, 1970), 575–81.
70. Zijderveld, *Reality,* 166–67.
71. Leslie Hotson, *Shakespeare's Motley* (New York: Oxford University Press, 1952), 33.
72. Robert Hillis Goldsmith, *Wise Fools in Shakespeare* (Lansing: Michigan State University Press, 1955), chap. 1.
73. Hotson, *Shakespeare's Motley,* 50–51.
74. Willeford, *The Fool,* 4.
75. Maximillian E. Novak, "The Wild Man Comes to Tea," in *The Wild Man Within: An Image in Western Thought from the Renaissance to Romanticism,* ed. Edward Dudley and Maximillian E. Novak (Pittsburgh, Pa.: Pittsburgh University Press, 1972), 183–221.
76. Brant, *Ship of Fools,* 9.
77. Edwin H. Zeydel, *Sebastian Brant* (New York: Twayne, 1967), 86–87.
78. Katherine Anne Porter, *Ship of Fools* (Boston: Little, Brown, 1945).
79. On female fools in social history, see John Doran, *The History of Court Fools* (1858; reprint, New York: Haskell House, 1966), chap. 3.
80. Brant, *Ship of Fools,* 43. John Van Cleve, *Sebastian Brant's The Ship of Fools in Critical Perspective, 1800–1991* (Columbia, S.C.: Camden House, 1993).
81. Brant, *Ship of Fools,* 12–13.
82. Ibid., 15, 366.
83. Swain, *Fools and Folly,* 118.
84. Zijderveld, *Reality,* 77.
85. Brant, *Ship of Fools,* 58.
86. Ibid., 59.
87. Ibid., 58.
88. Ibid., 60.
89. Ibid., 61.
90. Ibid., 125.
91. Ibid., 363.
92. Nicholas Cusanus, *Of Learned Ignorance,* trans. Germain Heron (London: Routledge and Kegan Paul, 1954), 8–9.
93. Anthony Ashley Cooper, Third Earl of Shaftesbury, *Second Characters, or The Language of Forms,* ed. Benjamin Rand (Cambridge: Cambridge University Press, 1914); and *The Life, Unpublished Letters, and Philosophical Regimen of Anthony, Earl of Shaftesbury,* ed. Benjamin Rand (London: Swann Sonnenschein; New York: Macmillan, 1900), 468–69, 472–74.
94. *Fools and Jesters: With a Reprint of Robert Armin's Nest of Ninnies,* ed. J. P.

Collier (London: Printed for the Shakespeare Society, 1842). Armin's book was originally titled *Foole upon Foole*.
95. See Donald Phillip Verene, "Technology and the Ship of Fools," in *Research in Philosophy and Technology*, ed. Paul T. Durbin, vol. 5 (Greenwich, Conn.: JAI Press, 1982), 281–98.
96. Erasmus, *Praise of Folly*, 43–44.
97. Ibid., 120. See Ecclesiastes 1:2 and 12:8.
98. On household fools, see Zijderveld, *Reality*, 95–99.
99. *Twentieth-Century Interpretations of the Praise of Folly*, ed. Kathleen Williams (Englewood Cliffs, N.J.: Prentice-Hall, 1969).
100. Erasmus, *Praise of Folly*, 71.
101. Ibid., 41.
102. Ibid., 26–27.
103. Ibid., 26.
104. Ibid., 13 n. 8.
105. Ibid., 42.
106. Immanuel Kant, *Critique of Practical Reason and Other Writings in Moral Philosophy*, trans. Lewis White Beck (Chicago: University of Chicago Press, 1949), 75 n; Immanuel Kant, *Werke*, ed. Wilhelm Weischedel, vol. 6 (Darmstadt: Wissenschaftliche Buchgesellschaft, 1968), 45 n.
107. Alasdair MacIntyre, "Does Applied Ethics Rest on a Mistake?" *Monist* 67 (1984): 498–513.
108. Iris Murdoch, *Metaphysics as a Guide to Morals* (New York: Allen Lane, Penguin Press, 1992).
109. Erasmus, *Praise of Folly*, 34. See the remarks on decorum in Chap. 4.
110. Donald W. Livingston, *Hume's Philosophy of Common Life* (Chicago: University of Chicago Press, 1984).
111. Richard Rorty, *Philosophy and the Mirror of Nature* (Princeton: Princeton University Press, 1979).
112. Ibid., esp. 389–94.
113. Ernesto Grassi and Maristella Lorch, *Folly and Insanity in Renaissance Literature* (Binghamton, N.Y.: Center for Medieval and Renaissance Studies, 1986).
114. Zijderveld, *Reality*, 60.

Chapter 3
Technological Desire

1. G. W. F. Hegel, *Phenomenology of Spirit*, trans. A. V. Miller (Oxford: Oxford University Press, 1977), 118; Hegel, *Phänomenologie des Geistes*, ed. Johannes Hoffmeister, 6th ed. (Hamburg: Meiner, 1952), 148–49.
2. Jacques Ellul, *The Technological System*, trans. Joachim Neugroschel (New York: Continuum, 1980); Ellul, *Le système technicien* (Paris: Calmann-Levy, 1977).
3. Jacques Ellul, *The Technological Society*, trans. John Wilkinson (New York: Knopf, 1964), 81.
4. Karl Marx, *Das Kapital: Kritik der politischen Ökonomie*, vol. 1 (Berlin: Dietz, 1973), 392.
5. Ellul, *Technological Society*, 19–21.
6. Hegel, *Phenomenology*, 114; Hegel, *Phänomenologie*, 144.
7. Hegel, *Phenomenology*, 292; Hegel, *Phänomenologie*, 345.
8. *Novum Organum*, in *The Works of Francis Bacon*, ed. James Spedding, Robert Leslie Ellis, and Douglas Denon Heath, vol. 4 (New York: Garrett Press, 1968), 47.
9. René Descartes, *The Passions of the Soul*, in *The Philosophical Writings of Descartes*, trans. John Cottingham, Robert Stoothoff, and Dugald Murdoch, 3 vols. (Cambridge: Cambridge University Press, 1984–91), 1:358.
10. *The New Science of Giambattista Vico*, trans. Thomas Goddard Bergin and Max Harold Fisch (Ithaca: Cornell University Press, 1984), par. 241.
11. Jean-Jacques Rousseau, *First Discourse*, in *The First and Second Discourses*, trans. Roger D. Masters and Judith R. Masters (New York: St. Martin's, 1964), 50.
12. Hegel, *Phenomenology*, 116; Hegel, *Phänomenologie*, 146–47.
13. Siegfried Giedion, *Mechanization Takes Command: A Contribution to Anonymous History* (Oxford: Oxford University Press, 1948), pt. 6.
14. Descartes, *Meditations on First Philosophy*, in *Philosophical Writings* 2:21.
15. Descartes, *The Search for Truth*, in *Philosophical Writings* 2:405.
16. Jacques Ellul, *La technique ou l'enjeu du siècle* (Paris: Colin, 1954). Ellul reports that the title of his 1954 work was influenced by the publisher: see Ellul, *The Technological Bluff*, trans. Geoffrey W. Bromiley (Grand Rapids, Mich.: Eerdmans, 1990), xi–xii; Ellul, *Le bluff technologique* (Paris: Hachette, 1988), 7–8. But it remains Ellul's title, and, as John Wilkinson comments, the subtitle "is a characteristically dark and difficult Ellulian phrase" (*Technological Society*, x).

17. Blaise Pascal, *Pensées* (French-English), trans. H. F. Stewart (New York: Pantheon, 1950), 121.
18. Ellul, *Technological Society*, xxv.
19. Ibid., 6.
20. Ibid., 110.
21. Ibid., 21.
22. Ibid., 80.
23. Julien Offray de La Mettrie, *Man a Machine* (French-English), trans. and ed. Gertrude Carnab Bussey et al. (La Salle, Ill.: Open Court, 1961).
24. *The Artificial Intelligence Debate: False Starts, Real Foundations*, ed. Stephen Graubard (Cambridge: MIT Press, 1988); Hubert L. Dreyfus, *What Computers Still Can't Do: A Critique of Artificial Reason* (Cambridge: MIT Press, 1994).
25. Karl Jaspers, *Man in the Modern Age*, trans. Eden Paul and Cedar Paul (New York: Doubleday Anchor Books, 1957), 62.
26. Nicolas Berdyaev, *The Fate of Man in the Modern World*, trans. Donald A. Lowrie (Ann Arbor: University of Michigan Press, 1961, 32–33).
27. John N. Findlay, *Hegel: A Re-examination* (London: Allen and Unwin, 1958), 113.
28. Hegel, *Phenomenology*, 238.
29. Ibid.
30. Ibid., 239.
31. Marshall McLuhan, *Understanding Media: The Extensions of Man*, 2d ed. (New York: Signet, 1966), 23.
32. Hegel, *Phenomenology*, 239–40.
33. Ibid., 240.
34. Herbert Marcuse, *One-Dimensional Man: Studies in the Ideology of Advanced Industrial Society* (Boston: Beacon Press, 1964), xvi.
35. Ellul, *Technological Society*, 83.
36. Hegel, *Phenomenology*, 241.
37. Ibid., 242.
38. Ellul, *Technological Society*, 97.
39. Hegel, *Phenomenology*, 250.
40. Ibid., 251.
41. Ellul, *Technological Society*, 74.
42. Hegel, *Phenomenology*, 251–52.
43. Ellul, *Technological System*, 107.
44. David Rothenberg, *Hand's End: Technology and the Limits of Nature* (Berkeley: University of California Press, 1993), 189.
45. Alvin Toffler, *Future Shock* (New York: Bantam Books, 1970), 263. The

standard criticisms of Ellul are reviewed by David Lovekin, *Technique, Discourse, and Consciousness: An Introduction to the Philosophy of Jacques Ellul* (Bethlehem, Pa.: Lehigh University Press, 1991), chap. 1.
46. Ibid., 264.
47. Ibid., 442.
48. Lewis Mumford, *Technics and Civilization* (New York: Harcourt, Brace, 1934); Aldous Huxley, *Ends and Means* (New York: Harper, 1937); Friedrich Georg Jünger, *The Failure of Technology* (Chicago: Henry Regnery, 1949).
49. Martin Heidegger, *The Question Concerning Technology and Other Essays*, trans. William Lovitt (New York: Harper and Row, 1977).
50. Pierre Ducassé, *Histoire des techniques* (Paris: Presses Universitaires de France, 1945).
51. Marcuse, *One-Dimensional Man*, 19.
52. Ellul, *Technological Society*, 319.
53. Jaspers, *Man in the Modern Age*, 123.
54. See, e.g., Samuel C. Floorman, *The Existential Pleasures of Engineering* (New York: St. Martin's Press, 1976); Albert Borgmann, *Technology and the Character of Contemporary Life* (Chicago: University of Chicago Press, 1984); Hans Jonas, *The Imperative of Responsibility: In Search of an Ethics for the Technological Age*, trans. Hans Jonas and David Herr (Chicago: University of Chicago Press, 1984); Don Ihde, *Technology and the Lifeworld: From Garden to Earth* (Bloomington: University of Indiana Press, 1990); Langdon Winner, *The Whale and the Reactor: A Search for Limits in an Age of High Technology* (Chicago: University of Chicago Press, 1986); Friedrich Rapp, *Analytical Philosophy of Technology*, trans. Stanley Carpenter and Theodor Langenbruch (Boston: Reidel, 1981).
55. *The Cantos of Ezra Pound* (New York: New Directions, 1991), Canto 33, p. 161.
56. James Joyce, *Ulysses* (London: Bodley Head, 1960), 547.
57. Henry Miller, *The World of Sex and the White Phagocytes* (London: Calder and Boyars, 1970), 60-61.
58. T. S. Eliot, "The Hollow Men," in *Selected Poems* (New York: Harcourt, Brace, 1964), 80; Pound, *Cantos*, Canto 74, p. 439.
59. Ernst Cassirer, "Form und Technik," in *Symbol, Technik, Sprache: Aufsätze aus den Jahren, 1927-1933*, ed. Ernst Wolfgang Orth and John Michael Krois (Hamburg: Meiner, 1985), 66. My translation.
60. Ernst Cassirer, *An Essay on Man: An Introduction to a Philosophy of Human Culture* (New Haven: Yale University Press, 1944), 26.
61. Ibid., 23. Cassirer is basing his views on the biology of Jakob von Uexküll.

62. Ernst Cassirer, *The Philosophy of Symbolic Forms*, trans. Ralph Manheim, vol. 3, *The Phenomenology of Knowledge* (New Haven: Yale University Press, 1957), 108, 124.
63. Dylan Thomas, "Fern Hill," in *The Poems of Dylan Thomas*, ed. Daniel Jones (New York: New Directions, 1971), 195.
64. Enrico Castelli, *Il tempo esaurito* (Rome: Bussola, 1947). See Ellul's use of this in *Technological Society*, 329 and 329 n. 2.
65. Ernst Cassirer, *The Myth of the State*, chap. 18. See also *Symbol, Myth, and Culture: Essays and Lectures of Ernst Cassirer, 1935–1945*, ed. Donald Phillip Verene (New Haven: Yale University Press, 1979), 233–67.
66. Ellul, *Technological Society*, 102.
67. Jacques Ellul, *The Political Illusion*, trans. Konrad Kellen (New York: Knopf, 1967), 17.
68. Jacques Ellul, *Propaganda: The Formation of Men's Attitudes*, trans. Konrad Kellen and Jean Lerner (New York: Knopf, 1965).
69. Carl Jung, *The Archetypes and the Collective Unconsciousness*, trans. R. F. C. Hull, vol. 9, pt. 1, of *The Collected Works of C. G. Jung*, 2d ed. (Princeton: Princeton University Press, 1968).
70. Walter Benjamin, "Das Kunstwerk im Zeitalter seiner technischen Reproduzierbarkeit," in *Illuminationen: Ausgewählte Schriften*, ed. Siegfried Unseld (Frankfurt: Suhrkamp, 1977), 136–69.
71. John O'Neill, *Plato's Cave: Desire, Power, and the Specular Functions of the Media* (Norwood, N.J.: Ablex, 1991).
72. Cassirer, *Myth of the State*, 289.
73. Ellul, *Technological Bluff*, xv–xvi.
74. Ellul, *Technological Society*, 95.
75. Napoleon A. Chagnon, *Studying the Yanomamö* (New York: Holt, Rinehart, and Winston, 1974).
76. Ellul, *Technological Society*, 89.
77. Umberto Eco, *Travels in Hyperreality: Essays*, trans. William Weaver (London: Picador, 1987), 7–8.
78. Marquis de Sade, *The Complete Justine, Philosophy in the Bedroom and Other Writings*, trans. Richard Seaver and Austryn Wainshouse (New York: Grove Press, 1965), 316–17; *Oeuvres complètes du Marquis de Sade*, vol. 3 (Paris: Au cercle du livre précieux, 1966), 499–500.
79. Lionel Rubinoff, *The Pornography of Power* (New York: Ballantine Books, 1967).
80. Ernst Cassirer, "The Influence of Language upon the Development of Scientific Thought," *Journal of Philosophy* 39 (1942): 309–27.
81. Ibid., 316.

82. Cassirer, *Philosophy of Symbolic Forms*, vol. 3, 281–314.
83. Cassirer, *Myth of the State*, 283–84.
84. George Orwell, *Nineteen Eighty-Four: A Novel* (New York: Harcourt, Brace, 1949), 215.
85. Jacques Ellul, *The Humiliation of the Word*, trans. Joyce Main Hanks (Grand Rapids, Mich.: Eerdmans, 1985), 128.
86. Anton C. Zijderveld, *On Clichés: The Supersedure of Meaning by Function in Modernity* (London: Routledge and Kegan Paul, 1979), chap. 2.
87. Thomas Hobbes, *De cive: The English Edition*, ed. Howard Warrender (Oxford: Clarendon Press, 1983), 29.
88. Thomas Hobbes, *Leviathan*, ed. C. B. Macpherson (New York: Penguin, 1968), 227.
89. Ibid., 420.
90. On Vaucanson, see Giedion, *Mechanization Takes Command*, 34–36.
91. Ellul, *Technological System*, 74.
92. Neil Postman, *Technopoly: The Surrender of Culture to Technology* (New York: Random House, 1993), 115.
93. Ellul, *Technological System*, 74.
94. Archibald MacLeish, *J. B.: A Play in Verse* (Boston: Houghton Mifflin, 1956), 147.
95. Ibid., 151.
96. Hobbes, *De cive*, 29.

Chapter 4
Philosophical Memory

1. *L'idea del theatro dell'eccellen. M. Giulio Camillo* (Florence: Lorenzo Torrentino, 1550), 7. My translation. The copy I have used is in the National Library in Florence.
2. See the analysis of Camillo's sources in Lu Beery Wenneker, "An Examination of *L'idea del theatro* of Giulio Camillo, Including an Annotated Translation, with Special Attention to His Influence on Emblem Literature and Iconography" (Ph.D. diss., University of Pittsburgh, 1970), 39–40, 360.
3. E.g., "He who has ears to hear, let him hear" (Matthew 11:15); "If any man has ears to hear, let him hear" (Mark 4:23); "As he said this he called out, 'He who has ears to hear, let him hear'" (Luke 8:8). See also Wenneker, "Examination," 360.
4. Lina Bolzoni, *Il teatro della memoria: Studi su Giulio Camillo* (Padua:

Livina, 1984), xiii. My translation. See also Bolzoni, "Lo spettacolo della memoria," in *L'idea del theatro*, ed. Lina Bolzoni (Palermo: Sellerio, 1991), 9–34.

5. Frances A. Yates, *The Art of Memory* (Chicago: University of Chicago Press, 1966), chaps. 6–7. See also Richard Berheimer, "Theatrum mundi," *Art Bulletin* 28 (1956): 225–47.

6. Yates, *Art of Memory*, chap. 6, contains a schematic drawing of the theater. See also Corrado Bologna, "Il *Theatro* segreto di Giulio Camillo: L'*urtext* ritrovato," *Venezia Cinquecento: Studi di Storia dell'Arte e Della Cultura* 1 (1991): 217–71.

7. Quoted in Yates, *Art of Memory*, 138; in Camillo, *L'idea*, 10–11. See also Eugenio Garin, "Note su alcuni aspetti delle retoriche rinascimentali e sulla 'Retorica' del Patrizi," *Archivio di Filosofia* (Rome and Milan: Fratelli Bocca, 1953), 32–35.

8. Quoted in Yates, *Art of Memory*, 131.

9. Paolo Rossi, *Clavis universalis: Arti mnemoniche e logica combinatoria de Lullo e Leibniz* (Milan and Naples: Ricciardi, 1960).

10. On "first philosophy," see Carl Page, *Philosophical Historicism and the Betrayal of First Philosophy* (University Park, Pa.: Pennsylvania State University Press, 1995).

11. *The New Science of Giambattista Vico*, trans. Thomas Goddard Bergin and Max Harold Fisch (Ithaca: Cornell University Press, 1984). Hereinafter cited as *NS*, followed by the paragraph enumeration common to the English and most Italian editions: see, e.g., Vico, *Opere,* ed. Andrea Battistini, 2 vols. (Milan: Mondadori, 1990).

12. On self-knowledge, see Ann Hartle, *Death and the Disinterested Spectator: An Inquiry into the Nature of Philosophy* (Albany: State University of New York Press, 1986), and *Self-Knowledge in the Age of Theory* (Lanham, Md.: Rowman and Littlefield, 1997).

13. Giovanni Pico della Mirandola, "Oration on the Dignity of Man," trans. Elizabeth Livermore Forbes, in *The Renaissance Philosophy of Man*, ed. Ernst Cassirer, Paul Oskar Kristeller, and John Herman Randall, Jr. (Chicago: University of Chicago Press, 1948), 235.

14. *Hermetica: The Greek Corpus Hermeticum and the Latin Asclepius*, trans. Brian P. Copenhaver (Cambridge: Cambridge University Press, 1992).

15. See Donald Phillip Verene, "Plato's Conception of Philosophy and Poetry," *Personalist* 44 (1963): 528–38.

16. Joyce told his friend Frank Budgen, "Imagination is memory." See Richard Ellmann, *James Joyce*, rev. ed. (New York: Oxford University

Press, 1982), 661. See also Donald Phillip Verene, "Vico as Reader of Joyce," in *Vico and Joyce*, ed. Verene (Albany: State University of New York Press, 1987), 221-31.

17. G. W. F. Hegel, *Phenomenology of Spirit*, trans. A. V. Miller (Oxford: Oxford University Press, 1977), 492-93.
18. G. W. F. Hegel, "Über Mythologie, Volksgeist und Kunst," manuscript in the Staatsbibliothek Preussischer Kulturbesitz, Berlin. See also Donald Phillip Verene, *Hegel's Recollection: A Study of Images in the Phenomenology of Spirit* (Albany: State University of New York Press, 1985), 36-37.
19. G. W. F. Hegel, "Das älteste System programm des deutschen Idealismus," in *Werke*, vol. 1 (Frankfurt: Suhrkamp, 1971): 236.
20. James Joyce, *Finnegans Wake* (London: Faber and Faber, 1939), 628.
21. Gianfrancesco Pico della Mirandola, *On the Imagination* (Latin-English), trans. Harry Caplan, Cornell Studies in English, ed. Lane Cooper, vol. 16 (New Haven: For Cornell University by Yale University Press, 1930), chap. 6.
22. Ibid., chap. 8.
23. Ernesto Grassi, *Renaissance Humanism: Studies in Philosophy and Poetics* (Binghamton, N.Y.: Center for Medieval and Early Renaissance Studies, 1988); Grassi, *Die Macht der Phantasie: Zur Geschichte abendländischen Denkens* (Königstein/Ts.: Athenäum, 1979).
24. Francis Bacon, *Sylva sylvarum, or A Natural History in Ten Centuries*, in *The Works of Francis Bacon*, ed. James Spedding, Robert Leslie Ellis, and Douglas Denon Heath, vol. 2 (New York: Garrett, 1968), 654.
25. See the remarks of Lane Cooper, *The Rhetoric of Aristotle* (Englewood Cliffs, N.J.: Prentice-Hall, 1960), xxii-xxiii.
26. Ernst Cassirer, *The Philosophy of Symbolic Forms*, trans. Ralph Manheim, 3 vols. (New Haven: Yale University Press, 1953-57), 3:191-204.
27. Ibid., 1:177-86.
28. See the discussion of Socrates and self-knowledge in Chap. 1.
29. See Donald Phillip Verene, "Giambattista Vico's 'Reprehension of the Metaphysics of René Descartes, Benedict Spinoza, and John Locke': An Addition to the *New Science* (Translation and Commentary)," *New Vico Studies* 8 (1990): 2-18.
30. R. G. Collingwood, *An Essay on Philosophical Method* (Oxford: Clarendon, 1933), 214.
31. On imaginative universals, see Donald Phillip Verene, *Vico's Science of Imagination* (Ithaca: Cornell University Press, 1981), chap. 3.
32. Barbara C. Sproul, *Primal Myths: Creating the World* (San Francisco: Harper and Row, 1979).

33. Cassirer, *Philosophy of Symbolic Forms* 2:60-70.
34. F. H. Bradley, *Appearance and Reality: A Metaphysical Essay* (1893; reprint, Oxford: Clarendon, 1930), x.
35. See, e.g., Bruno Snell, *The Discovery of the Mind: The Greek Origins of European Thought*, trans. T. G. Rosenmeyer (New York: Harper, 1960); F. M. Cornford, *Principium Sapientiae: A Study of the Origins of Greek Philosophical Thought*, ed. W. K. C. Guthrie (New York: Harper and Row, 1965); Henri Frankfort et al., *The Intellectual Adventure of Ancient Man: An Essay on Speculative Thought in the Ancient Near East* (Chicago: Chicago University Press, 1946).
36. Juan Luis Vives, "A Fable About Man," trans. Nancy Lenkeith, in *The Renaissance Philosophy of Man*, 387-93. See Donald Phillip Verene, "Vico and Vives on Humane Education," *New Vico Studies* 14 (1996): 47-63.
37. Alfred North Whitehead, *Adventures of Ideas* (New York: Macmillan, 1967), 221.
38. Ludwig Wittgenstein, *Tractatus logico-philosophicus*, trans. D. F. Pears and B. F. McGuinness (London: Routledge and Kegan Paul, 1974), 151.
39. Harold Bloom, *The Western Canon: The Books and School of the Ages* (New York: Harcourt, Brace, 1994), 23.
40. Claude Lévi-Strauss, *The Raw and the Cooked: Introduction to the Science of Mythology*, vol. 1, trans. John Weightman and Doreen Weightman (New York: Harper, 1969), 183.
41. Ellmann, *James Joyce*, 661 n.
42. Giambattista Vico, *On the Study Methods of Our Time*, trans. Elio Gianturco (Ithaca: Cornell University Press, 1990), 77.
43. Ibid., 78.
44. *The Autobiography of Giambattista Vico*, trans. Max Harold Fisch and Thomas Goddard Bergin (Ithaca: Cornell University Press, 1983), 199.
45. Giambattista Vico, *On Humanistic Education: Six Inaugural Orations, 1699-1707*, trans. Giorgio A. Pinton and Arthur W. Shippee (Ithaca: Cornell University Press, 1993), 138.
46. Vico, *Study Methods*, 48.
47. *The Digest of Justinian* (Latin text), ed. Theodor Mommsen and Paul Krueger, English trans. and ed., Alan Watson, vol. 1 (Philadelphia: University of Pennsylvania Press, 1985), bk. 1, sec. 1.1.
48. Vico, "The Academies and the Relation Between Philosophy and Eloquence," trans. Donald Phillip Verene, appendix to Vico, *Study Methods*, 89.
49. Ernst Cassirer, *The Philosophy of Symbolic Forms*, vol. 4, *The Metaphysics of Symbolic Forms*, ed. John Michael Krois and Donald Phillip Verene, trans.

John Michael Krois (New Haven: Yale University Press, 1996), 184.
50. Ibid., 185.
51. Ibid., 185–86.
52. *Justinian's Institutes*, trans. Peter Birks and Grant McLeod, with the Latin text of Paul Krueger (Ithaca: Cornell University Press, 1987), bk. 1. 1.1.3.
53. Alasdair MacIntyre, *After Virtue: A Study in Moral Theory* (Notre Dame, Ind.: University of Notre Dame Press, 1981). See also Albert William Levi, *The Highroad of Humanity: The Seven Ethical Ages of Western Man*, ed. Donald Phillip Verene and Molly Black Verene (Amsterdam: Rodopi, 1995).
54. *Tao Te Ching*, trans. Stephen Addiss and Stanley Lombardo (Indianapolis: Hackett, 1993), 5.
55. R. Johnson, "The Promethean Commonplace," *Journal of the Warburg and Courtauld Institutes* 25 (1962): 9–17.
56. Sources for Vico's account of the origin of human society, in addition to Cicero's *De inventione*, are likely Plato, *Laws* III. 676–82 and Lucretius, *De rerum natura*, bks. 5 and 6.

Credits for Illustrations

Page 9—In C. Kerényi, *Prometheus: Archetypal Image of Human Existence*, trans. Ralph Manheim (New York: Bollingen Foundation, 1962), pl. Xa. Reprinted by permission of Princeton University Press.

Page 19—In Johann Caspar Lavater, *Essays in Physiognomy*, trans. Henry Hunter, vol. 3 (London: John Murray, 1792), 252. Courtesy of the Woodruff Library Rare Book Collection, Emory University.

Page 50—In *René Magritte: Catalogue Raisonné*, ed. David Sylvester, vol. 2 (London: Menil Foundation, Philip Wilson, 1993), 268. Reprinted by permission of the Artists' Rights Society, representatives of Charley Herscovici.

Page 93—In William Willeford, *The Fool and His Scepter: A Study in Clowns and Jesters and Their Audience* (Evanston, Ill.: Northwestern University Press, 1969), pl. 1. Photograph by Frank Horvat. Reprinted by permission of Northwestern University Press.

Page 155—In Siegfried Giedion, *Mechanization Takes Command: A Contribution to Anonymous History* (New York: Oxford University Press, 1948), 97. Reprinted by permission of Oxford University Press.

Page 199—In D. M. Field, *Greek and Roman Mythology* (Secaucus, N. J.: Chartwell Books, 1977), 40. Reprinted by permission of Chartwell Books.

Index

Achilles, 58
Adam, 9
Aeschines, 229
Aeschylus, 1, 4, 7
Aesop, 80
Ahab, 2
Alberti, Leon Battista, 78-83, 86
Alcibiades, 230
Alcmena, 18
Alexander the Great, 92
Amphitryon, 18
Antisthenes, 229
Aoide, 36
Aphrodite, 80, 251
Apollo, 126, 204, 259
Apollodorus, 8, 12
Aquinas, St. Thomas, 53
Aratus, 198-99
Arbus, Diane, 101
Aristotle, 10, 51, 59, 63; and Momus, 79; on laughter, 108; on comedy, 117-18; and moral character, 131, 231-32; and moral choice, 167-68; and concept formation, 182-83; on imitation, 201; on memory and imagination, 207-11; on metaphor, 216; on wonder, 220-21; on melancholy, 227; on rhetoric, 240
Aristoxenus, 245
Armin, Robert, 128

Arnauld, Antoine, 49, 71
Asclepius, 114-15
Athena, 5, 11, 79-80
Atlas, 246, 249
Atomists, 51
Augustine, St., 18, 53, 111-12, 201-3

Babrius, 80
Bacchus, 124, 136
Bacon, Francis: on emblem, 7; on Prometheus, 29-30; influence on Lambert, 72; on laughter, 108; control of nature, 147-49; on imagination, 209
Bacon, Roger, 52-53, 68, 72
Badius Ascensius, 123
Bayle, Pierre, 65
Beatrice, 67-68
Beeckman, Isaac, 21
Behemoth, 188
Benjamin, Walter, 176
Berdyaev, Nicolas, 156
Bergson, Henri, 115, 121
Berkeley, George, 71
Bloom, Leopold, 172
Boccaccio, Giovanni, 6
Bolzoni, Lina, 193-94
Bosch, Hieronymus, 123
Bradley, F. H., 220
Brant, Sebastian, 94, 95, 102, 123-27, 129

Braudel, Fernand, 22
Brecht, Bertolt, 97
Brinker, Hans, 175
Browning, Elizabeth Barrett, 13
Bruno, Giordano, 243
Buddha, 113
Byron, Lord George Gordon, 13

Calliope, 201-3
Calvin, John, 193
Camillo, Giulio, 6, 192-97, 210, 242
Campanella, Thomas, 243
Caraja, 226
Cassirer, Ernst: on Prometheus, 28-29, 172; on Kant's third *Critique,* 60-61; on self-knowledge, 132; on technology, 172; on modern politics, 174, 177-78, 184-85; on concept formation, 182-84; symbolic pregnance, 213; on Socrates, 230-31
Castelli, Enrico, 173
Castiglione, Baldesar, 5-6
Cebes, 127, 242, 243
Cepheus, 249
Chaldeans, 246
Chaloner, Thomas, 129
Charmides, 76
Christians, 188
Christina, Queen of Sweden, 28
Cicero, 42, 248; and Prometheus, 1-2, 4; on reflection, 51-52; types of wit, 105; use of, by Camillo, 195; on Aratus, 198-99; on imagination, 208; *Ad herennium* and memory, 210; on nature of wisdom, 214; on melancholy, 227; on prudence and eloquence, 228-30; on decorum, 236-37; on Promethean commonplace, 238-40; on eloquence and rhetoric, 240; on Pythagoras, 248
Ciceronians, 193
Clio, 200-201, 203
Cock, the, 112, 114-15; as sign of fool, 90, 114, 122
Collingwood, R. G., 74, 216
Colvius, 18
Condillac, Étienne Bonnot de, 54
Condorcet, Marquis de, 171, 189
Corythus, 244
Crassus, 240
Critias, 75, 230
Crito, 114
Crotoniates, 244
cummings, e. e., 176
Cynics, 111-12

D'Alembert, Jean Le Rond, 15
Dante, 43, 67-68
Dardanus, 244
D'Avalos. *See* del Vasto
Death, 103-4
Dedalus, Stephen, 46, 171
Delphic oracle, 75-77, 204, 214, 231, 237
del Vasto, Marchese Alfonso Davalos, 193, 196
Democritus, 109-11, 117
Demosthenes, 228
Derridians, 101
Descartes, René (Cartesian; Cartesianism), 13-14, 68, 69, 143, 150, 205, 227; and modern society, 2-3, 15-35, 143, 189; Lavater's analysis of his features, 19-20, 117; on reflection, 45, 49-51, 54-55, 71; and Kant, 57-58, 77; and Vico, 68, 84; and

optics, 70; his evil genius, 99; on laughter, 107-8; on desire, 148; conception of truth, 152-53; contrast to Socrates, 224
de Sivry, Louis Poinsinet, 111
Devil, the, 118
Diderot, Denis, 15, 86
Dio Chrysostom, 32, 247
Diogenes Laertius, 112, 245
Diogenes of Sinope (Cynic), 111-13, 122
Dionysus. *See* Bacchus
Dionysus of Syracuse, 192
Druids, 246
Ducassé, Pierre, 170
Dürer, Albrecht, 123

Ecclesiastes, 128
Eco, Umberto, 117-19, 129, 181
Egyptians, 246
Eliot, T. S., 171, 172
Elizabeth, Queen, 128
Elizabeth of Bohemia, Princess, 27
Ellul, Jacques, 27, 143, 144, 151-52, 161-90 *passim*
Elpis (Hope), 11
Epicureans, 51
Epimetheus, 5, 8, 11, 29-31, 34, 37
Er, 116
Erasmus, Desiderius: on the *poêle*, 22; and Horace's spectator in empty theater, 88-89; on writing of *Moriae encomium*, 94; relation to Brant, 95, 123-24; on "true prudence," 96; Lucian's influence on, 111; on moral satire, 127; conception of folly, 128-30; on Momus, 129; on "foolosophers," 129, 136; on happiness, 131-32; and Camillo, 194

Erato, 201
Eros, 251, 254-55
Esperti, Abbé, 47
Eudoxus, 150
Euterpe, 201

Falstaff, 94
Farber, Marvin, 69
Farnese, Alessandro (Pope Paul III), 193
Fermat, Pierre de, 71
Ficino, Marsilio, 6-7, 193, 205
Findlay, John N., 98, 157
Folly. See *Moria*
Fool, Lear's, 94, 122
Foolosophers, 129, 136
Ford, Henry, 154, 168
Foucault, Michel, 102
Francis I, 193, 196
Franklin, Benjamin, 14
Fraser, Alexander Campbell, 71
Freud, Sigmund, 10, 115, 132
Fuller, Thomas, 108

Gadamer, Hans-Georg, 69, 97
Galileo, 20, 182-83
Gall, Franz Joseph, 117
Gargantua, 94
Ghert, Peter Gabriel van, 101
Gide, André, 33
Giedion, Siegfried, 170
Goethe, Johann Wolfgang von, 13, 28, 117
Gorgon sisters, 194
Grassi, Ernesto, 33
Grimm, Jacob, 102
Grimm, Wilhelm, 102
Guicciardini, Francesco, 46
Gyges, 83-84
Gymnosophists, 246

Haldane, Elizabeth S., 20
Ham-Cleaver, 92
Harlequin, 103
Hegel, Georg Wilhelm Friedrich: on Prometheus, 10; on the face as mask, 20; on skepticism, 64; criticism of reflection, 65–67, 68–69; on speculation, 73; on shamelessness, 86; inverted world and illusion, 86, 96–98, 100–106, 135; and phrenology, 112–13; humor of, 113; pun on *das Meinen,* 116; "Who Thinks Abstractly?" 119; on consciousness, 124–25, 132; on desire, 141–43, 146–50; *das geistige Tierreich,* 157–58, 162–65; on poetry and myth, 136; on individuals, 160, 162, 164–65; on philosophy, 191; on memory, 206–7; and bad infinity, 220
Heidegger, Martin, 170, 226
Hemingway, Ernest, 176
Hephaestus (Vulcan), 1, 5, 11, 14, 23, 79–80
Heraclides of Pontus, 248–49
Heraclitus, 110, 173, 245
Hercules, 1, 8, 112, 127, 186, 246–47
Herder, Johann Gottfried von, 116
Hermes (Mercury), 6, 7, 14, 18, 194, 250–52
Hermes Trismegistus, 192, 205
Hermotimus, 79–81
Hertz, Marcus, 73
Hesiod: conception of the Muses, 34–35, 37–38, 200–201, 203; on Momus, 79; and Homer, 205, 216
Hippocrates, 110

Hobbes, Thomas, 27, 29, 70, 108, 187–91
Hodge, 115
Holbein, Hans, 123
Homer, 58, 79, 198, 200, 205, 215, 216, 242
Horace, 12, 88, 120, 229–30, 237
Hume, David, 58–59, 132
Husserl, Edmund, 69
Huxley, Aldous, 170
Huygens, Christian, 27, 70
Hyperbius, 10

Iamblichus, 245
Isaiah, 245
Isocrates, 238–39

Jacques, 121
James, Apostle, 53
James, William, 78
Jaspers, Karl, 156, 170, 171
Jesus, 124, 192
Job, 115, 187–90
Jorge, 117–19, 129
Josephus, Flavius, 245
Joubert, Laurent, 110–11, 117
Jove (Jupiter, Zeus), 6, 7, 18, 23, 52, 223, 250–51; and Prometheus, 1, 4, 8–12, 14, 24, 30, 31–32; and the Muses, 34, 36, 198–200, 203, 215; and first humans, 64, 85, 217–18, 222, 240–42; and Momus, 80–81, 82
Joyce, James, 116, 171–72, 206–7, 227
Jung, Carl G., 34, 175
Jünger, Friedrich Georg, 170
Juno, 52
Jupiter. *See* Jove

Justinian I, 232
Juvenal, 110

Kafka, Franz, 174
Kant, Immanuel, 13–14, 69, 106, 154, 226; conception of reflection, 55–66; and Lambert, 72–73; and "I think," 77–78; on prudence, 130
Keats, John, 13
Kerényi, Carl, 30
Krull, Felix, 86

Lactantius, 245
Lambert, Johann Heinrich, 72
La Mettrie, Julien Offray de, 15, 156
Langer, Susanne K., 61
Lark, 92
Lavatch, 122
Lavater, Johann Caspar, 19–20, 116–17
Lawrence, D. H., 176
Lear, King, 122, 223
Le Cat, Claude-Nicolas, 4–5
Leibniz, Georg Wilhelm, 54–55, 94, 195
Lenin, Vladimir Ilyich Ulyanov, 161
Leon, tyrant of Phlius, 249
Leopardi, Giacomo, 14
Leviathan, 19, 187–89
Lévi-Strauss, Claude, 37, 226
Livy, 245
Locher, Jacob, 123
Locke, John, 27, 53–55, 71, 72, 205
Lucian, 14, 79–81, 92, 111, 250
Luke, St., 124, 193

Lycinus, 79–80
Lycurgus, 249

McCormick, Cyrus, 164
Machiavelli, Niccolò, 44–45
Mackerel, 92
MacLeish, Archibald, 190
McLuhan, Marshall, 158–59
Macrobius, 245
Magi, the, 246
Marcuse, Herbert, 161, 170
Mark, St., 124, 193
Mars, 10
Marx, Chico, 106
Marx, Groucho, 106
Marx, Karl, 14, 143–44
Matthew, St., 124, 193
Melete, 36
Melpomene, 201
Melville, Herman, 2
Memory, mother of the Muses. *See* Mnemosyne
Menippus, 113
Mercury. *See* Hermes
Mère-Folle, 136
Merleau-Ponty, Maurice, 69
Mersenne, Marin, 22, 28, 70
Metaphysic, Dame, 242
Miller, Henry, 172
Mneiai, 36
Mneme, 36
Mnemosyne (Memory), 34, 36, 136, 199, 203–4, 206, 210, 242
Momus, 78–84, 87, 129
Mondrian, Piet, 176
Montaigne, Michel de, 23
More, Thomas, 128
Moria (Folly), 128–29, 131, 136
Mother Earth, 175

Mumford, Lewis, 170
Muses, nature of, 34–38, 225, 241, 242; power of telling what was, is, and is to come, 134, 198–206, 209–12, 215, 232, 235, 237; and philosophy, 136, 198, 204–6, 237. *See also individual names*

Narcissus, 73–74, 83, 106, 250–52, 253
Nazis, 157, 165
Nestor, 249
Newton, Sir Isaac, 70
Nicholas of Cusa (Cusanus), 126
Nickles, 190
Nicolini, Fausto, 45
Nietzsche, Friedrich, 13, 226
Noah, 218
Notomisti, 193
Numa Pompilius, 245

Odysseus. *See* Ulysses
Ophelia, 112
Opossum, 226
Oresme, Nicolas, 15
Orpheus, 246
Orwell, George, 170, 185–86
Ovid, 12, 181

Pandora, 11, 30, 31, 36, 37
Pangloss, 94
Pantagruel, 89–90, 94, 120
Panurge, 89–91
Pascal, Blaise, 151
Pasiphae, 194
Peppi, 120–21
Peter, St., 124, 129
Petronius, 218
Pharisees, 171, 189

Philip II, 92
Phliasians, 249
Phoenicians, 246
Pico della Mirandola, Gianfrancesco, 209, 247
Pico della Mirandola, Giovanni 114–15, 193, 204, 205
Picot, Abbé, 28
Pirandello, Luigi, 98
Plato (Platonism, Neoplatonism), 5, 9, 45, 241, 249, 259; and Prometheus, 10, 12, 26, 33, 82; cave of, 51, 73, 87; and Momus, 79, 81–83; on laughter, 108; pun on "saved," 116; definition of man, 122; Academy of, 122, 199; world of becoming, 177; and Camillo, 192; quarrel with the poets, 206, 215–16; and imagination, 208; view of Socrates, 229, 231
Plautus, 18, 92
Pliny, 10, 26
Plotinus, 11
Plutarch, 4, 6, 7, 110, 199
Pod, 92
Polyhymnia, 201, 203
Porphyry, 246
Porter, Katherine Anne, 123
Poseidon, 79
Postman, Neil, 190
Pound, Ezra, 171, 172
Presocratics, 222
Prester John, 56
Prometheus (Promethean), 1–38 *passim*, 172, 194, 226, 238, 249; and Descartes, 45, 143–44; and Momus, 79–83; and laughter, 118–19; and "Promethean commonplace," 241–42

Propertius, 12
Protagoras, 8, 238
Pythagoras, 1, 114, 204, 244–47, 249, 259
Pythia. *See* Delphic oracle

Quintilian, 45, 197–98, 221–22, 228
Quixote, Don, 94

Rabelais, François, 89, 120
Radin, Paul, 24
Rembrandt van Ryn, 22
Rorty, Richard, 132–33
Rosenkranz, Karl, 102, 104
Rousseau, Jean-Jacques, 3–5, 7–9, 12, 31–32, 148
Ryle, Gilbert, 77–78

Saaz, Johannes von, 103
Sade, Comte Donatien Alphonse François de, 181
Sage, the, 235
Sandburg, Carl, 87
Sarah, 190
Sarpi, Paolo, 55
Scholastics, 123
Seneca, 110, 117
Servius Tullius, 245
Seven Sages, 204, 214, 245, 249
Seven Sephiroth, 194
Sextus Empiricus, 65
Shaftesbury, Anthony Ashley Cooper, 3d Earl of, 63, 127
Shakespeare, William, 94, 116, 121–22, 128, 186
Shelley, Mary Wollstonecraft, 13
Shelley, Percy Bysshe, 13
Sigismund August II, 88
Simonides of Ceos, 195

Socrates, 12, 230; and Prometheus, 8; and self-knowledge, 75–77, 101, 129, 204–5, 224; view of death, 114–15; and prudence, 126; and wisdom, 126–27, 214; Hobbes' view of, 191; and philosophy, 204–5; and memory, 210; on wonder and irony, 221; on moral philosophy, 229–32; Cassirer's view of, 230–31; as lover of learning, 231, 242
Solomon, King, 194
Sophocles, 1, 79
Sosia, 18–19
Sotto, 128
Spinoza, Benedict, 27, 107
Swift, Jonathan, 94

Tacana, 226
Tacitus, 47–48
Tanzan, 113–14
Tarlton, jester, 128
Terpsichore, 201
Tertullian, 110
Thales, 204–5
Thalia, 201
Thaumaste, 89–91, 120
Thomas, Dylan, 173
Thoth, 4
Tieck, Ludwig, 97–98, 101, 135
Titans, 1, 4, 7, 24, 35
Titian, 193
Toffler, Alvin, 167–68
Tomfool, 115
Tom Thumb, 175
Touchstone, 121
Trickster figure, 21, 24, 26, 226
Trojans, 244
Turnus, 52

Tuscans, 215
Typhon, 76–77

Ulysses, 12, 58, 85, 249
Unamuno, Miguel de, 25
Ungaretti, Giuseppe, 35
Urania, 200, 203

Varro, Marcus Terentius, 214–15
Vaucanson, Jacques de, 15, 189
Vergil, 52, 203, 215, 241
Vico, Giambattista, 18, 41–48, 62–64, 79, 87, 193; and barbarism of reflection, 42–43, 45, 78, 85, 148; and ideal eternal history, 46–47, 212, 233; and Descartes 68, 84; and laughter, 108–9, 129; *sensus communis*, 132; on the Muses, 200–203, 211, 215, 237; on memory, 206–7; poetic wisdom, 214–19; on irony, 221–22; on eloquence, 228–30; on Jove and the Promethean commonplace, 240–42
Viglius Zuichemus, 194–95

Virtue (goddess), 82
Vives, Juan Luis, 44, 223
Voltaire, François Marie Arouet de, 94
Vulcan. *See* Hephaestus

Whitehead, Alfred North, 223–24, 225
Wieland, Christoph Martin, 116
Wild Man of Borneo, 122
Willeford, William, 103, 122
William, 117–19
Winnebago Indians, 24
Wittgenstein, Ludwig, 225
Wyatt, John, 144, 189

Xenophon, 229, 231, 247

Yanomamö, 180

Zeus. *See* Jove
Zijderveld, Anton C., 95, 120–21, 134, 187
Zoroaster, 205